# Writing Between the Lines
## Composition in the Social Sciences

Douglas Flemons

Nova Southeastern University

W. W. Norton & Company

New York • London

For information about permission to reproduce selections
from this book, write to
Permissions, W. W. Norton & Company, Inc., 500 Fifth Avenue,
New York, NY 10110

Composition and book design by Paradigm Graphics.
Manufactured by Haddon Craftsmen.

Library of Congress Cataloging-in-Publication Data

Flemons, Douglas G.
Writing between the lines: composition in the social sciences /
Douglas Flemons.
p.   cm.
Includes bibliographical references (p. ) and index.
**ISBN 0-393-70263-4**
1. English language–Rhetoric.   2. Social sciences–authorship.
3. Academic writing.   I. Title.
PE1479.S62F58   1998
808'.0663–dc21     97-52365     CIP

W. W. Norton & Company, Inc., 500 Fifth Avenue, New York N.Y. 10110
http://www.wwnorton.com
W. W. Norton & Company Ltd., 10 Coptic Street, London WC1A 1PU

1  2  3  4  5  6  7  8  9  0

To Shelley, Eric, and Jenna

# Acknowledgments

Shelley Green, my wife and colleague, helped me persevere *and* take breaks, and she critically (and kindly) reviewed multiple drafts of each chapter. Eric, our son, often reminded me not to take anything (including him) too seriously. His and Shelley's love and laughter stayed with me while I wrote. Jenna, our new baby, thoughtfully allowed me to finish the manuscript before making her entry into the world.

Pat Cole suggested eight or nine years ago that I should offer a writing seminar for students in our department. Without her initial encouragement, I might never have approached my dean, Ron Chenail, with the audacious request to teach a subject in which I had much interest but no formal training.

The first group of students to sign up for my course helpfully nagged me to write down what I was telling them; the resulting document became the foundation for this book. Many of the additions and revisions I have made over the years have been inspired by the excellent questions my students have posed.

My editor at Norton, Susan Munro, stood behind me and my vision for the book, lent her expert eye to the manuscript, and graciously allowed me to put our other project on hold while I brought this one to completion. Carol Hollar-Zwick, also at Norton, made many helpful suggestions on an early draft.

Suzanne Ferriss combed the manuscript for errors, inconsistencies, and fuzzifications, and she laughed in all the right places. Steve Alford showed me how to make my writing leaner and more direct.

Kristin Wright allowed me to mangle a portion of her dissertation so I could show  (in Chapter 6) how *not* to develop ideas. Her generosity was matched only by her sense of humor at how I disarrayed her fine work.

William Rambo provided theological and historical information for Chapter 2. Dawn Shelton came up with the metaphors of "reader as tourist" and "writer as tour guide."

Stuart Horn, Kristin Wright, Herb Tavenner, Michael Greene, and Don and Bet Flemons critiqued various chapters. They, along with D'Aun Tavenner, Fern Weaver, Tom and Ward Flemons, Bill and La Claire Brown, Barry Duncan, Richard Ryal, Sandra Roscoe, and Bonny Cole, inspired me with their interest and enthusiasm.

Lee Shilts, Ron Chenail, and Elizabeth McDaniel helped me bring the book to a timely completion by approving a six-month sabbatical from my teaching responsibilities at Nova Southeastern University.

Thanks, y'all.

# Contents

# Introduction

Grammar is a piano I play by ear. All I know about grammar is its power.

—Joan Didion

I still have trouble identifying grammatical structures by name, though I know them as matters of usage.

—Robertson Davies

I know grammar by ear only, not by notes, not by the rules. A generation ago I knew the rules—knew them by heart, word for word, though not their meanings—and I still know one of them; the one which says—which says—but never mind, it will come back to me presently.

—Mark Twain

What is required is precise talk about relations.

—Gregory Bateson

In every structure we may distinguish the relation or relations, and the items related.

—Suzanne Langer

A biographer can best capture something of an individual's inner life by focusing outward—on the person's relationships with friends, enemies, and lovers. Similarly, a therapist can best grasp the significance of a client's symptom by viewing it within the context of the person's relationships with family, friends, and other caregivers. In both cases, *relationship* serves as the basis for knowing and understanding. But most of us don't think like biographers and therapists. We think and talk as if the world were made up of isolated *things*. As the communications theorist Gregory Bateson (1979) pointed out, this works fine when it comes to buying apples or selling cars, but it can get us into trouble (or land us in a heap of confusion) when we wish to explore anything having to do with *communication*.

Language, animal behavior, music, genetic codes: These are composed not of things, but of *relationships*. You can't get the sense of a poem by counting the number of letters in it, and a list of isolated notes—B♭, F, E♭, D, A♭—doesn't add up to a melody. Communicational phenomena, said Bateson, can only be understood relationally. He once commented that the standard way of teaching grammar—that is, that "a noun is the name of a person, place, or thing, and a verb is an action word"—is nonsense, for it defines each part of the sentence by isolating it. "[Children] are taught . . . that the way to define something is by what it supposedly is in itself, not by its relation to other things" (Bateson, 1979, pp. 16-17). However, if *relationship* were used as the basis for definition, then "any child could . . . see that there is something wrong with the sentence "'Go' is a verb" (p. 17).

Bateson said little else about the relational nature of language and nothing further about how a relational approach to teaching grammar would look; he made the comments I have quoted in passing, in a book he wrote on learning and evolution. Nevertheless, his ideas about language, however briefly discussed, have intrigued me for a long time and have shaped the way I teach people how to write. I offer a course on academic writing for advanced social science students who, for the most part, have not fared well in traditional composition classes.

Though bright, many students entering my course are spooked by discussions of dangling participles, subordinate clauses, tenses, compound predicates, and so on, and they recoil from most style manuals as if confronted with tomes on trigonometry. The technical language in such manuals acts as a barrier to their learning, a barrier most of the students feel incapable of crossing.

I begin my first class by underscoring the difference between ignorance and stupidity. This is an important distinction to make, particularly for people who feel embarrassed about their lack of necessary composition skills. Fear of ignorance drowns curiosity. I thus encourage the students to relax into their not-yet-knowing, and I offer them a vantage from which to approach the process of writing. As a teacher in the social sciences, I have neither the education nor inclination to manage a convincing impersonation of a bona fide composition instructor, so I don't try. I quote Joan Didion and Robertson Davies, each a renowned essayist and novelist, as evidence that people can learn to write well without fluency in grammarianese (see the epigraphs above); then, for the rest of the course, I demonstrate how it can be done.

This book is a reworked and refined version of a manuscript I originally etched out for my students. Its title, *Writing Between the Lines*, underscores Bateson's contention that ideas are formed and meaning is communicated *in relationship*—in the relationship between words, between sentences (i.e., between the lines), between paragraphs, between sections of a paper, and so on.[1] For ideas to be clearly articulated, the relationships shaping them, at all organizational levels of the text, must be clearly drawn. When this happens, readers experience the writing as transparent to the meaning it composes. This is surely an illusion, for language profoundly influences what and how we think, but writing that doesn't get in the way of itself (or, more accurately, in the way of the reader's reading) often seems to dissolve into the ideas it invites the reader to follow.

If you are like some of my students, you may presume that your thinking is localized in your head and that writing involves little more than typing already-worked-out notions into your word processor.[2] Not only is this a good recipe for writer's block (or, as I would say, "sticky writing"— see p. 8), but it also limits how and where you can invent ideas. In

---

[1] At the risk of stating the obvious, I should mention that all such relationships hold meaning only in relation to a reader.

[2] Some excellent writers—e.g., Wendell Berry, John Barth, Anne Tyler—compose with pen and paper. I write with a word-processing program on a computer, and I am assuming that you do too; if you prefer long hand, then your thinking goes on between you and your scribblings.

Chapter 1, I suggest that thinking, like all communicational phenomena, happens in relationship, particularly in the relationship between you and your word processor. Often the best way to discover what you know, believe, or understand is to edit your various attempts to tease apart and develop an idea in writing. As you refine your sentences and the transitions between them, you can more easily distinguish where clarity of thought gives way to confusion. Clear thinking and clear writing are recursively linked: Each depends on and inspires the other.

You can best *connect* your thinking and writing if you *separate* your creating and editing. Some writers can edit their sentences and paragraphs as they create them, but most people benefit from keeping the two processes distinct. Generating ideas can be a messy business, and it often helps if you don't tidy up too soon. Although editorial acumen is essential for a well-composed final product, unrelenting editorial vigilance can stifle your creativity. I offer suggestions for how to achieve an inspired, interactive balance between the art of inventing sentences (and ideas) and the rigor of editing them.

The literary critic Berni Benstock once told me he considered all novels to be mysteries. I trust he would forgive me for making his audacious claim still more extravagant. Why not approach essays and articles and nonfiction books, even those written by social scientists, also as mysteries? The mystery novelist and social science writer both engage the reader by offering compelling questions and, at the appropriate moment, providing satisfying answers. Readers of both sorts of literature are curious to find out who or what "dunnit" and how (and why) he or she or it pulled it off.[3]

This book is primarily intended for people writing social science mysteries, so I have devoted a chapter to explaining the idiosyncracies of the genre. Chapter 2 takes each section of a typical social science research paper—the *Abstract*, *Introduction*, *Literature Review*, *Method*, *Results/Analysis*, and *Discussion*—and offers suggestions for how to

---

[3]After writing this, I discovered that Harry Wolcott (1994) had used the same metaphor as a way of giving advice about writing qualitative research studies: "My final suggestion . . . is to organize and present qualitative studies as though writing a mystery novel. . . . The problem focus becomes the mystery to be solved. . . . Data are introduced in the manner of accumulating evidence, to be sifted, sorted, and evaluated according to their contribution to solving the mystery. The challenge (and reminder) is to write with a sense of excitement and discovery. How satisfying to have a reader say of a qualitative study, 'I just couldn't put it down'" (p. 22).

approach, structure, and relate it to the other sections. My comments are encompassing enough to be relevant for any paper you will likely find yourself writing. I pay particular attention to literature reviews—not only to their reasons for being and how to write them, but how to position yourself in relation to the works you are citing.

Of course, the mystery in a mystery needs to float at the proper contextual level: It should reside between the characters in the plot, *not* the characters in the sentences. The readers' questions should be, "Who really killed the heiress?" and "How did that change come about?" not, "What does this sentence really mean?" Chapters 3 and 4 demystify the process of crafting non-mysterious (i.e., unmuddled, non-confusing) sentences. I use the metaphor of *story* (with special attention, again, paid to mysteries) to explain how sentences, as mini-narratives, create coherent meaning. I describe how various sorts of *guiding words* (Chapter 3) work in conjunction with *punctuation* (Chapter 4) to help direct the reader along the narrative path of a sentence.

If the metaphor of *sentence as story* is taken seriously, grammarians can be appreciated as a species of literary critic. They have developed technical terms for critiquing the narrative integrity of sentences—for checking that the motives and actions undertaken by the characters in each "story" are consistent and sensible, that the narrative properly unfolds in time (i.e., that the sentence has a correctly tensed verb), and that the props and supporting characters respond as needed and expected. Grammarians explain how best to achieve consistent clarity.

Good writing *embodies* the rules grammarians set forth, and the same is true for good writers: They have the rules in their bones. Some writers are also conversant in the specialized language of the grammarians—they have, as it were, the rules on the tips of their tongues. If Robertson Davies and Joan Didion are any indication, however, bones are more important than tongues. In other words, you can understand and use grammatical rules and compositional ideas without knowing how to articulate them in grammarianese. In Chapters 3 and 4, I offer you a novel way of learning and applying rules of good composition, a way that makes use of your aesthetic eye and ear. By thinking relationally about the pattern and rhythm of sentences, you can learn how to provide readers with the necessary clues—via punctuation, word choice, and word placement—to follow your line of thought.

Stories unfold in time, which means that the writer of sentences must place each depicted event in the past, present, or future; must account for its state of continuance or completion; and must define its time span in relation to other events. Chapter 5 will help you develop skill in choosing the appropriate time, state, and duration of the storied sentences you write, without your having to be able to define, for example, *past perfect continuing tense*. Again, an appreciation of relationship can be most helpful when you are making time-choices for your sentences.

Readers get lost when they have to leap across gaps in the development of a story or argument, and, conversely, they get bored and irritated when new sentences recycle old ideas. In Chapter 6, I offer a set of "narrative-coherence" questions that you can pose to your manuscript as you write, questions that will help you assess the quality of your idea development at every level of your text: between words, between sentences, between paragraphs, between sections. For illustration, I take a clumsy introduction to a paper on death and dying and use the narrative-coherence questions to organize a series of revisions.

A good mystery needs airtight logic, but few people will read it if it isn't aesthetically appealing. A good social-science manuscript should similarly combine logical consistency and compositional elegance. After all, language is spoken, if only silently, and meaning is married to the music of its telling. Chapter 7 addresses issues of style—how you can better invite readers into your ideas by attending to the flow, rhythm, and pattern of your sentences.

If you are a student in an honors or a graduate program, you know (or soon will discover) how difficult it can be to write a thesis or a dissertation, even (or especially) with ongoing guidance from a committee of faculty members. In the Appendix, I make a number of brief suggestions for how to manage the personal and interpersonal complexities associated with such a significant undertaking.

If you wish to learn more about writing, turn to the Bibliography. It lists several excellent style manuals and writing guides, and it provides the URLs for some fascinating World Wide Web sites.

*Writing Between the Lines* invites you into the joys and challenges of writing social-science mysteries. The pleasures you derive from your efforts will be hard won and well-deserved, for it takes significant work and skill to write simply and elegantly about psychology, politics, society, culture, or economics. Still, as Gregory Bateson well knew, these areas of study all involve recognizing and analyzing *patterns of relationship*. Thus, the process of your writing can resonate with the *content*: You can learn to write relationally about relationships and, in so doing, develop the relational vision of the biographer, the therapist, the social scientist.

# Writing Between the Lines

*Composition in the Social Sciences*

# 1
# Composing: Creating and Editing

*How do I know what I think until I see what I say?*
                                                    —E. M. Forster

*I really do think with my pen, because my head often knows nothing about what my hand is writing.*
                                                    —Ludwig Wittgenstein

*When you write, you lay out a line of words. The line of words is a miner's pick, a wood-carver's gouge, a surgeon's probe. You wield it, and it digs a path you follow. Soon you find yourself deep in new territory. Is it a dead end, or have you located the real subject? You will know tomorrow, or this time next year.*

                                                    —Annie Dillard

*It still comes as a shock to realize that I don't write about what I know: I write in order to find out what I know. Is it possible to convey to a reader the enormous degree of blankness, confusion, hunch and uncertainty lurking in the art of writing?*
                                                    —Patricia Hampl

*Writing is thinking on paper. Anyone who thinks clearly should be able to write clearly—about any subject at all.*
                                                    —William Zinsser

> *The first-draft stupidity of great writers is a shocking and comforting thing to see. What one learns from studying successive drafts is that the writer did not know what he meant to say until he said it.*
>
> —John Gardner

> *The conventional wisdom is that writing reflects thinking. I am drawn to a different position: Writing* is *thinking. . . . Writers who indulge themselves by waiting until their thoughts are "clear" run the risk of never starting at all. . . . Writing is a great way to discover what we are thinking, as well as to discover gaps in our thinking. Unfortunately, that means we must be prepared to catch ourselves red-handed when we seem not to be thinking at all. . . . When the writing is not going well, we probably have nothing (yet) to say; most certainly we are not yet able to say it.*
>
> —Harry Wolcott

When Mozart committed one of his compositions to paper, he seldom made errors in his transcribing, for, at that point in his creative process, he had often worked out all the intricate musical details in his head. He simply wrote down what he already "heard." I know a few writers (and of a few more) who do a pretty fair Mozart imitation when they sit down to compose essays or books. Fingers fly, words flow, and sentences and paragraphs appear, as if by magic. But most of us are not so lucky or so blessed. Whenever I'm writing something that takes me to the edge of my understanding or my ability to describe, my crafting of ideas unfolds tentatively and gradually. My fingers are *able* to fly, but words seldom flow out of me, and my sentences and paragraphs often seem reluctant to be given form too quickly.

For most writers, composing is an ongoing trial-and-error process of false starts, inspirational bursts, and multiple revisions. I certainly can't develop ideas, descriptions, and explanations in my head and then, Mozart-like, transcribe them fully formed into my computer. Immaculate conceptualization lies beyond my reach. I begin with notions that have come to me in the shower, during my conversations or lectures, while I'm reading, and so on (more on that below), but they don't float in my head as complete sentences and well-shaped paragraphs. It takes a keyboard or a pen and paper for the ideas to begin to take coherent form.

As I begin to type, I search for ways of articulating my inklings and images. As I then read what I've written, new thoughts or different possible renderings present themselves, and I write them down too, trying them on for size, shape, aesthetics (see Chapter 7). If I like what I see, I go on to the next idea, the next sentence, the next paragraph. If not, I tinker. As I further refine what I've composed, I further define the shape of my thought, thus allowing me, if necessary, to return again, clearer still, to fiddle with the words in front of me. Back and forth I go, spinning out sentences and paragraphs, zigzagging between what I hear in my head and what I read in front of me, between listening and writing, reading and thinking.

At times I despair at my pace and method, but I garner some encouragement, if not inspiration, from Mozart. When he was treading into new territory (such as when writing his six "Haydn" string quartets), he too worked slowly and found it necessary to sketch his ideas on paper, scratching out those that didn't work. Just about everything I write in my areas of academic interest and expertise challenges me in some significant way, so I seldom compose with brisk abandon.

When you are writing about something familiar or straightforward, you may well be able to proceed smoothly, making few revisions along the way. But if you don't quite yet know what you think or all you want to say about a topic, and/or if you are trying to say something involved or complex, you can't expect your sentences to spill out of you. Scholarly writing requires you to write thoughtfully and think "writefully"—that is, it necessitates your adopting something like the string-quartet, trial-and-error method of composition I have been describing.

At first you may be dismayed to discover how long it takes you to write a sentence that elegantly says something meaningful. With wise practice, the process becomes faster and easier, but I, for one, have found it helpful to readjust my expectations and priorities. I know I must allow ample time to compose a well-honed manuscript, and I care much more that my words flow smoothly for the reader than effortlessly from me. I also find it fascinating to discover what I think by reading what I write.

# Freedom and Form

*No one can hope to write well if he has not mastered—*
*absolutely mastered—the rudiments: grammar and syntax,*
*punctuation, diction, sentence variety, paragraph structure,*
*and so forth.*

—John Gardner

*Let her go! Be careless, reckless! Be a lion, be a pirate! Write*
*any old way.*

—Brenda Ueland

*Rigor and imagination[:] the two great contraries of mental*
*process, either of which by itself is lethal. Rigor alone is par-*
*alytic death, but imagination alone is insanity.*

—Gregory Bateson

*The reason to perfect a piece of prose as it progresses—to*
*secure each sentence before building on it—is that original*
*writing fashions a form. It unrolls out into nothingness. It*
*grows cell to cell, bole to bough to twig to leaf; any careful*
*word may suggest a route, may begin a strand of metaphor*
*or event out of which much, or all, will develop. . . .*

*The reason not to perfect a work as it progresses is that,*
*concomitantly, original work fashions a form the true shape*
*of which it discovers only as it proceeds, so the early strokes*
*are useless, however fine their sheen.*

—Annie Dillard

As a writer in the social sciences rather than the creative arts, you may
have considered your writing primarily as a means to an end, as a way
of getting across essential details about a research project, a theoretical
exploration, a clinical case study. This is a limiting assumption, for
ideas and the language of their expression are not separate: *How* you say
something influences *what* you are able to say. Linguistic dexterity is
essential when refining a conceptual tool, describing a complex
research design, and so on. Such facility with language requires not
only knowledge of the rules of *composition*, but competency in the act

or process of *composing*—that is, with the art of inventing (or receiving) ideas and with the craft of revising sentences and paragraphs.

Writing good scholarly prose is necessarily a *creative* endeavor, requiring a keen eye and an aesthetic ear. Every time you draft a paper for a class, write up a research study for a journal, or compose a thesis or dissertation, you have the opportunity to invent new combinations of words and sentences, new descriptions, new ideas. But creative writing—whether it be of short stories or social science manuscripts—doesn't come cheaply. Demanding as it is rewarding, it requires you to think clearly on paper (or computer screen) and to use this clarity to say something fresh, something that matters.

To write creatively, you must balance *freedom* and *form*. Your thinking needs to be loose enough to let go and invent sentences and ideas, and, conversely, it must be strict enough to demand grammatical, logical, and narrative coherence in whatever you produce. Balance between the two is best achieved by honoring the importance and integrity of each, by not letting one intrude on or limit the other. If you keep your loose and strict thinking relatively distinct, you can, as you write, move back and forth between them in a trial-and-error fashion that jeopardizes neither. When you enter *creation mode*, you free yourself up for the loose thinking of your creative imagination, for insight and inspiration. You save your most rigorous, careful discernment for when you switch over to *edit mode*. Once there, your creative imagination can take a coffee break while you focus on the strict-thinking application of the rules of good form (see chapters 3-7).[1]

Writers vary considerably in how often they zigzag between modes. Some produce a confusing, almost incomprehensible first draft of an entire paper before beginning the process of cleaning it up. Others zip back and forth between loose thinking and strict thinking every time they compose a new sentence. Neither way is better or worse than the other, but each has attendant benefits and drawbacks. By freely creating pages and pages of text before looking back with a discriminating eye, you give your imagination a wonderful opportunity to fly. However, when you return to earth and begin editing, you may find it

---

[1]The two modes necessarily overlap. If, when you are in creation mode, you write in anything approaching grammatically correct sentences, you are wisely allowing compositional rules to shape your imagination. Similarly, you can be creative in your editing process.

next to impossible to organize the results. You can avoid this problem by moving sooner from creation to edit mode; however, if you move too soon, you might prematurely reject a phrase or incipient idea that, with a little more time and freedom to develop, could have been shaped into something significant.

To clarify further the distinction between creating and editing, I will, below, talk about each under a separate heading, offering suggestions and illustrative examples and stories. I will then go on to discuss issues relating to the *combination* of the two modes, that is, to the process of *composing*. Some of what I say may work for you, some may challenge or encourage you to try something different, and some, no doubt, will not work at all. I know of no universal, "right" way to produce a manuscript. Thus, my suggestions are just that—suggestions. They are intended to help you experiment with new writing practices and fashion a flexible, personal approach to creative, scholarly composition.

# Creating

*Writing is no trouble: you just jot down ideas as they occur to you. The jotting is simplicity itself—it is the occurring which is difficult.*

—Stephen Leacock

*Drift, wait, and obey.*

—Rudyard Kipling

*When I'm trying to control the story and make it do something, it doesn't work. When I quit trying, when I let the story tell me what it is, I get to a whole deeper level in my writing. Letting your work do itself this way requires, of course, an extremely intense, alert attitude. It's not passive; it's actively passive, passively active.*

—Ursula LeGuin

*Young people . . . often ask, with youthful bluntness, "Where do you get your ideas from?" My usual, perfectly honest reply is, "I don't get them; they get me."*

—Robertson Davies

> *Nothing helps one to concentrate so well as gazing for a long*
> *time at running water. One remains perfectly still oneself and*
> *all the necessary diversion is provided by the water, which is*
> *never the same for a single instant.*
>                                           —Italo Svevo's Zeno

Some people would argue that writing a paper for a class is less challenging of your imagination than penning a short story. After all, you
don't have to make up characters with names and motives and tangled
histories, and you needn't choose an appropriate setting for the action
or fashion an engaging plot line. Still, you must adopt a theoretical perspective, organize a literature review, link and slice up concepts, and
develop and shape ideas with an eye to narrative and logical coherence.
These too are acts of imagination, and acknowledging them as such
may help you enhance the creative part of your writing process. The
following suggestions concern some physical preparations and mental
practices that can help you receive and capture insights as they come
near. Ever heard of a social-science epiphany?

### ➡ Don't wait for inspiration
If you've been waiting around for inspiration and nothing is happening,
try *writing around* for it instead. The word *inspiration* comes from the
Latin *in* + *spiro*, to breathe in. Just as you must breathe out before
breathing in, you may need to get some ideas out of your system—expire
them—before breathing in some new ones. And the best way to do that
is to write, to try out multiple versions of a sentence or a passage or an
idea, multiple ways of getting something said. By trying, and then eliminating, different attempts, you prepare yourself for inspiration.

### ➡ Stir your mind
The mathematician Norbert Wiener used to stare at a breeze-rippled
curtain while working out his ideas. He liked to bring his thought
experiments to a brain already in motion, stimulated visually by the
movement of the curtain (see Bateson, 1991, pp. 271-275). You can
keep *your* mind in motion, even while playing with a still point in your
writing, by bringing some kind of movement into your work space. Try
holding a problematic sentence or idea in mind as you follow the dance
of a fan-stirred mobile or the melodic line of a piece of music.

## ↠ Keep a journal of ideas

As you work on a manuscript, you necessarily switch back and forth between creation and edit modes innumerable times as you try out new descriptions, make revisions, and develop new drafts. As an adjunct to this zigzag composition process, you may find it helpful to engage in some no-editing-allowed, stream-of-consciousness thinking-writing. You will find it easier to keep your editing ear and eye from adversely affecting the freedom of these creation-mode jottings if you preserve a separate place for them, a place where you can play, knowing you don't have to clean up afterwards. Write down ideas regardless of their apparent irrelevance, and juggle notions that refuse to be pinned down.

Sometimes for this purpose I have tried using hard-bound books full of blank pages, but their formality scares me a little, making my pen shy. I prefer to record my musings directly into my word processor, in a separate "journal" marked *notes* or *ideas*. My fingers are faster than my pen, I can write with my eyes closed if need be, and I then have my descriptions in the computer, so I can copy portions and paste them into the current draft of the paper or chapter I am working on.

Most word-processing programs allow you to keep multiple documents open at a time. Keep your "journal" file active whenever you are writing; you never know when some tangential idea or phrasing will come to you, asking to be written down. Promising yourself to jot it down later is like promising to take out the garbage after dinner: If you don't do it immediately, you will probably forget. And though ignored trash will always stick around to remind you of your lapse, an ignored inkling may up and leave.

## ↠ Suffer from sticky writing instead of writer's block

I don't like the term *writer's block*, because, like all psychological diagnoses, it reifies, and thus dignifies, a description as a condition. If your writing feels stuck *and* you define this feeling as writer's block, then you have two problems, not one, to solve. You have to find a way to get your words flowing again, but to do so, you have to be somehow "cured" of your psychological "affliction."

Rather than suffering from writer's block, try "sticky writing" on for size. Sticky writing comes from not knowing where to go or what to do next in your manuscript *and* being afraid of your not knowing. The solution is simple: Trade your fear for absorbed interest, and the stickiness will disappear.

I once knew a two-year-old girl who was terrified of thunder. Whenever a storm hit, her mother held her close, shielding and comforting her, but the fear refused to be mollified. I suggested to the mother that, in the future, she try loosening her grip a little and saying to her daughter after each thunderclap, "Wow! That was a loud one! I wonder when the next one will come? Do you think it will be even louder?" The approach worked. Once the mother engaged her little girl's anticipation and sense of wonder, fear gave way to curiosity.

Rather than getting a grip on yourself, try relaxing it. Embracing uncertainty is a challenge, but if you never get lost, you'll never stumble across discoveries, surprises, and epiphanies. Try asking yourself what your manuscript is failing to tell you, what you still don't understand, or where the ideas seem to eddy rather than edify. Such questioning needs to be done with the correct tone of voice, though. Read on.

### ➡ Treat yourself and your manuscript with respect

When the words aren't coming and the ideas aren't sparking, do you ever begin questioning yourself, wondering what array of psychological shortcomings could be causing your malaise?

> Am I afraid of graduating? Afraid of success? Lazy? Afraid of getting published? Creatively blocked? Not bright enough? Not disciplined enough? Not mature, knowledgeable, well-read, academic, _____ (fill in the blank) enough?

Such questions, and any answers they might inspire, steal your focus away from your writing, making it that much more difficult to look where your gaze is most needed: toward your text. You can't get much work done while you are recoiling from yourself. So instead of holding your psyche at arm's length, peering at it with dismay, try holding your manuscript close. Become fascinated by its intransigence. If it has been refusing to be written, its integrity deserves your admiration. Ask the text to explain what it needs; it will tell you if you are willing to listen with care and respect.

### ➡ Treat your ideas like a novelist's characters

As the epigrams above suggest, something curious happens to many fiction writers when their imaginations are humming. At some point in their story-creation process, their characters quit "belonging" to them. The narrative takes on a life of its own, and the characters become (seemingly) independent, making their own decisions and acting (for their creator at least) in unpredictable ways. The wise author, at this point, stops trying to dictate what will happen to whom and, instead, lets the characters take the lead in unfolding the story.

Such active passivity, as Ursula LeGuin calls it, needn't be limited to the writing of fictional stories. You can relate to your ideas much like the novelist relates to his or her characters, listening intensely to the quiet voices inside your head and paying respectful heed to what they have to say. If you listen well, you might hear them whisper something you didn't know you knew. And if you write that wisp of an idea down and read it over a number of times, you can then ask it what it thinks needs to be said next. If the idea is kind enough to tell you, then, as Rudyard Kipling says, "obey." If it stays silent, then drift, wait, listen, and ask again.

### ➠ Write like a painter painting

Here's another, more visual, way of describing the receptivity necessary for the creation of ideas. A painter's first brush stroke on a new canvas constrains the choices for color and placement of the next; and these two strokes, combined, similarly limit choices for the third. The painter must stay "in conversation" with his or her canvas, repeatedly "asking" it for guidance in the placement of the next bit of paint. The painting, as much as the painter, determines what can happen next.

You are in much the same position as a painter. Having written a sentence, or even just part of one, you are limited in what you can say next. Rather than trying to do all the figuring out yourself, you can ask your manuscript what stroke, what color and shape it now needs, given what is already in place.

### ➠ Hallucinate a reader

Hung up on whether you need more or less detail, more or less background information? Sometimes writing gets sticky when you don't know how much or little you need to say. Try hallucinating an ideal reader—an intelligent, friendly, reasonably well-read person in your discipline who is interested in your topic, but who lacks your intimate familiarity with it. When you write, write for this person, and when you don't know what to include, request a consultation.

## ➹ Dream up solutions

Sometimes I write myself into a corner. I get to a place in a manuscript where I can't keep going in the direction I've been heading, but all other forward-heading pathways also seem blocked. If this happens to you and it is late enough at night, try going to bed. Just as you are drifting off to sleep, pose the question, "I wonder what solution I will dream up?" When you wake, go straight to your computer and reread the passage that was giving you trouble. If your experience is at all like mine, you will be delighted, and perhaps embarrassed, by how quickly you find a way out of your "no-exit" dilemma. (I must admit that I haven't subjected this compositional method to scientific scrutiny. I can't say how important the question is to the process because I haven't tried *not* asking it as I nod off.)

## ➹ Listen to your body

If your writing is sticky but you are not sleepy enough for bed, here is another idea. You may think it a little odd, but you can always, in the name of science, give it a try anyway. Walk away from your desk, find a spot on the floor where you can feel reasonably comfortable (a carpet or thick rug helps) and lie down on your back. Close your eyes, pose the "I-wonder-what-solution?" question to yourself, breathe comfortably, and wait. Don't actively search for an answer, just let yourself float for a while and wait for some part of your body to twitch. It might be a finger, a muscle in your leg, an eyelid. As soon as you feel a jerk, get up and go back to your keyboard. Reread the section you've been struggling with and see if you now know what to do with it.

# Editing

*Easy reading is damned hard writing.*
> —Nathaniel Hawthorne

*For artists, writing has always meant, in effect, the art of endless revising.*
> —John Gardner

*The essence of writing is rewriting.*
> —William Zinsser

*Creation mode* works best when you can get inside the logic and flow of your manuscript, so far inside that you see your thoughts in what you write and hear your writing in what you think. When you and what you are writing feel "of one mind," you know you are on the right track. But *edit mode* requires a very different relationship with your text. You must be able to read what you've written with a critical eye and an uncompromising ear, and you can't do this while your thoughts and your document are so inextricably connected. If you read with *familiarity*, recognizing the words as yours and knowing what is going to happen next, you won't catch textual rough spots and narrative gaps. You will find yourself following along and nodding at the gist of your argument— "Yeah, okay, sure, that's pretty much what I had in mind"—rather than assessing its integrity. To edit your work well, you need to find ways to *defamiliarize* what you've written. Can it stand on its own? You won't know until you read it from a distance—as an outsider, a stranger.

## ➡ Change hats

Put on a hat, print off your manuscript, sit in a different chair, use a special pen, change the background music or your shoes or your glasses— do whatever is necessary to transform yourself into the role of editor. By demonstrably shifting the context of your reading into edit mode, you can help alter your relationship to your text. The more you feel like a stranger to the words in front of you, the easier it will be to replace the question, "What did I mean here?" with the more helpful query, "What does this paragraph manage or fail to say?"

## ➡ Give it time

One of the simplest, but not always most practical, ways to engineer distance between you and your words is to put your manuscript away for a week or two. When you pick it up after such a break, both of you will feel fresh again, and you can better evaluate what is there on the page. Read it straight through, from start to finish, circling, along the way, places where you get lost, confused, bored, or irritated. Don't stop and go over problematic sections on that first read-through—you must race to keep ahead of your familiarity. Later, you can go back and figure out how and why this sentence or that paragraph doesn't work, demanding the same clarity you would from something written by someone else.

You may not have enough leeway in your schedule to allow for such time away from your entire manuscript, but you can achieve a similar effect by letting part of your paper sit—perhaps overnight—while you shift to writing another section. As you focus *here*, you can forget, for a little while, the particularities of what you wrote *there*.

## ➜ Give it voice

To edit well, you must focus not on what you *wanted to say*, but on what you *actually wrote*. Were you repetitive? How clumsy was your phrasing? Any nonsensical abstractions? You will more easily catch such problems when you can *hear* your sentences articulated. So you have a choice: either develop your capacity for auditory hallucination, or, if you can put up with ridicule from those within earshot, read your work aloud. Let your ear help your eye. And who knows? If your social science aspirations don't develop as hoped, at least you will have done some preparation for a career on the stage.

## ➜ Take a bicycle ride

Prior to starting a major project on our house or yard—painting, planting new trees, landscaping our garden—my wife and I ride our bicycles through our favorite neighborhoods, looking for ideas. We go in search of particularities. This time it might be house colors; next, the placement and variety of trees or flowers. As we ride along, looking at familiar homes with our defined, pre-chosen blinders, we always notice details that had previously escaped our attention. Such filtered viewing helps us see with a sensitivity and specificity that would otherwise be difficult to achieve. On one outing, instead of trees, we notice pine, live oak, seagrape, foxtail or queen palms; on another, instead of flowers, we see pentas, blue daze, lantana, hibiscus, impatiens.

When you enter edit mode, you can't pay attention to everything at the same time. Your sensitivity can be heightened by taking numerous bicycle trips through your manuscript, each time with a different predefined filter to delimit your viewing. Identify each of your weaknesses—misplaced, misused, or missing punctuation marks; sentence structure; typos (although many can now be caught by computers, their are still those that escape the notice of a spell checker, such as *their* earlier in this sentence); citations; tenses; idea development; whatever—and then make a number of blindered rides through your manuscript, each one devoted to looking for a special kind of potential problem.

## ⟶ Give Katherine a red pen

Remember your hallucinated reader, the one for whom you write? Let's say you've decided her name is Katherine. (Who says only fiction writers get to make up characters and names?) If you respected Katherine's advice back when you were trying to decide what needed saying, why not let her voice an opinion on how well you said it? Give her a red pen and ask her to comment. Given all you have written for her, doesn't she owe you a favor?

## ⟶ Seek outside criticism

If you are enrolled in a traditional psychology program or you work with people who know their DSM, you might not want to talk too much about Katherine. A useful and more socially acceptable, albeit more prosaic, way of getting an outsider's perspective is to give drafts of your work to flesh-and-blood people. Don't be surprised, though, if you receive contradictory criticism. Whenever more than one person reads a draft of your work, you will likely get divergent suggestions for needed changes. You might be able to dismiss some such comments as symptomatic of sloppy reading, ignorance, or bad intent, but don't rush to interpret diversity of opinion as evidence of the unreliability of your reviewers. Consider the possibility that the source of confusion lies not in your readers but in your writing. Before you begin making substantive alterations, look carefully at the quality of your sentences and the clarity of your ideas.

A friend in graduate school gave each of his dissertation committee members a draft of his dissertation proposal, hoping they would approve his setting a date to defend it orally (that is, to discuss his research question, review the literature relevant to his study, and outline his proposed research methods). To his dismay, they told him he wasn't ready, and they gave him numerous recommendations for changes to his manuscript. Unfortunately, many of the suggestions contradicted one another, so my friend felt trapped. He didn't know how to satisfy one committee member without dissatisfying another (see the Appendix for more on the pragmatics and politics of writing a thesis or dissertation).

I found the proposal interesting, but I noticed many awkward sentences and fuzzy ideas. I helped my friend improve the quality and clarity of his writing, and when the proposal read much more smoothly, he took it back to his committee for a second look. He hadn't yet made any of the substantive content changes they had requested, but they no longer thought them necessary. Each committee member had offered ideas for how to improve a confusing manuscript, but no one believed his or her suggestions to be the only solution. Once the proposal was clear, all were satisfied, and my friend got his defense date.

## Creating and Editing: Composing

*The artist Paul Klee once told his students that "art is exactitude winged by intuition." I like that equally as a definition of good writing.*

—William Zinsser

*Everybody is talented, original, and has something important to say.*

—Brenda Ueland

*A careful first draft is a failed first draft.*

—Patricia Hampl

*For many years I have done my serious writing, that intended for publication, almost exclusively during morning hours, from nine to noon or half past twelve. . . . About one and a half manuscript pages constitute my daily stint. This slow method of working springs from severe self-criticism and high requirements in matters of form.*

—Thomas Mann

*I have come to the conclusion that the majority of writing problems I encounter in student papers should not be considered problems so much as symptoms. I reached this conclusion after observing how miraculously most of them disappeared after one genuine problem had been treated: the failure to think well. Thinking well, in this case, means thinking the way a skilled writer thinks.*

—John Trimble

*A lot of people have the mistaken conception that writers sit down at the computer and words just flow. Most of the process of writing is the process of thinking, which is not always done at the computer. It may even look like wasting time.*

—Barbara Ehrenreich

Whether you move back and forth between creation and edit modes frequently or intermittently, the challenge is the same: to evolve a personal, compositional process that allows for both invention and scrutiny. When you write with such a balance, you can learn as much or more from your writing as you do from your reading.

## ➡ Don't ask

My wife and I both cherish putting our young son to bed, and we have always alternated nights. However, when he was two years old, he went through a period when he would only grant the privilege to his mother. I wasn't fond of the arrangement, but neither my wife nor I could budge him from his decision. Not wanting to force him to let me tuck him in, I would pose the possibility as a question. Every night as I kissed him goodnight, I asked, "Daddy put you to bed?" "No," he would reply firmly, "Mommy."

One night at bedtime I tried something new. Rather than *ask* him, I *told* him what was going to happen, and I gave him a chance to prepare. "Tonight," I said, "Mommy puts you to bed, and tomorrow night, Daddy." "Okay," he said contentedly. The next night we reminded him it was my turn and he happily agreed. The situation was resolved simply by turning a question into a statement of fact.

If you don't ask a two-year-old whether you can put him to bed, you won't need to be told "no." And if you don't ask yourself the question, "Should I start (or keep) writing now?" you won't need to choose "no."

One of my students once commented on how disciplined I am about writing. The description didn't fit for me. Composing with words would hold no allure if I needed to order myself to "sit down and stay put!" I prefer to feel pulled, not pushed, toward my computer (see below).

You can take some of the discipline out of your writing process by setting a time to start and then simply keeping to it. You don't wrangle or negotiate with yourself about whether to show up at work on time, you just do it. Once the decision is made, waffling is a superfluous luxury. Writing takes no discipline, just commitment.

## ➤ Let your curiosity pull you

I'm hopeless when engrossed in a novel. I live to get lost in it and to find out what happens next, and, to that end, I'm quite willing to let other parts of my life slide or stack up (as the case may be). I find it easier to turn pages than write them, so I mostly avoid novels while I'm working on demanding manuscripts. Instead, I redirect my curiosity to wondering what will happen next in the piece that I'm writing. Posing that question, I feel drawn to my computer. The satisfaction of finding out the answer doesn't come as quickly as with novels, but it keeps me writing and it lasts longer.

## ➤ Keep climbing

When I was younger, living alone, I did my best writing in 12- to 16-hour chunks. I would sometimes walk around and eat and so on, but like an actor staying in role when off the set, I held my focus even when I wasn't sitting in front of my computer. By immersing myself in and staying with a set of ideas for an extended period, I could reach a place where new ideas, new ways of saying things, would come to me. All I had to do was be ready to write them down.

If you lengthen your writing time, you might discover something new about your ability to create. Say you typically give yourself a couple of hours to get something down on paper, and if nothing is happening, you stop and do other things. But what if, like me, you need three or four hours of concentrated immersion before your imagination even begins to wake up? You may have been short-circuiting your creativity by quitting too soon.

I once heard a mountain climber describe his ascent to the top of Everest: "I climbed and climbed and climbed to the point of absolute exhaustion, to where I knew I couldn't take one more step (long pause) and then I continued climbing for another 14 hours." When you keep going beyond your limit of endurance, new possibilities sometimes open up. Like the round-the-clock labor negotiators who achieve breakthroughs in talks after too many hours "at the table," you may get a breakthrough after too many hours at your computer. And if you hold the mountain climber's Everest experience in mind, you will know what to do when you get too tired: Check your fingers and toes for frostbite and resume typing.

## ✺ Wake up

As an undergraduate, I loved writing into the early morning—it fit my lifestyle and accorded with my definition of myself as a "night person." But while writing my master's thesis, I started noticing that my best ideas were coming to me upon waking or while taking my morning shower. I thus began turning my computer on as soon as I woke up; when I emerged from the shower, I could go over and start writing, sometimes while still dripping. Since then, I have continued to favor mornings for composing, so much so that I've evolved into a "morning person."

Question your assumptions about the time of day or night when you are at your creative best, and try writing when you least expect to be awake, never mind alert.

## ✺ Schedule writing appointments with yourself

With my family and my teaching responsibilities, I now don't have the luxury to write for extended periods, so I have adopted a "quality time" strategy. I can now do more with eight hours than I could before, and I can even make good use of a two-hour period by devoting the first 10 or 15 minutes to soaking myself in whatever I was last working on. (I've tried unsuccessfully to write in one-hour blocks, so I avoid frustration by using such time for reading or taking notes.)

I can only make these shorter times productive, though, when I protect myself from potential distractions. The easiest way I've found to do this is to schedule writing appointments with myself. Here is the reasoning. When I schedule a meeting with a student or a client, I block that time out, and once the person arrives, all of my attention is focused on our conversation. I don't take or make telephone calls, and I don't interrupt our time to chat with other people. I decided at some point that if I can accord such respect to people, why not to my writing? I thus schedule meetings with my computer, during which time my manuscripts and I engage in uninterruptible conversations.

## ✺ Give priority to your writing

Some people take care of their correspondence and e-mail before getting started for the day (or night) on their current writing project. This works for me if I'm writing to others about the ideas I'm presently developing, but otherwise I find it distracting—it keeps me from settling in. I save my freshest time for me.

## ➡ Settle in

Chick Corea, one of the most gifted of jazz pianists, likes to transition into a song by improvising a preparatory prelude. "In the jazz music that I come from," he says, "piano introductions have always been a way to settle in, to connect with yourself and summon up the song" (in Scherman, 1996). As you begin to write, you too must connect with yourself and summon up your as-yet-unfinished composition. Consider, then, looking for preparatory rituals that can invite you across the threshold of your manuscript, that can help you gather your thoughts and settle in. Just don't get too carried away. Most of us, like the novelist and essayist Barbara Kingsolver (1995), can't afford the luxury of self-indulgence:

> My jaw drops when I hear of the rituals some authors use to put themselves in the so-called mood to write: William Gass confesses to spending a couple of hours every morning photographing dilapidated corners of his city. . . . [Diane Ackerman] listens to music obsessively, then speed-walks for an hour, every single day. "I don't know whether this helps or not," she allows. . . . "My muse is male, has the radiant, silvery complexion of the moon, and never speaks to me directly."
>
> My muse wears a baseball cap, backward. The minute my daughter is on the school bus, he saunters up behind me with a bat slung over his shoulder and says oh so directly, "Okay, author lady, you've got six hours till that bus rolls back up the drive. You can sit down and write, *now*, or you can think about looking for a day job." (pp. 95-96)

## ➡ Take care of your body

Jack London, the novelist, held many manual jobs in his life, including shoveling coal on a steamer and working in a sawmill, but he said that the worst backache in his life resulted from sitting down at his brother-in-law's typewriter. Physical discomfort often precludes playful improvisation, so it makes sense to attend to your chair, the position of your keyboard, the light in the room, and so on.

I took up running when I started my doctoral dissertation, and it helped not only my physical well-being but also my state of mind. When I felt too overwhelmed and discouraged to write, I would go jogging. During the last stretch of the run, my muscles tired and my breathing labored, I would, of course, want to stop. Instead, I picked up my pace and let the metaphoric significance of that wash over me. I could then come back to my manuscript, my body revitalized, my determination renewed.

A theorist I know runs marathons, and he tells me that he generates his best ideas while running. I need a keyboard or a pen if I'm going to do any refined thinking, so that doesn't work for me, but you might give it a try.

## ➻ Play with mediums and settings

When I purchased my first computer in the second year of my master's program, I had only recently taught myself how to touch type. I had always successfully composed my papers long-hand, so I'm not sure why I decided to experiment with writing directly onto the computer, but I gave it a try—and immediately hated it. It felt unnatural, sterile, and clumsy, and I came very close to retreating to my fountain pen. But I persevered, and once my fingers could keep up with my thoughts, I was hooked. I now write almost everything with my keyboard, but I haven't thrown away my pen. Sometimes the best way to loosen an idea or tighten a description is to take it and some paper and go sit for a while in a coffee shop, at the beach, or under a tree. It helps me to use a pen that writes well and feels good in my hand, but I avoid paper that looks too elegant. I want to feel comfortable making a mess of the page as I try to sort out the mess in my head.

## ➻ Keep your voice and sense of humor

Some of my students complain that the conventions of academic prose stifle their creativity. Attempting to become upstanding members of the social scientific community, they feel themselves losing their voice, their unique perspective, their sense of humor.

As the author of the only article listed in PsycINFO with "zucchini mush" in its title (Flemons, 1987) and someone who finds scholarly writing a most satisfying creative pursuit, I am hard pressed to lend a sympathetic ear to such moaning. As Bateson makes clear in the epi-graph on page 4, all forms of creative expression—including those of the arts—involve some kind of *rule-bound* play of the imagination.

I must admit that social science authors can sound dour, sterile, and pretentious at times, but you needn't aspire to this standard. Our field needs your wit, your appreciation for irony, and, most especially, your distinctive and creative voice.

## ➤ Exercise patience

I use my computer and a projection unit to help me teach my writing course, displaying the output from my word processor on a large screen so everyone can see what I'm doing. I once took all three hours of a class to demonstrate the reworking of a paragraph. Although devoting this much time to a few sentences isn't at all unusual for me, it was new for many of the students. As I narrated my process, describing my dilemmas and explaining my choices, they developed an appreciation for the kind of time and commitment it can sometimes take to say something well.

## ➤ Stand by your words

I can play casually with an idea in my head and in dialogue with my colleagues and students, but I can't play seriously until I'm writing, until I'm composing on paper or computer screen. I have to read (and hear) what I've written before deciding whether an idea is viable and contextually relevant. When I decide that an idea can stand on its own and can stand in relation to other ideas, then I'm willing to stand by *it*. As the poet Ezra Pound realized, the Chinese word meaning *trust* is a picture of a person 亻 standing by his or her word 言 : 信. I keep revising my work until I believe what I have written, until it rings true to my ear.

## ➤ Back up to go forward

Sometimes as I'm composing a sentence, I can already hear the next one, can already feel it tingling on the tips of my fingers, impatiently waiting to be typed. More frequently, I am the one who waits. Having completed a sentence, finished a thought, I hear only silence, feel only the keyboard.

To prepare for the arrival of more words, I back up a bit and reread what I've written, up to end of the sentence I have just completed—to the border between what I have so far thought and have yet to think. Again and again I back up and read forward, arriving expectantly at the brink of my unfolding narrative, asking the manuscript to tell me what next to write down. When a composable idea presents itself, I fit it into place and then use it as the new launching edge for the question, "What next?" If, after much patience and many iterations of my back-and-forth process, I don't get an answer, I pose a different question to my manuscript: "Where am I?" This is a scarier one to ask, because of the potential for hearing that most unsettling of replies: "You are lost."

#### ⚬ Lose your way, then get your bearings

If you develop a detailed outline in advance of starting to write and you follow it closely, it can sometimes keep you from getting lost. But blithely following pre-ordained pathways also keeps you from thinking. Mindful writing—writing as a form of thinking—will always take you off course, because as you compose your sentences, new ideas are formed and evolved, and you can never know in advance just where they will steer you. To write creatively—thoughtfully—you need the freedom to get disoriented. However, you also need the ability to regain your bearings, lest you wander aimlessly, rambling on without direction or purpose.

Losing your way, finding it, losing it again—this is how to proceed, how to discover what you think, what you have to say. And when this groping takes you in unanticipated directions (as it always will), pause every so often and survey your current position. Look at what you've written from the vantage of your outline, examine your outline from the vantage of what you've written, and then make some assessments and choices. If you are off track, try adapting your outline to accommodate the new direction you've taken. You may be able to keep your meanderings if you can construct a transition from where you are to where you need to get. Be careful, though, that you don't end up with a narrative route too tortuous for your readers to follow—you don't want to solve your problem of being lost by foisting your confusion on your readers. (See Chapter 6 for a method of assessing and improving the coherence of your idea development.) Alternatively, your "detour" might work well as a footnote, or, with some further development, as its own section. Most dramatically, if, on the way to losing your way, you've managed to say something significant, you might restructure your entire outline so that your minor detour becomes a main thoroughfare.

## ➬ Disentangle your narrative thread

Sometimes I know I haven't lost the thread of my narrative, but I feel tangled up in it, unable to move to the next paragraph or the next section. If this ever happens to you, take the paragraph that seems most troublesome and try playing around with the wording and rhythm of the sentences and the sequence of ideas. By changing how the narrative is woven, you may happen on a way of unsnarling your paper and your thinking. For example, see what happens if you rewrite the first sentence of the paragraph. Does this allow you to say something different in subsequent sentences? Or move the third or fourth sentence of the paragraph up to the beginning and shift the first sentence down, perhaps to the end. Does this loosen any knots?

## ➬ Look for solutions across the road

My friends David and Kathee love books almost as much as they love their daughter, Sarah. They started reading to her when she was just a baby, and, delighting in her growing interest in words and stories, they continued their daily ritual for many years. Sarah was obviously a bright child, so her parents were understandably puzzled when, by third grade, she still hadn't started reading on her own. They tried encouraging and cajoling her, and they talked seriously with her, but nothing helped. Finally, after months of worry and failed efforts, they asked Sarah's teacher for names of remedial tutors and learning specialists. Instead, she gave them an odd suggestion: "Let her cross Victoria Drive by herself."

David and Kathee had been reluctant to let their young daughter negotiate alone the traffic on this busy street, but they were ready to try anything, so they followed the teacher's advice. Within a week, Sarah was reading at grade level.

"Why did the girl cross the road?"

"To get a bachelor's in English."[2]

And what does this story have to do with writing? If you are stuck at some point in your manuscript and all your focused efforts prove fruitless, try looking for a solution some place other than where you would

[2]And she did, from the University of Victoria.

expect to find it. More than once I have fixed a major problem on, say, page 15 by tinkering with something small back on page 7 or 8. You might also reflect on Harry Wolcott's point, quoted in the epigram at the beginning of the chapter: Words won't come if you don't yet have anything useful to say. When multiple attempts at writing aren't helping you work out your ideas, try reading more and/or thinking away from your computer screen. You might find a solution to that conundrum on page 2 by crossing the road—to the library, the gym, or the park.

### ⚬ Try film-director avoidance strategies

No doubt your home is the cleanest when you have a blank computer screen staring you in the face and a deadline hanging over your head. Messy kitchens and dusty floors look ever so inviting when you feel stuck, and, indeed, sometimes the clutter in your head can be cleared up by bringing some order to your living space. But if you keep looking for one more closet to clean, or you start volunteering to spruce up your neighbor's yard, you might try a different kind of avoidance behavior.

Instead of walking away from the computer when you are stuck at a particular place in your manuscript (unless you are on your way to sleep, lie on the floor, exercise, or do some pen-and-paper thinking), try taking a break from your frustration by emulating a film director. When the shooting of a particular scene isn't going well, a director may try multiple takes, but if the actors are pushed too far, frustrations can reverberate throughout the rest of the production. Since the scenes of a film are shot out of sequence anyway, the director can stay on schedule and avoid complications by putting a difficult scene on hold and moving on to others less challenging. Later, he or she can return to it, once success has been achieved elsewhere.

### ⚬ Treat your confusion like a dead canary

A student once gave me an intriguing paper that confused me. I am typically bothered by confusion, so I kept reading until I could put my finger on the source of her problem. When I met with her, I asked if she had noticed anything awry in what she had written. She said that she had known something was wrong all along, but she couldn't figure out what it was, so she had given up looking, hoping no one else would notice.

Miners once used canaries as an early warning system. A keeled-over bird signaled a gas leak or an oxygen problem, and the workers would then know to exit the mine immediately. If they ignored the canary, they imperiled their lives.

As you write, treat your confusion as if it were a dead canary. Well, almost—don't respond to it by running for oxygen. Instead, consider your confusion an early warning system for your readers. Trust that if you are puzzled by what you've written, your readers will be utterly perplexed. By ignoring your muddle, you imperil the logic of your paper and the good humor of your readers.

When my student and I sorted out the source of the confusion in her paper—it had to do with using a central metaphor in two or three different, conflicting ways—she was able to reorganize and rewrite her work so as to highlight and clarify the very point she had earlier tried to fudge.

Try sorting out a muddled passage in a paper by reading the passage again and again, each time using one of the following questions to focus your scrutiny (see also Chapter 6):

- Is each sentence grammatically correct? Can it stand alone?
- Are any of the sentences vague?
- What are the relationships between the sentences? Between the ideas?
- What explicit assumptions does the passage make? Implicit?
- How many times does the passage make each point?
- Can the explanation be simplified?
- What ideas does it lump together?
- At what point do I get lost? What am I saying just before then?

## ➡ Restart fresh

If you get a paper or a chapter back from a professor or editor with a request to "make substantial revisions before resubmitting," try starting fresh. Read all the comments closely, get clear on what didn't work, and then set the critiqued draft aside. Treat it like an abandoned gold mine—an interesting spot to visit and to pick up the odd shiny bit of treasure, but not a place to spend a considerable amount of time.

This approach may initially seem riskier, as well as more difficult and time-consuming, than tinkering with what you've already done, but if your manuscript requires significant changes, you need the freedom to find a different way of putting it together. The next suggestion proposes that you adopt an attitude that allows you such freedom at *all* levels of your composing.

## ◆ Let go

When the Zen Buddhist teacher Mu-nan was getting close to death, he named his student Shoju his successor. Calling Shoju to him, Mu-nan handed him a treasured possession, a symbol of his new position as Master—a book that had been passed down from teacher to teacher for seven generations. Shoju took the book and threw it onto the burning coals of a brazier. Mu-nan, looking in horror as the flames devoured the revered text, shouted, "What are you doing?!"

Shoju yelled back, "What are you saying?!" (see Reps, 1957, pp. 80-81).

If you aren't familiar with the philosophical tenets of Zen Buddhism, Shoju's actions may appear disrespectful and inappropriate. Actually, they aptly demonstrate his grasp of and respect for Zen and his suitability as a teacher. Shoju put into practice the Buddhist commitment to non-attachment: He threw away a book that would have told him how to throw away books.

You needn't become a Buddhist to become a good writer, but it helps to act like one while you are composing. If you work hard on a sentence for a few hours, a paragraph for a day or two, or a paper for a couple of months, you will naturally feel attached to what you have composed. This isn't a problem unless the sentence doesn't fit, the paragraph doesn't flow, or the paper as a whole doesn't cohere. Unfortunately, unless you write papers like Mozart wrote symphonies, you will always encounter such problems, because your work will always require revision. How then do you respond to criticism (your own or someone else's), and, more importantly, what do you do with the words, the ideas that feel so much a part of you? Who wants to undergo corrective surgery, or worse, amputation?

When I had finished an initial polished draft of the first 40 or so pages of my master's thesis, I handed them to the chair of my committee with a sense of relief and anticipation. I liked what I had done, and, as I waited for him to get back to me, I imagined his responding with all sorts of glowing remarks. He didn't. He thought I had gotten off on the wrong foot and with the wrong tone of voice. I needed to try again, he said, virtually from the beginning.

I learned a lot about attachment that day and over the next few weeks. Although I trusted my chair and respected his criticism, I still struggled to preserve as much of the 40 pages as possible. Trying my best to rescue this sentence and that paragraph, I created a patchwork mess. Finally, *finally*, I took a deep breath, put it all aside, and started again. What a difference that simple act of non-attachment made! Rethinking the logic and structure of the entire thesis, I streamlined the organization, clarified my ideas, and changed my tone. From that point on, the writing proceeded with relative ease.

It takes courage to look your treasured words in the eye and say, "No, I can't use you here." You foster courage by committing yourself, as you evaluate your work, to the quality of what you read rather than the quantity of or fondness for what you've written. By cultivating Shoju's ability to let go of valuable possessions, by practicing non-attachment as you write, you gain in freedom and clarity what you lose in pages and time.

## ◆ Hang on

I enjoy cooking, particularly when I can create a new dish by combining leftovers from different meals. I'm not sure whether this proclivity was influenced or occasioned by an analogous writing habit, but the same principle governs my involvement in each activity: I assume that yesterday's tidbits can add much to today's creation, but, before I use them, I check for mold.

Yes, I know, I just got through suggesting that you practice "letting go." But allow me to add a small addendum: After earmarking a sentence or passage as unworkable, but before hitting the *delete* key, put it aside for a while, in a place where you can find it if you need it.[3]

Here's how I typically do it: Rather than writing a whole first draft of something, I usually compose sentence by sentence, paragraph by paragraph. I try a version of a sentence and when it doesn't work, I move it down the screen a way and go back and try again. On a day when nothing is clicking, I may stack up two or five or more rejected versions before I get something I like. I continue in this fashion, sen-

---

[3]Unfortunately, adopting this suggestion will mean giving up the romantic act of crumpling your rejected prose into a ball and throwing it into your recycling bin.

tence by sentence, until I have a paragraph that works, then I go and read through all my rejects, looking for better words or phrases—tid-bits—than those I used in my finished version. When I'm satisfied that I've got the best paragraph possible, I delete all the early-draft sentences and go on.

The next time I sit down to write, I begin by reading what I last produced. The text almost always needs further tidying up, but sometimes portions of it require significant revision. Before embarking on a rewrite, I copy and paste troublesome passages to another place in the document (sometimes to just below the section I'm working on, sometimes to the last page), just in case my efforts make matters worse. If still more extensive revisions are needed, I save the current manuscript as *draft1* and then create a new document (*draft2*) where I can make and house my changes. Once I've finished my final draft, I skim through my cast-off paragraphs and earlier drafts before deleting them. I don't want to throw out anything that isn't yet moldy.

## •• Back up

If photocopy machines and word processors had been available when the novelist Malcolm Lowry was writing (he died in 1957), the curse on his manuscripts might not have been so calamitous. The only typescript of *Ultramarine*, his first novel, disappeared when the briefcase of one of the publisher's directors was stolen; *In Ballast to the White Sea* was destroyed when Lowry's house burned down; and the manuscript of *Under the Volcano* was lost (but later found). But who knows whether Lowry would have bothered to safeguard his work even if he could have easily duplicated it?

I know of a former doctoral student who could have easily made copies of his research data and his almost-completed dissertation, but he never quite got around to it. Using the trunk of his car as his safe-deposit box, he kept his data and manuscript with him at all times. This worked fine until some Lowry luck struck: His car was stolen and his many years of work, along with his Lowry pluck, was lost for good. He abandoned his research and never finished his doctoral degree.

Draw a picture of Lowry hunched over his typewriter, rewriting *Ultramarine*, and tape it to the bottom of your computer monitor. Or buy a small dye-cast car at a toy store and use it, trunk open, as a paper-weight. Do whatever it takes to acquire the habit of backing up your documents *before* your hard disk crashes, *before* someone steals your car.

Even though my word processor automatically backs up the on-screen file every ten minutes, I still manually save my work whenever I write a sentence or two that I like. In addition, I copy my files from the hard drive to a floppy disk whenever I get a good paragraph or page written. Before turning my computer off at the end of a writing session, I double check that my floppy copies are as current as those on my hard disk, and I may even print off the day's work. I keep at least three updated versions of my manuscripts (some on disk, one on paper) in at least two different locations. This is my insurance against Lowry luck—fire, theft, computer failure, human (my) error, or human (my children's) curiosity.

### Write for you

Wynton Marsalis, a jazz (and classical) trumpeter highly regarded for his impeccable technique, tells the story of one his more significant learning experiences. As a high school student, he learned how to dazzle audiences with pyrotechnic improvisations. But his father, Elias, himself a jazz pianist, remained unimpressed: "Son," he said to Wynton, "those who play for applause, that's all they get" (Marsalis, 1995, p. 134).

Receiving an "A" on a paper feels great, and getting an article published is uplifting, but if you write for a grade, for a professor's admiration, or for your colleagues' respect, that's all you'll get. Write for yourself, your understanding, your pleasure, your own clarity of thought, and your writing will continue to mean something to you after the course is over, after you graduate, after the applause dies down.

# 2
# Social Science Papers

*Scientific writing [is] a form of rhetoric, meant to persuade.*
—Howard Becker

Each of the subgenres of social science writing—quantitative and qualitative research reports, meta-analyses and other reviews, case studies, theoretical investigations, descriptions of training protocols—has relatively distinct conventions governing the content and structure of manuscripts. Some of these conventions, most notably those for empirical research reports, are more standardized than others, but all are designed to help readers easily follow and evaluate the author's logic, scholarship, and method.

Style manuals, such as *The Publication Manual of the American Psychological Association* (a.k.a. the *APA Manual*), as well as various introductory research texts, provide useful protocols for organizing different kinds of papers. However, the best way to learn the necessary conventions is to go to the library and search out the top journals in your (or a related) discipline. Read 10 or 20 or 30 articles of the kind you are preparing to write and track how the authors present their material:

- What do they *leave out* of their abstract?
- How do they introduce their study?
- What subheadings do they use?
- When and how do they talk about literature relevant to their work?

- How do they discuss the generation and analysis of their data?
- Where do they present their criticisms of their own work?
- How conservative/daring are they in the conclusions they present?
- What questions are they better able to ask by the end of their paper?

Pose such queries while reading a stack of articles, and you will learn much of what you need to know about your subgenre of choice. Below I offer some ideas and suggestions to augment this learning. But first I would like to talk briefly about mastering all those persnickety rules from your discipline's style manual (such as the *APA Manual*).

A social scientist I once knew asked me to read a paper he was about to send off to a journal for review. The manuscript was interesting and well written, but it was full of small APA errors—everything from the layout of the title page and the placement of page numbers to the citation of sources and the formatting of the reference list. When I pointed out the glitches, he said that he had purposefully left them in place. He reasoned that niggling details would distract the reviewers' attention, making it less likely that they would notice more significant lapses in the manuscript. I suspect that the author's strategy was more an excuse for laziness than a psychologically sophisticated master plan, but he had a good publishing record, so who knows? Nevertheless, my experience as a reviewer of journal submissions and a reader of student papers does not support his speculation. If I encounter too many careless errors, I start grinding my teeth, and this inevitably affects my assessment of a paper's content, coherence, and relevance.

I suggest you thoroughly learn the nuances of your discipline's stylistic conventions (and if you are submitting a paper for publication, any idiosyncratic divergences requested by the journal to which you are sending it). The better you attend to small details, the more you communicate to your readers that you are fully versed in their academic culture and that you care about your work.

Of course, if you fancy yourself a compositional descendent of someone like George Herbert Mead, you might be able to claim that the work of inventing marvelous ideas leaves you no time to bother with trifling stylistic conventions.[1] But then, like him, you will need a

---

[1]Charles Morris, in his preface to George H. Mead's *Mind, Self, and Society*, said, "His thought was too rich in internal development to allow him to set down his ideas in ordered array. His genius expressed itself best in the lecture room" (Mead, 1962, p. vii).

group of devoted students to write down your lectures and turn them into books. Short of that, you might try learning the necessary rules. Besides, are you sure you *aren't* a "detail person"? If you can recognize particular makes and years of cars, identify individual instruments within a symphony, remember batting averages and draft picks, or distinguish between Coke and Pepsi, Bud and Coors, or a merlot and a cabernet, then you have all the discernment necessary for learning the fine points of preparing your manuscript.

## How to Write Social Science Manuscripts

Sophisticated readers of mysteries (that is, readers who know the genre well) come to new novels with pre-set expectations, established by their previous reading. As the plot unfolds, they anticipate learning about a victim of an unsolved crime, a sleuth and motivated suspects, an investigation, a series of seemingly unrelated clues, a solution that connects these unconnected dots, and an explanation that clarifies what happened and whodunnit. In a sense, readers pose an ongoing series of questions of the text—Who was killed? How was it done? Who wanted to do it? Why? Who knew about it? How did the killer get away with it?—and their satisfaction grows as the text responds to their curiosities.

Sophisticated readers of social science mysteries also come to new manuscripts with pre-established expectations and a desire for answers. You can expect their curiosities to remain relatively consistent, regardless of the type of paper you have written (empirical investigation, clinical case study, ethnography, organizational or political analysis, review of other studies, theoretical investigation, etc.), or the topic, method, or approach you took. As you write, it might be helpful to keep in mind the sorts of questions your readers are probably going to be asking, if not explicitly, then implicitly, as they follow your plot.

### During the Introduction
- What is this paper about?
- What is the historical/philosophical/scientific context of the work?
- What specifically is the author seeking/exploring?
- Why this particular study? How is it relevant?

- Is the topic researchable?
- Do the topic and approach make sense?

**During the Literature Review**
- Who else has conducted related research?
- What did these other authors find/discover/invent?[2]
- Is the author balanced and thorough in his or her discussion of these studies?
- How does this study relate to (fit with and depart from) these others?
- What gap does this study fill?

**During the Method**
- How was the research conducted?
- Does the mode of inquiry match the research question(s) posed?
- How credible was the research? Can it be trusted?
- Can the author be trusted? Does he or she recognize limitations of and problems with the study?

**During the Results/Analysis**
- What did the author find/discover/invent?

**During the Discussion**
- What does the author make of the results?
- Why do the results matter?
- How do the results relate to those of earlier studies?
- Implications and ramifications?

If you can anticipate the queries your manuscript is likely to inspire, you can organize it accordingly. Do your best to provide readers with the information they require or desire just as—or just before—they begin formulating a question about it. In so doing, you will be like a good host, anticipating the needs of valued guests.

Writers of fiction can afford to tease, frustrate, and unsettle their readers from time to time. But you don't have this luxury, even if you have the skill to pull it off. Social-science readers want straightforward clarity, not beguiling ambiguity. Of course, you can never be completely forthcoming, at least not all at once. You are limited, like all writers,

[2]The version of the question asked will depend on the philosophical assumptions held. A positivist will pose a different question from a constructivist or social constructionist.

by the linear structure of language. Thus, your ideas must be offered sequentially, and your readers must be willing to wait in suspense to find out where you will go next.

Just where and how comprehensively you answer your readers' emerging questions will depend, in large part, on the kind of manuscript you are writing. Arraying your answers within the standard empirical-research progression—*Introduction, Literature Review, Method, Results, Discussion*—makes sense if you are writing, say, a paper about a laboratory experiment or a survey you conducted. But if your paper is theoretical in nature, or if you are using a case-study approach to illustrate your clinical work, you may need to format your manuscript more idiosyncratically.

For simplicity, I have organized the following discussion of social science manuscripts along traditional lines, offering suggestions about writing each of the components listed above, as well as your title and the *Abstract*. I focus most on the process of researching, organizing, and writing your *Literature Review*, as it is, in many ways, the most complex part of your paper to compose.

Keep in mind that just as your research method should fit the type of research question you pose, your paper's organization and subheadings should accord with the nature of your study. If a traditional structure works, then use it, along with the attendant subheadings; however, if it doesn't, adapt or change it as necessity—not whim—dictates.

## Title

*[Your title] is your reader's introduction to your paper.*
*A pedestrian title is about as welcoming as a burned-out motel sign.*

—John Trimble

I don't belong to the science-must-be-boring school of thought, especially when it comes to choosing titles for manuscripts, but I'm also unwilling to sacrifice descriptive accuracy for the sake of panache. A good title captures the essence of the paper it names and piques the curiosity of potential readers. Try for something evocative and descriptive rather than either glitzy or pretentious.

Some writers start their title with a something catchy and follow it with a colon and an expository phrase.

*Truth or Care?: The Therapist's Role with Court-Referred Patients*

or

*Short Fuse: A Discourse Analysis of Bomb-Squad Arguments*[3]

This structure, one I've used (too) many times myself, helps achieve a balance between style and description, but it has become an academic cliché. Many titles of published articles would benefit greatly from a colonectomy.[4]

Sometimes the title for a manuscript comes to me before I sit down to write. More commonly, I must read my completed, untitled paper over a few times, listening for a phrase or idea that captures an important aspect of the work. I then develop three or four versions, whittling away superfluities and changing word order and word choices, before settling on one. Here's an example:

*A Study of Gender Stereotypes in
Computer Games that are Marketed to Children*

This needs to be streamlined; the first three words and four of the last seven aren't necessary.

*A Study of Gender Stereotypes in
Computer Games that are Marketed to Children's*

The revision is more succinct,

*Gender Stereotypes in Children's Computer Games*

but it sounds flat. Some added fizz might help,

*Dungeons, Dragons, and Daughters:
Gender Stereotypes in Children's Computer Games*

but does it help enough to warrant the use of the colon? Maybe, depending on the intended audience. But some readers might consider the title too slick, and others might not recognize the reference to the computer game *Dungeons and Dragons*. Before settling on a final version, I would want to survey the opinions of several colleagues.

---

[3] The *APA Manual* wisely advises against using such phrases as "A Study of" or An Experimental Investigation of" in titles. In this case, I think the use of "A Discourse Analysis of" is warranted, given that a *specific* research method is being named.

[4] In addition to removing the colon, authors would, of course, also need to conduct surgery on the words.

Once you have chosen a title, ensure that it accurately reflects the content of your paper. I have read several manuscripts in which the body of the text failed to live up to the promise offered in the title or where the title didn't do justice to the excellent paper it named.

# Abstract

An abstract must be concise *and* inclusive, distilling 15–20 (or more) pages of text down to 4–7 sentences.[5] Like your title, it should invite people's interest, and, like the blurb on the jacket of a mystery novel, it should touch on the highlights of the plot. If your paper is published in a professional journal, the abstract tells potential readers what to expect in terms of content and style. Some people, such as those using psycINFO or an analogous electronic bibliographic reference source, will have initial access only to your abstract. Their subsequent decision to track down and read your article will be based on what they can glean from your few lines of summary and invitation.

If you write your abstract after completing the rest of your paper, you will solve two problems at once. First, you will find it much easier to compose. Use subheadings from your manuscript for organizational inspiration, and reread key sentences from your different sections for content inspiration. Be sure, though, that the result doesn't read as a pastiche—along with the rest of your paper, your abstract needs coherence and flow. Recognize, too, that you can't just copy the first paragraph of your introduction and use it again as your abstract. As I discuss below, those first sentences in your introduction should establish the *context* for your study; your abstract is not an introduction in this sense, but rather a *summary* of your entire paper.

Second, by writing your abstract last, you won't be tempted to treat it as a substitute for your introduction, that is, as *part of* rather than *separate from* the rest of your manuscript. Your abstract should be isolated on its own page as a stand-alone entity—don't try to create a transition between it and the body of your paper. Let's say, for illustration, that in your abstract you include, among other things, the following statement:

[5]Most journals give writers 100, 120, or at most 150 words to summarize the major points of their article. APA stipulates a limit of 960 characters and spaces, which translates into approximately 120 words.

> The author[6] conducted content analyses of four speeches by President Clinton, one before and one after the 1992 election, and one before and one after the 1996 election.

Now, the first time you mention these speeches in your introduction, *do not* assume that readers are already acquainted with them.

> ✗ By comparing Clinton's four speeches, I have been able to . . .

Your paper *starts with your Introduction*; thus, regardless of what you said in your Abstract, you must, in the body of your paper, introduce the speeches from scratch:

> ✓ Of the many hundreds of speeches delivered by President Clinton during his two terms in office, I have chosen to focus on four. The first, given a few days prior to his 1992 election, . . . .

Your abstract is not the first section of your paper, it is *about* your paper. The mystery writer doesn't treat the jacket blurb as the first paragraph of his or her novel, right? Thus, don't tell readers what you *will do* in your paper; tell them what your manuscript *does* and what you (and/or the people in your study) *did*.

> ✗ This article will present national survey data on the marital consequences of "virtual affairs." The author will describe how a sample of 1140 Internet subscribers rated their levels of sexual and emotional involvement in sexually-oriented chat rooms and how they responded to questions about the effects of this involvement on their marriages.

>> ✓ This article presents national survey data on the marital consequences of "virtual affairs." A sample of 1140 Internet subscribers rated their levels of sexual and emotional involvement in sexually-oriented chat rooms, and they responded to questions about the effects of this involvement on their marriages.

---

[6]The *APA Manual* advises authors to use third person ("the author") in the abstract and first person ("I") in the body of the text.

# Introduction

*The beginning of a novel is a threshold, separating the real world we inhabit from the world the novelist has imagined. It should therefore, as the phrase goes, "draw us in."*
                                                                    —David Lodge

I write my introductions at least twice—once when I'm first starting a paper, to help me figure out what I want to say (and thus, to some extent, what the paper will be about), and again after I have finished everything else, when I know what I have said. As I discussed in Chapter 1, writing thoughtfully means that you can't predict on page 1 where your writing will take you. Once you get to the end and find out where you went, you can go back and better orient readers to where they will be going.

Like your abstract, your introduction tells readers what to expect out of your manuscript, but it has other responsibilities, such as setting the context for, and explaining the relevance of, your study, introducing your research problem, and so on. It also establishes the direction for all that follows, and it presents "coming attractions": "Soon-to-be-discussed topics in a paper near you."

The first duty of your introduction, though, is to invite your readers into your manuscript, to orient them to your work. Where and how do you begin? Imagine yourself as a film director, shooting a movie that follows a young couple through the course of their three-month relationship, from their first blind date to their last fight. You shoot the first scene in an old, dimly lit pizza parlor, where, amid the soft clatter of dishes and strains of Italian music, the two about-to-be lovers are trying to separate a couple of slices of pizza from each other and from the pie on the table between them. But the mozzarella is still too hot and thick to be cut, so, as they pull their slices apart, long liquid strings of cheese create a suspension bridge across the table.

Okay. You manage to shoot the scene without a hitch, and although it looks great and the symbolism works nicely, you later worry that you can't open the film with it. You decide that you need to show the audience something else first, something to create a context within which the stretching mozzarella can be understood and appreciated. You could do this by backing up in time, depicting events in each person's life during the preceding hours (getting ready for the date), months (living alone), or years (growing up). Alternatively, you could open your film with a shot of the pizzeria from across the street. Slowly, as the credits roll, the camera could move forward, through the traffic and up onto the sidewalk, closer and closer to the restaurant, until the couple could be seen through the window, laughing at their table. Or you could bring the camera forward from the edge of the neighborhood, or, still farther, from the edge of the city, or from above the city, or from outer space.

In whatever way you choose to introduce your mozzarella-stretching scene, you must decide how far to back up. How far is too far? Does the audience really need to see baby pictures? Do you really need to establish that the restaurant is located on planet earth? If you start too far back from the couple and their pizza, you risk drowning the significance of the scene in irrelevant details. However, if you start in the time-or-space vicinity of the pizzeria, if you *stay within the neighborhood* of the important action, then the hot mozzarella will still be hot (i.e., significant) by the time the audience gets to see it.

As a social-science writer, you must contend with analogous context-setting questions every time you work on the first sentences and paragraphs of a new manuscript. How much background should you provide? How much do you need to prepare your readers before you move on to describe the main point of your paper? Here is a guideline for making opening-scene decisions, for drawing in and orienting your readers:

➥ **Start in the neighborhood:**
   **Get to the mozzarella while it is still hot**
By "start in the neighborhood," I mean "open your paper within the ideational and/or temporal vicinity of your main topic." If you start not too far away from where you want to get, you can more quickly and smoothly orient your readers to the focus—the "hot mozzarella"—of your work. My Texas-born-and-bred wife would probably render this advice still more succinctly (and slightly less metaphorically) by telling you to "cut to the chase."

I once read a 20-page paper that didn't let me know what it was about until page seven. The information on those first pages was inter-

esting, but until I understood how it was relevant, I felt lost and confused. Your readers should know what they can expect of your manuscript by the time they reach the end of your first or second paragraph.
(If you are writing a longer work, such as a thesis or dissertation, you
might be able to keep readers waiting until the end of three or four
paragraphs, but don't try their patience.)

Let's say, for illustration, that you have written a clinical case study
describing how you use letter-writing as a way of offering therapeutic
suggestions to clients, and you are trying to write an introduction. Here
are some potential opening sentences:

> 1  The Sumerians invented writing some 5000 years ago in
> southern Mesopotamia, and, ever since, people have been
> writing down ideas, ideas needing to be remembered and
> communicated. It is only natural, then, that therapists
> would recognize the potential in writing down their inter-
> ventions and sending them to their clients. These "inter-
> vention letters" may not have the lasting power of
> Sumerian clay tablets, but they are more permanent than
> the spoken word, and they can thus help clients remember
> what matters in times of crisis.

> 2  Since the time of the Pony Express, people in this coun-
> try have been writing letters as a way of staying in touch.
> However, recently, a small number of therapists have begun
> putting pen to paper with a more specific focus in mind.

> 3  Therapists have been writing letters to clients for years,
> but only recently have they recognized the interventive or
> therapeutic possibilities of doing so.

> 4  The therapeutic value of *talking* to clients has been
> widely acknowledged since the time of Freud, but few ther-
> apists have recognized the potential therapeutic benefits of
> *writing* to them.

> 5  Therapists commonly suggest to clients that they write
> letters: letters of reconciliation to estranged family mem-
> bers; letters of accusation or forgiveness to abusers; letters
> of confession to those they have abused; letters of mourn-

ing to deceased lovers, relatives, and friends. But few therapists have considered the therapeutic possibilities of clients *receiving* letters, specifically, of their receiving letters written by their therapists.

If the hot mozzarella of your paper has to do with the therapeutic uses of letter writing with clients, then orienting readers with references to the Pony Express or, worse, Sumerian clay tablets, can only trivialize the significance of the work to be described. Such broad-sweep contextualizing introduces readers to your work from far beyond the reaches of the paper's neighborhood—that is, beyond the notion of therapists communicating with clients or therapists therapeutically intervening with their clients. It also leaves you with two unsatisfactory options. First, if you take the necessary time to properly discuss the differences, and possibly the developments, between the disparate times, places, and practices being juxtaposed, the mozzarella will be long cold by the time you have done a thorough job. Second, if you zoom forward in time as quickly as was done in the first two examples, you will leave the reader dazed and confused (and unintentionally amused).

The third introduction leaves the temporal context vaguely defined ("for years"), and it demarcates the borders of a more restricted ideational neighborhood than any of the other examples. In this example, the neighborhood (therapist-to-client correspondence) is only slightly more encompassing than the focus of the paper (therapeutic letter-writing). This makes for hot mozzarella because you can get to the point of your paper very quickly, but it doesn't provide a rich or interesting context within which to understand your work.

By invoking the name of Freud, the fourth version draws readers in at the edge of a defined, albeit rather large, neighborhood. The temporal range—100 years—is manageable in this case, though, partly because the ideational scope is so sharply drawn. The dichotomy between therapeutic talking and therapeutic writing moves the reader toward the mozzarella both quickly and effectively.

The fifth version makes no mention of the temporal context of therapeutic letter writing (by clients *or* therapists), thus eliminating the need for you to decide how much history to include (5000 years? 200? 100? 20?). In this example, the edges of the contextual neighborhood are defined by the variety of applications of therapeutic writing. Smooth, efficient movement toward the mozzarella is again facilitated by a clearly distinguished dichotomy, but here a contrast is created between client-generated and therapist-generated letters rather than between therapeutic talking and writing.

For the reasons I have just outlined, you would be wise to hit the delete key on the first three of these examples. Who needs empty profundity, cold mozzarella, or a boring neighborhood? The last two versions have potential, but how do you decide between them? Into which neighborhood should you invite your readers?

> 4  The therapeutic value of *talking* to clients has been widely acknowledged since the time of Freud, but few therapists have recognized the potential therapeutic benefits of *writing* to them.

> 5  Therapists commonly suggest to clients that they write letters: letters of reconciliation to estranged family members; letters of accusation or forgiveness to abusers; letters of confession to those they have abused; letters of mourning to deceased lovers, relatives, and friends. But few therapists have considered the therapeutic possibilities of clients *receiving* letters, specifically, of their receiving letters written by their therapists.

You could always toss a coin, or make an aesthetic judgment, but you can't decide which version is more *contextually* appropriate by only comparing back and forth between them. You must make your choice in relation to the rest of your paper, most particularly *in relation* to your literature review.

## ●● Match the scope and focus of your introductory paragraph(s) with the scope and focus of your literature review

The first sentences of your introduction and the entirety of your literature review share a similar responsibility: Both help readers appreciate and assess the relevance of your scholarship by placing the focus of your work within a broader context of understanding, within a more encompassing neighborhood of previous and current ideas, trends, practices, and/or research. Your introductory sentences rough out, with a few broad brush strokes, the contextual boundaries of your study. These boundaries should accord with those defined by the fine-brush detail of your literature review. For example, version #4 would work well with a historically structured literature review, one that discusses developments in talk-based therapy over the last 100 years, surveying the kinds of techniques that therapists have used to offer new ideas to clients, from, say, dream analysis to bibliotherapy (where clients are given books to read). The review would best conclude with a focused discussion of the various therapists who have used letter-writing as a means of reaching out to and intervening with clients. To match the introductory sentences of version #5, a literature review would need to begin with a survey of case studies and clinical books, each describing a particular therapeutic application of client-generated letter-writing. This referenced commentary could then transition into a discussion of those practitioners who have made good use of therapist-generated letters.

Sometimes your literature review can be woven into your introduction; however, if you have a substantial number of works to discuss (such as when you are writing a thesis or dissertation), it may be more organizationally effective to locate your review under its own subheading.

## Literature Review

*Use the literature, don't let it use you.*
                                        —Howard Becker

When you write a paper for the social scientific community, you lend your voice to one or more ongoing conversations between researchers, theoreticians, and clinicians—dialogues that started before you arrived and will continue after you fall silent. Through your literature review, you acquaint your readers with what you consider to be the recent (and perhaps historical) highlights of those portions of the conversation(s) relevant to your study, and you clarify how you will be contributing to the unfolding of the discussion. By the end of your paper, your voice may provide support for other voices, contradict what they have maintained, highlight what they haven't yet mentioned, or offer a new perspective on what they have concluded.

But you are faced, as you begin preparing to write your literature review, with the same kinds of questions that wait for you when you are looking for a starting point for your introduction. The social science literature, taken as a whole, is a cacophony of voices, a muddle of conversations about ideas and findings. Which ones do you listen to? Which ones do you isolate and use to set the context for your work?

Your literature review reassures your readers that you know what you are talking about, that you are familiar with what others in your field have been saying, and that you are not going to blunder, unprepared and ignorant, into the conversation. By recapping highlights from other studies, you define the parameters of your own, preparing readers to understand and critically examine what you have done.

The following series of suggestions offers a step-by-step procedure for thinking about, researching, preparing to write, and finally composing your literature review. The method is time-consuming, especially in the beginning, but it will help you find a clear and interesting narrative path through the piles of studies stacked on the floor around your desk.

### ➡ Define your audience

In Chapter 1, I talked about the benefits of hallucinating (and even naming) an ideal reader, someone who is well-versed in your field but unfamiliar with the specific subject matter of your study. This imaginary person (I call her Katherine) can be particularly helpful when you are planning your literature review, for she can tell you what and how much background information she requires. Let her help you find a balance between stating the obvious and taking too much for granted.

### ➡ Define your topic

Write down your topic as succinctly as possible. If you have a title or a problem statement worked out, use it to help you get something down on paper. Here are some examples:

- AIDS among the elderly
- The effects of trauma on memory retrieval
- Nonverbal indicators of lying
- Homosexuality and Protestant doctrine
- The "glass ceiling" for women in federal politics
- The language of oppression among the oppressed
- Conflict resolution among school children
- Cybercrime
- Inside the Bloods

**•◦ Identify and circle the components of your topic**

Most studies can be viewed as a meeting point or interface of two or more ideas, variables, groups, or areas of knowledge. How many different subject areas does your research bring together? Look carefully at your topic and circle each of the components comprising it.

- (AIDS) among the (elderly)
- The effects of (trauma) on (memory retrieval)
- (Nonverbal indicators) of (lying)
- (Homosexuality) and (Protestant doctrine)
- The ("glass ceiling") for (women) in (federal politics)
- The (language of oppression) among the (oppressed)
- (Conflict resolution) among (school children)
- (Cyber)(crime)

For some studies, though, you may only be able to identify one component.

- (Inside the Bloods)

**•◦ Use topic components to help you define parameters and create an outline of your literature review**

The components of your topic provide an excellent starting point for choosing appropriate parameters for your literature review. Using a few of the research-study examples above, I will show how the *topic components*—first alone and then combined—can help you decide what kind of information to include in your literature review.[7] Of course, the extent, level of sophistication, and depth of your review in each area will always depend on your intended audience and on the scope of your project. A literature review for a thesis or dissertation will be much more extensive than one for a term paper or a brief report.

### • AIDS among the elderly

If your topic has two components, your literature review can be organized most simply into three sections—one for each component (in this case, *AIDS* and the *elderly*) and a third for their combination (*AIDS-and-the-elderly*). To decide what sort of information to look for within each area, ask yourself what Katherine, your ideal reader, would

[7]My colleague Ron Chenail (Chenail & Gale, 1993) uses Venn diagrams with his dissertation students to help them make these sorts of decisions.

need/want to know. What details and research results from other studies would provide her with an interesting and comprehensive tour of the subject? Here is an outline of what you might include (I have erred on the side of thoroughness):

## AIDS

- An explanation of how HIV is contracted, how it replicates within the body, and how it compromises the person's immune system.
- A definition of AIDS.
- A brief history of AIDS in North America.
- A description of the typical complications from which persons with AIDS suffer and die.
- An overview of the various groups most at risk of contracting the HIV virus.

## Elderly

- A definition of the term *elderly*.
- An overview of health-related issues for the elderly.
- A survey of current social behaviors among the elderly, including drug use and non-monogamous and widow/widower sexual activity.

## AIDS-and-Elderly

- A differentiation between two groups—(a) persons with AIDS who have lived long enough to be classified as elderly, and (b) previously healthy elderly persons who have recently contracted the disease.
- A description of the unique attributes of elderly persons' immune systems.
- A summary of statistical information on the growing incidence of HIV and AIDS among the elderly.

Having created an outline for your review, the next step (which I will be discussing shortly) is to go to the library and begin (or continue) your search of the literature. Look for the empirical, historical, and theoretical studies from which you can learn and with which you can reference your narrative.

To further illustrate the process of using topic components to develop subject areas and an outline for your literature review, I have included a second illustration of the process:

### • Homosexuality and Protestant doctrine

This topic also has two components, so you would again need to cover at least three areas in your literature review: *Homosexuality, Protestant doctrine*, and their combination (*Homosexuality-and-Protestant doctrine*). Again, you would need to consider Katherine when making breadth-and-depth content decisions. Be sure you cover whatever historical and/or ideational background material necessary to inform and interest her and to prepare her for understanding your study. Possible subjects for the three sections would include those listed below; greater refinement of your outline would come once you had defined a specific research problem:

### Homosexuality
- A summary of the current state of the nature/nurture debate.
- An exploration of the implications of recent DNA studies on the issues of sexual choice and sexual identity.
- A brief history of the gay/lesbian movement in America since Stonewall.
- A brief account of how the American Psychiatric Association came to decide that homosexuality should no longer be considered a psychiatric disorder.
- A description of the increased visibility of gays and lesbians in contemporary American culture.

### Protestant Doctrine
- A brief recounting of Luther and Calvin's contributions to the launching of the Protestant Reformation in the early 1500s.
- An overview of early Protestant doctrine on sin and salvation.
- A survey of the differences in interpretation of Protestant doctrine among contemporary Protestant denominations.

### Homosexuality-and-Protestant-Doctrine
- An examination of Old and New Testament references to homosexuality, with particular attention paid to Paul.
- A discussion of translation and interpretation controversies.
- A history of contemporary Protestant responses to gay and lesbian church members.
- A history of contemporary Protestant responses to gay and lesbian church leaders.

- A survey of current debates within and among Protestant denominations regarding the acceptance of members and the ordination of ministers.

➡ **To expand your outline further, identify broader categories within which your components can be classified**

Sometimes Katherine (or a professor) will tell you that the background information you plan to offer in your literature review is too sparse or that the contextual boundaries you have etched out for your literature review look too constricted (such as when you can identify only one component within your topic area—e.g., "Inside the Bloods"). If this happens to you, use the following procedure for fleshing out or expanding your review. The process will help you derive more encompassing categories for your topic.

For illustration, let's assume that your paper on homosexuality and Protestant doctrine worked out so well that you've decided to use it as a pilot study for your dissertation. You plan to maintain your focus but expand the scope of your research, so, accordingly, the contextual boundaries provided by your literature review will also need to be enlarged. But how? One way is to take each of your topic components—in this case, *Homosexuality* and *Protestant doctrine*—and find answers to the following questions:

> **1. "To what larger context(s) does this component belong?" (or, put differently, "Of what category or categories is this component a subcategory or a subset?")**
>
> *Homosexuality* can be viewed, for example, as a subset of the more encompassing context *human sexuality*. Similarly, *Protestant doctrine* can be considered a subcategory of *Christian doctrine*, which, in turn, can be deemed a subcategory of *Western religious doctrine*.

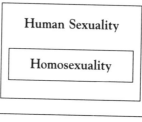

## 2. "What other comparable subsets or subcategories fit within these larger contexts or categories?"

Sometimes your answer to the first question will help you figure out an answer to this one; however, the reverse may also prove true—finding comparable subcategories may be a good first step to figuring out an appropriate larger context. Let's assume here, though, that you have already decided on your broader categories. Within the context of *human sexuality*, you could, for the purposes of this proposed dissertation, identify three subsets or subcategories: *heterosexuality*, *homosexuality*, and *bisexuality*. Similarly, within *Christian doctrine*, you could juxtapose *Protestant doctrine* and *Catholic doctrine*, and within *Western religious doctrine*, you could identify three subcategories: *Christian doctrine*, *Jewish doctrine*, and *Islamic doctrine*.

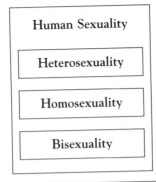

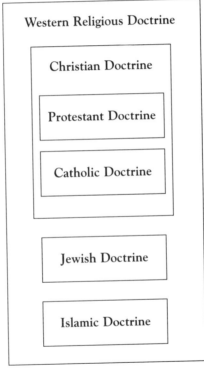

I want to underscore that these larger contexts and comparable sub-categories are just one way to classify the topic components. Depending on the focus of your research, your academic discipline, and your philosophical/political orientation, you might categorize these topics very differently. For example, taking a historical perspective, you could classify *homosexuality*, along with *Jewish blood* and *Gypsy blood*, as a subcategory of *attributes vilified by Nazis*; and you could, following Max Weber, classify *Protestant doctrine*, along with *capitalist doctrine*, as a subset of *individualistic belief systems*. The larger categories chosen for this proposed dissertation—*human sexuality; Western religious doctrine; Christian religious doctrine*—along with their respective comparable subcategories—*heterosexuality / homosexuality / bisexuality; Jewish doctrine / Islamic doctrine / Christian doctrine; Catholic doctrine / Protestant doctrine*—are appropriate for this particular research study, but they aren't "true" or "correct" in any objective sense.

With the broader categories and comparable subcategories figured out in this way, you could now develop an outline for a much more extensive literature review for your topic, "Homosexuality and Protestant doctrine." Your research problem and method wouldn't necessarily need to change (though they might); you would simply be providing your readers with a richer understanding and broader appreciation of the relevance of your work by touring them through a much larger neighborhood. Here is a new, expanded outline:

### Human Sexuality
- A brief summary of the current state of the nature/nurture debate.
- A brief survey of the range of human sexual expression.

#### Heterosexuality / Homosexuality / Bisexuality
- An exploration of the implications of recent DNA studies on the issues of sexual choice and sexual identity.
- A summary of the controversies regarding definitions of hetero-, homo- and bisexuality in this and other cultures.
- A history of the gay/lesbian movement in America since Stonewall.
- An account of how the American Psychiatric Association came to decide that homosexuality should no longer be considered a psychiatric disorder.
- A description of the increased visibility of gays and lesbians in contemporary American culture.
- A discussion of stigma: how heterosexuals stigmatize homosexuals and homosexuals stigmatize bisexuals

### Western Religious Doctrine
- An overview of the historical connections between Islam, Judaism, and Christianity.

#### Islamic Doctrine
- An overview of the Koran.

#### Jewish Doctrine
- An overview of the Old Testament

#### Christian Doctrine
- An overview of the New Testament.

##### Catholic Doctrine
- A brief discussion of St. Augustine and his writings.
- An explanation of the role of the priest in granting salvation.

##### Protestant Doctrine
- A brief recounting of Luther's and Calvin's contributions to the launching of the Protestant Reformation in the early 1500s.
- An overview of early Protestant doctrine on sin and salvation.
- A survey of the differences in interpretation of Protestant doctrine among contemporary Protestant denominations.

### Human-Sexuality-and-Western-religious-doctrine
- An examination of the way each of the religious traditions approaches sexual relationships.
- A discussion of the textual references to homosexuality in the Koran and the Old and New Testaments.
- A focused discussion of Paul in the New Testament.
- An overview of translation and interpretation controversies within each religion.
- A discussion of contemporary Islamic responses to homosexuality.
- A discussion of contemporary Jewish responses to homosexuality.
- A discussion of contemporary Christian responses to homosexuality, including both Catholic and Protestant thinking.

- A history of contemporary Protestant responses to gay and lesbian church members.
- A history of contemporary Protestant responses to gay and lesbian church leaders.
- A survey of current debates within and among Protestant denominations regarding the acceptance of members and the ordination of ministers.

You can begin your library/Internet search long before you have prepared a detailed outline of your literature review; however, the more detailed your plan, the more focused you can be in seeking studies within particular areas or subjects.

### ⟿ Use "Snowball Sampling" to Help You Search for Sources

In his book, *Qualitative Evaluation and Research Methods*, Michael Quinn Patton (1990) distinguished a variety of purposive sampling strategies that qualitative researchers can use for locating knowledgeable "informants"—that is, people in an organization or culture who possess important information. One of these strategies Patton called *snowball sampling*, a process that involves asking well-situated people to recommend possible informants. These individuals are contacted and interviewed, and then they, in turn, are asked to suggest names of others who possess key information. "The snowball gets bigger and bigger as you accumulate new information-rich cases. . . . The chain of recommended informants will typically diverge initially as many possible sources are recommended, then converge as a few key names get mentioned over and over" (Patton, p. 176).

You can use this same approach for finding articles and books relevant to your topic. Start by asking professors and friends to recommend studies; search PsycINFO and related databases; thumb through recent issues of key journals in your discipline; nose around in the stacks in your school's library (checking out books and journals in the vicinity of any you have found interesting); search the Internet with key words related to your topic; and ask for suggestions from people on listservs in your discipline. Once you get your hands on some useful studies, use their literature reviews and reference lists to direct you to articles and books with which you are not yet familiar. Once you find these new sources, repeat the process: Use *their* literature reviews and reference lists to help you look still further. Continue snowballing your way through the library until you stop finding new documents or until you determine that the new authors you are uncovering aren't saying anything you haven't already heard.

How much time have you got for writing your literature review? Be assured that some wonderful article or book is, at this very moment, sitting on a shelf just outside your purview, patiently waiting to be discovered, and you may never find it. An exhaustive search could take you many months, and because of the numbers of studies continually being published, you will never be able to track down *everything*. The breadth and depth of your searching must depend on the scope of your study (a dissertation requiring, as I mentioned above, a much more in-depth review than a term paper or brief report), the intensity of your curiosity, the demands of your professor(s) or reviewers, and the limits of your time, money, and energy. Adjust the size of your snowball accordingly.

## ➥ Know When to Let the Snowball Melt

The better acquainted you are with the literature on your topic, the better prepared you will be to write your review and to conduct a study that doesn't reinvent the wheel. Allow me, though, to add one caution about excessive source sleuthing. This advice isn't for everyone. It doesn't apply to you if you typically bristle at suggestions from others (professors, journal reviewers) that your literature reviews look malnourished. However, if you worry incessantly that you might have overlooked a key article somewhere, despite your intensive, thorough efforts, if you find it easier to hang out in the library than to sit down in front of your computer, then consider this: Yes, good scholarship depends on a comprehensive grasp of your sources, but don't use your reading to avoid writing.

If you have used a snowball search technique, you no doubt will have already located a number of key sources—landmark studies that are cited again and again. Once you have a good handle on these primary works, you can safely begin organizing your literature review in the manner I describe below. If, after you have begun writing, you come across something new and important, you most likely will be able to assimilate it within the outline you have already created (or accommodate to it by tinkering a little with your layout). If you wait to start writing until you are completely prepared, you will die of old age in some dark, cramped corner of the library.

## ❧ Photocopy and Highlight

When you locate relevant articles and chapters, make photocopies for yourself, and go through and underline or highlight passages that seem generally applicable and interesting. Alternatively, you can bring your index cards or laptop to the library and work directly from the original documents. I hope, if you choose not to photocopy, that you treat the books and journals you read as wilderness—that is, that you leave no trace of your having been there. I had a friend in college who could only read with a ruler and a pencil in hand, and he acted as if library documents were his personal possessions: a litter-ary bug of the first order.

## ❧ Create Files for Quoting, Paraphrasing, and Making Notes

Create a new file on your word processor for each of the articles/books/dissertations you think you might wish to reference, paraphrase, or quote in your manuscript. Alternatively, depending on the length of your sources and of the notes you will be taking, you might want to cluster topic-related sources together. For example, you could include together in one file your quotes and notes on a group of recent sociological studies of teenage suicide but devote a separate file to Durkheim's book, *Suicide*.

At the top of each file you create (or at the top of a new page if you are grouping sources within one file), type the reference for the source, using your discipline's format for reference lists (e.g., APA). Now go back to the passages that stood out for you and type verbatim whatever seems most important. If, as you are typing, you get some ideas of your own, or if you wish to paraphrase (rather than quote) what the author is saying, type your comments and paraphrases within square brackets. Later, when you are reading your notes, you will know that anything not inside brackets is a direct quote.

Each time you start a quote (or paraphrase) from a new page in the article or book you are reading, type the page number, indent a bit, and start typing. If a quote spans two pages, indicate mid-sentence (within square brackets) where the new page starts. That way, if you later use a portion of the quote for your manuscript, you will know exactly the page or pages on which it was located.

To illustrate, I have included a few excerpts from some notes on Erving Goffman's *The Presentation of Self in Everyday Life*.

*the reference, APA style* ↘ *—it can be copied and pasted directly into a reference list*

Goffman, E. (1959). <u>The presentation of self in everyday life</u>. Garden City, NY: Doubleday Anchor Books.

*page no.* ↘     *direct quote* ↘

17  When an individual plays a part he implicitly requests his observers to take seriously the impression that is fostered before them. They are asked to believe that the character they see actually possesses the attributes he appears to possess.

*page no.* ↘     *paraphrase* ↘

18  [People who don't believe their own acts and don't care whether others believe them can be termed "cynical"; people who believe their performances are "sincere."]

*page no.* ↘     *clarifying note* ↘     *direct quote of Park* ↘

19  [Goffman quotes Robert Ezra Park]: The word person, in its first meaning, is a mask. It is rather a recognition of the fact that everyone is always and everywhere, more or less consciously, playing a role. . . .

*direct quote from the Oxford English Dictionary* ↘ *—to cross check Park's claim*

[The OED says this]: **Person** from the Latin <u>persona</u>—a mask used by a player, a character or personage acted (<u>dramatis persona</u>), one who plays or performs any part, a character, relation, or capacity in which one acts. . . . The sense <u>mask</u> has not come down into Eng.

*page no.* ↘     *back to Goffman* ↘

19  In so far as this mask represents the conception we have formed of ourselves . . . this mask is our truer self. . . . In the end, our conception of our role becomes second nature and an integral part of our [20] personality.

↖ *new page no.*

*planning notes* ↘

[Might be able to make some connections with Ken Gergen's <u>Saturated Self</u>. See also his 1985 paper in <u>American Psychologist</u>.]

[Possible epigrams for the paper: Juxtapose Park's quote with something from one of Patricia Highsmith's <u>Tom Riley</u> mysteries.]

If, at a later time, you reread an article or book from which you have previously taken notes and you see more than you did the first time, you can always add new quotes and comments.

**⊷ Reorganize your sources thematically**

Once you have exhausted most of your sources (and/or yourself) and finished typing most of your quotes, paraphrases, and thoughts into your word processor, you are ready to begin formally organizing your literature review. Open a new file, title it something like *themeorg* (for thematically organized sources), and use your earlier-developed outline to help you create and array a first-draft set of subheadings. Type each one, in bold, on a separate line. You will probably be adapting your outline (and thus your subheadings) based on the literature you have found; thus, don't worry about coming up with the "right" organization at this point. Simply lay out some subheadings that can help you organize diverse sources under common themes.

Imagine that you are working on a literature review for a study on the effect of trauma on memory retrieval. Let's assume that, drawing from your outline and your reading, you have created the following broad subheadings and have typed them into your *themeorg* file:

**Trauma**
    **Physical Trauma**
    **Psychological/Social Trauma**
**Memory**
    **Metaphors of Memory**
    **Encoding/Storage/Retrieval**
    **Theories of Memory**
    **Implicit/Explicit Memory**
**Forgetting**
    **Amnesia**
    **Dissociation**
    **Repression**
**Effects of Trauma on Encoding/Storage/Retrieval**

Go now to your source file(s) and scroll, paragraph by paragraph, through all the notes you have taken. If you are working with many sources, and/or if your memory is as unreliable as mine, you may find it helpful to add reference information (author and publication date) to the beginning of *every* paragraph you intend to copy-and-paste into your *themeorg* file. Without such tracking information, you may forget who in which article or book said what. For example:

> Garry, M. & Loftus, E. (1994). Pseudomemories without hypnosis. <u>International Journal of Clinical and Experimental Hypnosis, 42</u>, 363-378.

*copy and paste this* ➘ *to the front of each paragraph you intend to transfer*

> (Garry & Loftus, 1994) 367 [Traditional understanding of memory: once information is in long-term memory, it remains there forever, and forgetting is merely an inability to retrieve the information.]

*without this here* ➘ *you might later forget who had quoted Piaget*

> (Garry & Loftus, 1994) 373 [Quote from Piaget]: One of my first memories would date, if it were true, from my second year. . . . I was sitting in my pram, which my nurse was pushing in the Champs Elysees, when a man tried to kidnap me. . . . [My nurse] received various scratches, and I can still see vaguely those on her face. . . . When I was about fifteen, my parents received a letter from my former nurse. . . . She wanted to confess her past faults. . . . She had made up the whole story. . . . I, therefore, must have heard, as a child, the account of this story, which my parents believed, and projected into the past in the form of a visual memory.

Next, copy- (don't cut-) and-paste passages from your source files into your *themeorg* file, delivering each paragraph to an appropriate location under one of the subheadings. When you have finished with all the transfers, your source files will still be intact and your literature review "data" will be organized thematically: Diverse quotes, paraphrases, and notes will be juxtaposed in conceptually linked groupings. For example, each of the following four passages, copied-and-pasted from their respective original files, have been brought together under the subheading *Metaphors of Memory*:

### Metaphors of Memory

*memory: like reconstructing a dinosaur from fragments & expectations*

(Schacter, 1996)   69 [Schacter paraphrasing Neisser]: Retrieving a memory is like reconstructing a dinosaur from fragments of bone. For [70] the paleontologist, the bone chips that are recovered on an archeological dig and the dinosaur that is ultimately reconstructed from them are not the same thing: the full-blown dinosaur is constructed by combining the bone chips with other available fragments, in accordance with general knowledge of how the complete dinosaur should appear. Similarly, for the rememberer, the engram (the stored fragments of an episode) and the memory (the subjective experience of recollecting a past event) are not the same thing.

*memory: not like a computer; like weaving a story*

(Baker, 1990) 192  Our memories are not like computers or phonograph records, but more like the village storyteller. Our brain doesn't passively store the facts and nothing but the facts; instead, it takes the facts and weaves them into a plausible and coherent story that, surprisingly enough, is recreated with each telling.

*memory: like writing a book from fragments*

(Kihlstrom, 1994)  341 Memory is not so much like reading a book as it is like writing one from fragmentary notes. . . . Any particular meaning is only partly derived from trace information encoded at the time of the event: In the process of remembering, trace information combines with knowledge, beliefs, and inferences derived from other sources.

*memory: not like a video recorder*

(Pettinati, 1988)  278 Normal memory production is inexact. That is, memory is not like a video recorder that can provide instant replays at the push of the appropriate buttons. Rather, following from the tradition of Sir Frederic Bartlett (1932), memory is reconstructive, not reproductive.

## •◆ Read any new sources with your themes in mind

Don't stop searching for new references once you are ready and organized to write, but change the way you relate to them. When you locate articles or books that you haven't seen before, don't approach them with open-eyed wonder. Squint your eyes and scrutinize them through the lens of your themes, looking to see if the authors can add anything to what you already know.

## •◆ Look for comparisons and contrasts

A popular how-to-lead-your-life book takes the position that all the necessary rules for negotiating our way successfully through the world were taught to us in kindergarten: share, take naps, don't hit, and so on. In fact, the author, Robert Fulghum (1988), used this charming idea as his book's title: *All I Really Need to Know I Learned in Kindergarten*. I would like to make a similar, if somewhat less sweeping, claim—maybe one that I could use some day as the title of a new book:

> *All You Really Need to Know about Writing Literature*
> *Reviews You Learned in Elementary School and Junior High*

Not best-seller material, perhaps, but the truth it conveys is deep and abiding. Remember being asked to read two stories or poems or essays and then to write a report that would "compare and contrast" them? Literature reviews are little more than extended versions of such assignments. You may be teasing out similarities and differences among 20 or 200 sources instead of between just 2, but the logical structure of the exercise remains the same.

### ➤ Summarize and illustrate similarities and differences among sources

The length and detail of your literature review will depend on the overall length of your manuscript and the number of references with which you have to work. If you are writing a short paper or a brief report, or if you have many more references than you have space to describe them, you will be restricted to pointing out general similarities and differences among your sources. For example, the following two sentences summarize the four quotations on memory cited above:

> Researchers have proposed a variety of analogies for characterizing the nature of memory (e.g., Baker, 1990; Kihlstrom, 1994; Neisser, as cited in Schacter, 1996; Pettinati, 1988); however, the differences in metaphor reveal a common understanding. Memory, as Bartlett pointed out in 1932 (Pettinati, 1988), is reconstructive, not reproductive.

If you don't have to worry so much about the length of your manuscript, and/or if you have only a limited number of sources to discuss, you can afford to provide a more detailed commentary:

> Researchers have offered a variety of metaphors in keeping with Bartlett's contention (cited in Pettinati, 1988, p. 278) that memory is *reconstructive*, not *reproductive*. Our brains do

not store experiences in the same way that computers store data (Baker, 1990, p. 192) or VCRs record pictures and sound (Pettinati, 1988, p. 278); thus, we can't just push a button and passively watch an accurate replay of some past event. The person remembering is like a paleontologist piecing together a dinosaur from bone fragments (Neisser, 1967; cited in Schacter, 1996, pp. 69-70) or like an author writing a book from fragmentary notes (Kihlstrom, 1994, p. 341).

When space permits (such as when you are writing a long paper or a thesis or dissertation) and the quality and importance of your sources warrant it, flesh out your comparisons and contrasts with illustrative quotes:

> Researchers have offered a variety of metaphors for characterizing the inexact nature of memory. As Sir Frederic Bartlett said as far back as 1932, memory is *reconstructive*, not *reproductive* (Pettinati, 1988, p. 278). Our brains do not store experiences in the same way that computers store data (Baker, 1990, p. 192) or VCRs record pictures and sound (Pettinati, 1988, p. 278); thus, we can't just push a button and passively watch an accurate replay of some past event. As Baker put it, our memories are like a village storyteller, weaving facts "into a plausible and coherent story that . . . is recreated with each telling" (p. 192).

> Kihlstrom (1994) also considered remembering to be a process of creative weaving:

> > Memory is not so much like reading a book as it is like *writing* one from fragmentary notes. . . . In the process of remembering, trace information [encoded at the time of the event] combines with knowledge, beliefs, and inferences derived from other sources. (p. 341)

> Schacter (1996), drawing from Neisser, used a different metaphor to make a similar point. He likened the process of retrieving a memory to that of

> > reconstructing a dinosaur from fragments of bone. . . . The full-blown dinosaur is constructed by combining the bone chips with other available fragments, in accordance with general knowledge of how the complete

dinosaur should appear. Similarly, for the rememberer,
the . . . stored fragments of an episode . . . and the memory . . . are not the same thing (pp. 69-70).

**•• Tell an intriguing, informative story**

Your memory may be a kind of story teller, but so are you. By pointing
out interesting similarities and differences among your sources, you provide your readers with an engaging narrative path through the neighborhood of your study. Upon reaching the end of your literature review,
your readers should understand the context of and rationale for your
work and be adequately prepared to assess the balance of your paper—
your method, results, and discussion. However, wouldn't it be great if
they were also intrigued?

**•• Foster dialogue**

If you are writing a theoretical piece that develops your argument in
counterpoint with other authors' work, your literature review will be
interspersed throughout your paper, and your voice will weave through
and around the voices of those you cite. But if you are writing, say,
about an empirical study you have conducted, then you would be better off saving your voice until after you have demonstrated, via your
results, that you have something to contribute to the conversation you
are entering. In a more conventionally structured paper, you should be
highlighting, in your literature review, other authors' ideas, results,
conclusions, insights and, if appropriate, shortcomings.

Somewhere near the end of your review, you need to talk about how
your study fits with and departs from the others you have been citing.
Avoid gushing about or trashing other people's work—neither helps
foster dialogue. Build a rationale for your research that underscores the
contributions of others and illuminates an area that deserves more
attention or a different kind of approach.

**•• Vary the ways you introduce quotations**

I once read a 50-page literature review for a dissertation that introduced every quotation in precisely the same way:

Lovejoy (1964) stated, ". . ."
Lévi-Strauss (1962) stated, ". . ."
Toulmin (1972) stated, ". . ."

By page 3, I wanted to scream; by page 20, I was ready to either call it quits or tear my (remaining) hair out. Would you like to help prevent high blood pressure, depression, and premature baldness among your readers? Here are a few suggestions:

**➣ Find appropriate alternatives for your stock phrases**
- ✓ Lovejoy (1964) noted, ". . . ."
- ✓ Lévi-Strauss (1962) commented, ". . . ."
- ✓ Toulmin (1972) concluded, ". . . ."
- ✓ Wilden (1980) argued, ". . . ."
- ✓ Marx (1964) clarified, ". . . ."

2 **Precede your quotes with suspense devices** (see Chapters 3 and 4)
- ✓ As Lovejoy (1964) noted, ". . . ."
- ✓ According to Lévi-Strauss (1962), ". . . ."
- ✓ As Toulmin (1972) put it, ". . . ."
- ✓ In Wilden's (1980) view, ". . . ."
- ✓ For Marx (1964), ". . . ."

**➣ Use the word *that* to help readers slip smoothly into quotes**
- ✓ Lovejoy (1964) argued that "rationality, when conceived as complete, as excluding all arbitrariness, becomes itself a kind of irrationality" (p. 331).
- ✓ Wilden (1980) pointed out that "the supreme value of remaining silent when you have nothing relevant to say is not a recognized academic virtue" (p. xlix).
- ✓ Arendt (1968) contended that "the central concept of Hegelian metaphysics is history" (p. 68).

Strictly speaking, you should reserve the word *that* for describing (in your own words), *not quoting*, what an author has said.
- ✓ Lovejoy (1964) argued that rationality, if taken to an extreme, reverses on itself, becoming a kind of irrationality.
- ✓ Wilden (1980) pointed out that silence in academia is never golden. Professors continue to profess even when they have nothing relevant to say.
- ✓ Arendt (1968) contended that history lies at the center of Hegelian metaphysics.

However, in illustrative examples of how to handle direct quotations, both the *APA Manual* (1994) and *The Chicago Manual of Style* (1993) use *that* to introduce quotes (pp. 95 & 361, respectively). You thus have a couple of precedents to refer to should anyone object to your doing the same. Don't insert a comma before the quotation:

   ✗   Lovejoy (1964) argued that, "rationality, when conceived as complete, as excluding all arbitrariness, becomes itself a kind of irrationality" (p. 331).

### ➥ Avoid dagger-in-the-back attributions

   ✗   As Lovejoy (1964) admitted, ". . . ."
   ✗   Lévi-Strauss (1962) confessed that ". . . ."
   ✗   Toulmin (1972) conceded: ". . . ."
   ✗   Wilden (1980) purported that ". . . ."
   ✗   As Marx (1964) whined, ". . . ."

Let the authors you quote speak for themselves; if you wish to criticize them, do it directly.

### ➥ Avoid introductory phrases altogether

You can sometimes place a quote in context without using any introductory phrase.

   ✓   When taken to its logical extreme, rationality reverses on itself, becoming its own opposite: "Rationality, when conceived as complete, as excluding all arbitrariness, becomes itself a kind of irrationality" (Lovejoy, 1964, p. 331).

   ✓   Silence in academia is never golden. Professors, by definition, must profess: "The supreme value of remaining silent when you have nothing relevant to say is not a recognized academic virtue" (Wilden, 1980, p. xlix).

   ✓   For Plato, truth resides beyond the sphere of human affairs; for Hegel, truth reveals itself *within the process of time*: "The central concept of Hegelian metaphysics is history" (Arendt, 1968, p. 68).

### ➥ Take care not to create awkward or ungrammatical quotations

Once you have chosen a passage to quote, check to ensure that your introduction to it doesn't render the first sentence awkward, redundant, or ungrammatical. For example,

✗ Thorndike eventually concluded that "it became clear that the assumption of inner thought-processes was not required" (Skinner, 1953, p. 60).

The close proximity of the two *thats* makes for an awkward sentence.

✓ Thorndike eventually concluded that "the assumption of inner thought-processes was not required" (Skinner, 1953, p. 60).

✗ In describing the shaping of operant behavior, Skinner (1953) said that "operant conditioning shapes behavior as a sculptor shapes a lump of clay" (p. 91).

This sentence includes two similar phrases expressing the same idea: *the shaping of operant behavior* and *operant conditioning shapes behavior*. By eliminating your preamble, you can avoid redundancy:

✓ Skinner (1953) said that "operant conditioning shapes behavior as a sculptor shapes a lump of clay" (p. 91).

✗ Skinner's objection to inner states was not based on: "they do not exist, but that they are not relevant in a functional analysis" (p. 35).

Readers of this sentence trip twice, once when first encountering the quotation (*they do not exist*), and again when reaching the phrase *but that they*. The preamble doesn't prepare readers for the beginning of the quote, and it doesn't set up the necessary structure for a comparison between *not existing* and *not being relevant*. Here is an easy fix:

✓ According to Skinner (1953), "The objection to inner states is not that they do not exist, but that they are not relevant in a functional analysis" (p. 35).

✗ Skinner (1953) objected to inner states, not because "they do not exist, but that they are not relevant in a functional analysis" (p. 35).

In this case, the introduction to the quotation fails to set up a parallel structure for the two components being compared (*not existing* and *not being relevant*). The parallel relationship can be rescued by replacing the *that* in the quotation with *because*:

✓ Skinner (1953) objected to inner states, not because "they do not exist, but [because] . . . they are not relevant in a functional analysis" (p. 35).

**⟶ Make editorial insertions to *clarify,* not *alter,* the original author's meaning**

You can use square-bracket insertions to modify or augment a quotation so that it reads more smoothly, or so that the reader will understand an unclear reference, but you can't change the author's meaning to better suit your purposes. Say you are starting with the following quote from Norman O. Brown (1959), and you want to make it shorter:

- "Negation, as the dialectical logicians recognize, and as Freud himself came to recognize when he wrote the essay 'On Negation', is a dialectical or ambivalent phenomenon, containing always a distorted affirmation of what is officially denied" (p. 160).

You can do this:

- ✓ "Negation, as . . . Freud . . . recognize[d] when he wrote the essay 'On Negation,' is a dialectical or ambivalent phenomenon, containing always a distorted affirmation of what is officially denied" (p. 160).

Or this:

- ✓ "Freud . . . came to recognize . . . [that negation] is a dialectical or ambivalent phenomenon, containing always a distorted affirmation of what is officially denied" (p. 160).

But you can't do this:

- ✗ "Negation, as . . . [psychoanalysts recognize], is a dialectical or ambivalent phenomenon, containing always a distorted affirmation of what is officially denied" (p. 160).

Or this:

- ✗ According to Brown (1959), psychoanalysts, following "Freud[,] . . . came to recognize . . . [that negation] is a dialectical or ambivalent phenomenon, containing always a distorted affirmation of what is officially denied" (p. 160).

You might be writing about psychoanalysts in general, but you can't leave your readers with the impression that Brown was too, even if you wish he had. You could, however, say something like this:

- ✓ According to Brown (1959), "Freud . . . came to recognize . . . [that negation] is a dialectical or ambivalent phenomenon, containing always a distorted affirmation of what is officially denied" (p. 160). Freud's sophisticated understanding of negation proved to be one of his most significant contributions to 20th-century psychoanalytic thought.

Or, better yet, this:

✓ According to Brown (1959), Freud eventually realized that negation "is a dialectical or ambivalent phenomenon, containing always a distorted affirmation of what is officially denied" (p. 160). Freud's sophisticated understanding of negation proved to be one of his most significant contributions to 20th-century psychoanalytic thought.

**➡ Remember that *recent* is relative and times change**

Consider the following statements:

• Recent developments in neoclassical microeconomic theory have opened the way for orthodox economists to offer analyses of criminal behavior and to outline optimal approaches to prevention and punishment (Gordon, 1974).

• Anthropologists and communication researchers are relying more and more heavily on kinesics—human body motion—in their study of culture-specific interaction. According to Birdwhistell (1970), "as anthropologists have become increasingly aware of the importance of comparative body motion studies, evidence has accumulated to support the proposition that 'gestures' are culture linked both in shape and in meaning" (p. 79).

Paraphrasing Gordon on theoretical applications in microeconomics would have been fine had you been writing in 1974 or 1975, and you might even have been able to use this passage in 1978 if you could have cited a more recent source that said much the same thing. Similarly, the quote from Birdwhistell could have been introduced in this way back in the early 1970s. However, both statements would compromise your scholarship if you were to use them today as they stand. You can't support a claim about the current state of affairs with a source that was current yesterday. You can, however, place the statements in historical context:

✓ Developments in the late 1960s and early 1970s in neoclassical microeconomic theory opened the way for orthodox economists to offer analyses of criminal behavior and to outline optimal approaches to prevention and punishment (Gordon, 1974).

✓ Anthropologists and communication researchers have long relied on kinesics—human body motion—in their examination of culture-specific interaction. Birdwhistell, who pioneered the study of kinesics in the 1950s and 60s, noted as early as 1970 that "anthropologists ha[d] become increasingly aware of the importance of comparative body motion studies, [and that] evidence ha[d] accumulated to support the proposition that 'gestures' are culture linked both in shape and in meaning" (1970, p. 79).

## ➻ Cite research and researchers, not *the literature*

Having spent so much time immersed in and writing about *the literature*, you may find yourself concretizing or personifying it. Whatever you do in the privacy of your own mind is your business; don't, however, let your confused thinking seep into your writing. Keep your delusions—or, as the lit-crit folks would say, your *pathetic fallacies*—to yourself.

✗ The literature has described . . .
✗ The literature has demonstrated . . .
✗ The literature has provided . . .
✗ The literature has examined . . .

Authors and researchers and studies can describe, demonstrate, provide, and examine, but the literature is incapable of performing these or similar actions.

✓ Polyani (1962) described the personal involvement of the knower in . . .
✓ Recent studies have demonstrated a link between . . .
✓ Harré and Secord (1972) provided a theoretical account of . . .
✓ Researchers (e.g., Cebula, 1997; Haug, 1995) have examined the impact of the federal deficit on . . .

## ➻ Double check your quotations

Once I'm finished with copying, pasting, and paring down all the quotations for my literature review, I go back and make sure that I have accurately quoted and cited my sources. I invariably find a wrong page reference or date, or a misspelled name.

## ⟶ Know the difference between paraphrasing, quoting, and plagiarizing

Don't risk getting accused of plagiarism: The consequences are almost always dire. If you draw on the ideas of another writer, you must cite the source of your influence.

✗ Intimacy only becomes possible once a person's individual identity has taken form.

✓ As Erikson (1968) pointed out, intimacy only becomes possible once a person's individual identity has taken form.

If you use an author's *words*, you must cite the source, use quotation marks, and provide a page reference.

✗ It is only when identity formation is well on its way that true intimacy—which is really a counterpointing as well as a fusing of identities—is possible.

✗ As Erikson (1968) pointed out, it is only when identity formation is well on its way that true intimacy—which is really a counterpointing as well as a fusing of identities—is possible.

✓ As Erikson (1968) pointed out, "it is only when identity formation is well on its way that true intimacy—which is really a counterpointing as well as a fusing of identities—is possible" (p. 135).

You can't just delete or alter a few words in a passage and treat the result as if it were a paraphrase.

✗ As Erikson (1968) pointed out, it is only when identity formation is well on its way that true intimacy—which is really an entwining as well as a melding of identities—is possible.

✗ As Erikson (1968) pointed out, it is only when one's identity is well formed that true intimacy—that is, the entwining and melding of identities—is possible.

✗ As Erikson (1968) pointed out, it is only when identity formation is well on its way that true intimacy is possible.

You must either quote the source (with or without deletions) directly—

✓ As Erikson (1968) pointed out, "it is only when identity formation is well on its way that true intimacy—which is really a counterpointing as well as a fusing of identities—is possible" (p. 135).

> ✓ As Erikson (1968) pointed out, "it is only when identity formation is well on its way that true intimacy . . . is possible" (p. 135).

—or rewrite the original in *your* words.

> ✓ As Erikson (1968) pointed out, intimacy only becomes possible once a person's individual identity has taken form.
>
> ✓ If a person's identity has not yet taken form, intimacy is impossible (Erikson, 1968).
>
> ✓ Intimacy is not the opposite of identity. Indeed, if a person's identity formation is not well developed, intimacy is impossible (Erikson, 1968).

If you paraphrase or quote another writer's work without acknowledgment, or if you cite an author but make a verbatim or slightly altered quotation from his or her work look like a paraphrase (i.e., by not including quotation marks and a page reference), you are plagiarizing.

# Method

Assuming this many beats of musical time per minute and this key signature, play this note (with this kind of attack) at this volume, starting here and ending there, and then, after a pause of this length, begin playing these two notes simultaneously, stopping the higher one at this point and letting the lower one sustain this much longer, stopping just before the downbeat at the beginning of the next bar.

Cream the butter and sugar together and then add the eggs, beating well after each addition. Stir in the melted chocolate. Combine the flour, baking powder, salt, and cinnamon. Stirring continually, alternately add the buttermilk and the dry ingredients to the chocolate mixture. Slowly stir in the hot coffee and the vanilla. Pour the batter into two prepared pans and bake 25–30 minutes.

Like a piece of sheet music or a recipe for chocolate cake, your method section should be readable as an elaborate set of instructions for repeating the steps you took in setting up and conducting your research. You need to provide your readers with the background and details necessary for replicating (or, at least, approximating) your study, should they choose to do so. Short of actually carrying out your procedures, they should, at least, be able to walk through them in their imaginations, assessing, along the way, the logic of and care with which you conducted your investigation and made your comparisons.

In describing your method, attend in some way to each of the following relationships:

- The relationship between your question and your approach
- The relationship between your audience and your approach
- The relationship between your research participants (subjects) and some larger (or different) population
- The relationship among the research participants
- The relationship between you and the research participants
- The relationships among the data (the analysis)
- The relationships among reliability, internal and external validity, and objectivity; or among dependability, credibility, transferability, and confirmability

☞ **The relationship between your question and your approach**

Too often research questions are twisted, scrunched, and otherwise deformed by the Procrustean bed of the researcher's desired method of analysis and/or the available technology. You can always decide in advance that you want to perform, say, analysis of variance on data generated by a survey instrument, or to analyze ethnographic interviews with a particular qualitative-research software package such as NUD·IST or HyperQual, but I suggest, instead, that you reverse your decision-making process. If you base your methodological decisions on the type of question you are interested in pursuing, you have a better chance of generating worthwhile data.

☞ **The relationship between your audience and your approach**

If you are writing for an audience acquainted with the assumptions underlying your method, then you probably won't need to provide much, if any, justification for it; however, if you are introducing something new—for example, a qualitative study within a discipline or a department whose members are more comfortable or familiar with quantitative research—then outline the philosophical tenets and/or historical precedents of your approach.

☞ **The relationship between your research participants (subjects) and some larger (or different) population**

The relevance or generalizability of your findings to anyone outside of the particular participants or subjects in your study depends, in part, on the quality of your sampling procedures. Describe the procedures by which your sample was chosen.

☞ **The relationship among the research participants**
If you are using some kind of experimental or quasi-experimental design, describe how you assigned your subjects to comparison groups. If you are conducting, say, ethnographic interviews, describe the similarities and differences among your informants.

☞ **The relationship between you and the research participants**
Experimental researchers take great pains to ensure that they do not unknowingly influence their results in some systematic way, that is, that they do not unwittingly bias the sensitivity and accuracy of their research instruments. If you are doing ethnographic research, you similarly need to guard against any unintended and problematic influence on the people you are studying; however, since *you* are your primary research instrument, the issue of bias must be handled much differently. Either way, you will need to account for what you did, how you did it, and how you kept from deluding yourself. If you used a questionnaire, describe it, and include a copy in an appendix. If, say, you conducted semi-structured interviews, explain your format and your rationale.

☞ **The relationships among the data (the analysis)**
If you are doing quantitative research, describe the procedures by which your data were analyzed (analysis of variance, multiple regression, factor analysis, etc.). If you are using a qualitative method, outline the steps by which you developed your thematic categories and chose exemplary passages from the raw data to illustrate themes or concepts.

☞ **The relationships among reliability, internal and external validity, and objectivity; or among dependability, credibility, transferability, and confirmability**
All researchers must demonstrate their concern for the trustworthiness of their data. If you are conducting quantitative research, you will do this by reporting the reliability of your instruments and the internal and external validity of your results. If you are involved in a qualitative research project, demonstrate how you have attended to what Lincoln and Guba (1985) call credibility, transferability, dependability, and confirmability.

# Results/Analysis

*Basic to scientific evidence (and to all knowledge-diagnostic processes including the retina of the eye) is the process of comparison, of recording differences, or of contrast.*
                    —Donald Campbell and Julian Stanley

Near the end of a typical murder mystery, the sleuth, in a climactic scene, reveals the identity of the murderer and explains how he or she committed and covered up the crime. Near the end of a typical social science mystery, the author reveals the complex relationships between one or more independent and dependent variables (in the Results section of a quantitative-research study) or among thematic categories (sometimes presented in an *Analysis* section of a qualitative-research study). In all cases, the readers' curiosity, which has been building from the outset, is finally satisfied.

If you are writing up a quantitative research study, you can get excellent advice from the *APA Manual* on what your *Results* section should include (such as an overview of your data, the statistical tests you performed on them, and the findings that resulted from your efforts). Your narrative should be brief and to the point, organized in keeping with your original hypotheses, and each claim you make should be illustrated with your statistical results. Consider augmenting your discussion with tables and/or figures.

If you are writing up a *qualitative* research study, you can't turn to the *APA Manual* for advice (it remains silent on such matters), so I will include a few suggestions here. You might wish, in your *Analysis* section, to imitate the data-presentation conventions of quantitative researchers, especially if you think your readers will then be more likely to take your work seriously (i.e., as an example of "good science"). Alternatively, you could emulate the rigor of your quantitative colleagues but present your results in a way that best fits the type of data you have gathered and analyzed. You don't need to account for variance (as you do when doing quantitative research); rather, your responsibility when conducting most qualitative studies is to explore *categories of meaning*. Your narrative can still benefit from judiciously used tables and figures; however, *thematic* relationships generally require a more elaborate discussion than *statistical* relationships.

The method I explained earlier in the chapter for organizing and writing your literature review can also be used for analyzing and presenting the results of qualitative research studies. The presentation of your analysis of your qualitative data, like the discussion of sources in your literature review, involves making thematic connections and distinctions. In a literature review, you organize your discussion according to similarities and differences among the sources you cite. In a qualitative data analysis, you similarly offer comparisons and contrasts among the data you have collected—interviews with various research "informants," transcripts of some kind of cultural interaction (such as therapy sessions, police interrogations, political speeches), different historical documents (letters, diaries, government reports), etc.

In your literature review, quotations from your sources help to enrich and illustrate the points you make. They serve an analogous function in your data analysis. Quotations (or, as they are typically called, "exemplars") from your raw data contextually ground your analyses, thereby keeping your categorical statements from becoming meaningless abstractions.

The narrative path of your analysis may make explicit use of your categories, for example, as subheadings. Alternatively, you might use your categories to organize your discussion but keep them implicit, thus allowing your narrative to flow more like a story. In the absence of universal protocols for presenting qualitative-data analyses, you must balance the demands of your data with those of your readers. Do your best to protect the contextual integrity of your work, but don't ignore the expectations and concerns of those who will be assessing it.

If you are writing a case study or something descriptive or theoretical, you may not be able to circumscribe your "results" and "analysis" enough to locate them in a stand-alone section. But even if you have interspersed your analysis throughout your manuscript, you should plan your narrative so that it comes to some kind of climax, to a place where your readers' curiosity can be satisfied. You may wish to avoid making any conclusive statements, but you can still offer readers some understanding of how your work ties together.

# Discussion

When Mr. Patterson, my ninth-grade homeroom teacher, wasn't offering stock-market investment strategies or extolling the genius of Miles Davis and John Coltrane, he would, among other things, teach our class how to deliver effective speeches. One piece of advice has stayed with me, one that I have heard many times since: "Tell your audience what you are going to say, say it, and then tell them what you told them."

I have let my stock-market understanding slip away, but I continue to listen to jazz, and I would still recommend repetition as a rhetorical tool. Recapitulating salient points at the end of a speech can help your audience recall the steps in your argument and appreciate the whole of what you had to say. But a wrap-up summary is more important for *listeners* than *readers*, more necessary for those who can't flip back a few pages to review a detail or reread a complex passage.

I suggest, then, that you not use the last page(s) of your manuscript to rehash what you have already said. You may wish (and, indeed, need) to mention earlier-made points as you bring your paper to a close. But an abbreviated reference to the previous information may be all that is necessary:

- ✓ As I mentioned earlier, researchers have recognized, if not completely understood, the *reconstructive* nature of memory since at least the early 1930s.

- ✓ In my introduction, I differentiated two groups of elderly persons with AIDS—those who had had AIDS since they were younger (long-time infected elderly persons—LTIEPs), and those who became infected with HIV after the age of 65 (recently infected elderly persons—RIEPs).

Your *conclusion* or *discussion* section is primarily a place to look forward, to extrapolate from what you have done and to speculate on next steps; however, if you were testing a hypothesis in your study, you should begin this section by clarifying whether your results supported it:

- ✓ As I hypothesized, LTIEPs scored significantly lower on measures of psychosocial stress than RIEPs; however, when I controlled for gender and sexual orientation, the difference between the two groups was no longer significant at $p < .01$.

Try standing at the 25-mile-marker of a 26-mile marathon. When you see a runner, say a woman, approach, dash out and jog the last mile with her. As you run together, ask her to reflect on her accomplishment, ask her to comment on what she plans to do differently in her next competition, and ask her to offer some good advice for others who might wish to try something similar. And then get out of her way before she spits on you.

As a dissertation chair, I have often found myself asking such questions to almost-finished students who are too tired to be reflective, too exhausted to speculate on possibilities for future research. All they (think that they) want to do is to get to the finish line (the oral defense of their work). My job is to get their focus off the imminent end to (what at the moment they think of as) their misery and back onto the course of their journey. I try to inspire and encourage them, and, from a safe distance (in case they confuse extrapolating and expectorating), I suggest that they address a number of important issues. I ask them to explain the meaning, relevance, implications, and ramifications of their work for others (and, if they are doing qualitative research from a constructivist perspective, for themselves); to discuss the limitations of their study and how they are constrained in what they can say; and to offer suggestions for new applications of their method, new areas to explore, or different ways of approaching the problem they originally identified.

You will have more resilience near the end of writing a paper than you will near the end of a dissertation, but 5K and 10K runners still approach the finish line of races feeling depleted and wanting to stop. Allow me to pose some questions for you, questions that may help you get a second (or third or fourth) wind. You might imagine Katherine, your ideal reader, asking them of you:

- **What do your results *mean*?** Put your results in context. How do they relate to the neighborhood of ideas that you discussed in your introduction? How do they contribute to the larger social-scientific conversation that you, with this research, have now entered?

- **So what?** Explain to me why I should care about or be interested in your findings. What relevance should they hold for me and for others? Help me appreciate why I didn't just waste my time reading your work. If you are writing within the positivist tradition, go to the next question, but if your research is informed by constructivist/postmodern ideas, then tell me about your relationship with your results. Why did you not waste your time conducting your research? What has it meant for you? What did you learn about yourself?

- **What do your results *not* mean?** You have already analyzed your results; you know what you have. Now, tell me, what do you *not* have? What is missing from, troublesome, or anemic about your analysis? Why? What error variance crept in? What biases did you bring to your research? If you could start again from scratch, what would you do differently? What conclusions can you *not* draw?

- **What next?** Offer some suggestions for next steps. And please don't just mumble that pat phrase, "More research is needed." Try some educated extrapolating. What better question(s) can you now pose? If I were to give you a small grant to continue your work, what would you do next? Where would your curiosity take you? What if I were to give you a major grant? How would you expand/extend/elaborate the focus/breadth/method of your work?

As you search for answers to these questions, strike a balance between humility and hubris. You need to let your voice be heard, but don't get carried away and subject your readers to a violin-accompanied soliloquy.

Once Katherine is satisfied with your answers, take a deep breath and go back to your *Introduction*. What is missing? What did you not say the first time? Rewrite it so that it properly prepares your readers for what you ended up saying, clean up any remaining rough spots throughout the rest of your manuscript, put together your *Abstract*, and double-check your citations against your reference list. Okay, you're done.

# 3
# How Sentences Work

*The basic unit of language behavior is the sentence. A word has no meaning except as part of a sentence.*
—Walker Percy

*When we reflect that "sentence" means, literally, "a way of thinking" (Latin:* sententia*) and that it comes from the Latin* sentire, *to feel, we realize that the concepts of sentence and sentence structure are not merely grammatical or merely academic—not negligible in any sense. A sentence is both the opportunity and the limit of thought—what we have to think with, and what we have to think in. It is, moreover, a* feelable *thought, a thought that impresses its sense not just on our understanding, but on our hearing, our sense of rhythm and proportion. It is a pattern of felt sense.*
—Wendell Berry

*A writer is not someone who expresses his thoughts, his passion or his imagination in sentences but someone who thinks sentences. A Sentence-Thinker.*
—Roland Barthes

*People . . . think in terms of stories. . . . This is indeed how people think.*
—Gregory Bateson

For a sentence to be a sentence, it must accomplish two tasks simultaneously: It must tell a story, and it must (implicitly) tell readers how to follow the story. Typed on a page, a sentence is just a succession of words; however, when it is *read*, it becomes a *web of relationships*. Punctuation marks, along with various words and word clusters, offer directional guidance, telling readers how and where to make connections between words, preparing them for forthcoming events or details, and helping them remember what has already been said.

I begin this chapter with an explanation of how you can tell the difference between a story and non-story—that is, between a complete and incomplete sentence. I then distinguish three kinds of relationships that words and word groups combine to create: *narrative relationships*, *parallel relationships*, and *referential relationships*. Finally, I describe how various words in a sentence cue readers to go in the right direction at the right time, helping them to keep track of these intra-sentence (and sometimes inter-sentence) relationships. The first part of the chapter may, at times, seem too basic; however, I suggest you read it anyway, if only quickly, because it lays the groundwork for the rest of the book.

## Stories and Sentences

For a story to be a story, something must take place: A narrative must unfold, involving a main character (or two or three), perhaps some props, and some action. Some stories are more sedate (less action-oriented) than others, developing characters or circumstances more than the plot; however, to pass muster as a story, *something* has to happen. The same is true for sentences. For a sentence to be considered "complete," something must occur—a main character (i.e., the subject of the sentence) must be involved in something happening. In a highly plotted sentence, the action is easily recognizable:

> The ethnographer *swaggered* over to his blue Suzuki, *straddled* the seat, and casually *glanced* at the tattooed people he had come to study.

Sometimes the "happening"—the action—in a sentence is less dynamic, more a description of a state of being than of a process. But relating what someone or something "was," "is," or "will be" is still a legitimate way of providing the necessary action for a sentence to be considered complete:

- His polyester pants *had been* on sale.
- Participant observation can *be* difficult.
- The bikers *were* not impressed.

Note that the main character in a sentence need not be human or even alive. In the stories above, "polyester pants" is a thing and "participant observation" is an *abstraction*, and yet each is the main character, or subject, of the sentence.

An incomplete sentence is an incomplete story. If you have a main character and no plot (a subject without a verb), you may have set a scene, but you haven't told a tale:

- ✗ The black Harleys gleaming in the sun.
  (What about them? What happened to them?)
  - ✓ The black Harleys gleaming in the sun sent a shiver up the ethnographer's spine.
- ✗ An ethnographer wanting to blend into a new culture.
  (Yes? What about him or her?)
  - ✓ An ethnographer wanting to blend into a new culture should learn as much as possible about it before beginning his or her study.

Conversely, a plot without a main character (a verb without a subject) is just empty action:

- ✗ Found himself in a sticky predicament.
  (Who found himself in the predicament?)
  - ✓ The ethnographer found himself in a sticky predicament.
- ✗ Was complicated by many factors.
  (What was complicated?)
  - ✓ The encounter with the bikers was complicated by many factors.

Also, if you introduce suspense into a story (via what grammarians identify as subordinate clauses or prepositional, verbal, and absolute phrases), you must resolve it. If you don't, the reader is left hanging and the sentence is left incomplete, even if you have both a main character and some action. Good plots (and complete sentences) demand the resolution of suspense:

- ✗ Whereas the ethnographer's helmet was orange.
  (Yes? What about the other side of the comparison?)
    - ✓ Whereas the ethnographer's helmet was orange, the bikers' helmets were black.
- ✗ Before he took off his brown jacket.
  (Yes? What did he do?)
    - ✓ Before he took off his brown jacket, the ethnographer loosened his tie.
- ✗ The biker who had been staring at the ethnographer the most intently.
  (Yes? What did he do?)
    - ✓ The biker who had been staring at the ethnographer the most intently took off his sunglasses and began to laugh.

A main character without a plot, a plot without a main character, or unresolved suspense: Each gives you what the grammarians call a *sentence fragment*. For a sentence to be complete—for a story to be a story—one of two things needs to happen. Either someone or something needs to do (or be) something—

- ✓ The ethnographer surreptitiously scribbled field notes.
- ✓ The situation was unfortunate.
- ✓ A Suzuki is not a Harley.

—or something needs to happen to someone or something:

- ✓ The bikers were offended by the ethnographer's color preferences.
- ✓ The ethnographer was roughed up.
- ✓ His helmet may have been destroyed.

When someone or something *does* (or *is*) something, that is, when the main character (the subject of the sentence) *acts*, grammarians say the verb is in the *active voice*. When something *happens* to someone or something, that is, when the main character (the subject of the sentence) is *acted upon*, grammarians say the verb is in the *passive voice*.[1]

---

[1] See pages 84–85, 128, and 183 for more information.

Either way, the narrative rule for assessing the integrity of sentences is the same:

No plot? No main character?—No story.
No story?—No sentence.[2]

## Relationships Within Sentences

A simple sentence tells a simple, though not necessarily simplistic, story. Unfolding without suspense or appended descriptions, without multiple characters or multiple themes, its narrative follows a straight-line trajectory.

- Postmodern social scientists argue that "raw"data do not exist.
- The study was funded.
- Keynes underestimated the importance of capital accumulation.
- John Locke believed sensing to be a passive activity.
- Dr. Rogers interviewed Gloria.

Add characters, actions, suspense, and/or descriptive details to these sentences, and you can tell more elaborate stories:

- Pointing to the constructive nature of perception, postmodern social scientists argue that "raw"data do not exist, that all data are, at best, "parboiled."
- The study was funded by government and foundation grants.
- Influenced by the events of the Great Depression, Keynes underestimated the importance of capital accumulation and oversold the benefits of spending.
- John Locke believed sensing to be a passive activity; the mind, according to Locke, could neither refuse nor blot out transmissions from the sense organs.
- Drs. Rogers, Perls, and Ellis, in separate demonstrations of their

[2]This rule about the necessary ingredients for a story or sentence is itself not a complete sentence: The plot is missing. However, it echoes the well-known admonition, "No shirt, no shoes, no service," and thus has more "bite" than something like, "In sum, without both plot and character[s], you have no sentence." Sometimes, if readers trust you know the difference between a story and a scene—between a complete sentence and a sentence fragment—they will accept such a non-story as a purposefully-composed message, rather than an ill-conceived mistake. But even if they assume you intended to write what you did, most social science readers, particularly professors and editors of journals, will tell you to be more conservative. You need neither shirt nor shoes to do good science, but complete sentences help.

respective therapeutic approaches, interviewed Gloria, a woman who had agreed to have three therapy sessions filmed for training purposes.

These elaborated sentences may be more complicated than those in the previous group, but if you look at the *relationships among the parts* configuring them, you will discover not complexity but *organizational simplicity*. Every part of every sentence connects in some way with at least one other part, and this connection can take one (or in some cases, two) of three forms: a *narrative relationship*, a *parallel relationship*, or a *referential relationship*.

## Narrative Relationships

The parts of a sentence that, in combination, contribute to the unfolding of the story can be viewed as being in a narrative relationship with one another. As I mentioned above, every story includes some kind of act, as well as either the actor responsible for it, the person or thing acted upon, or both:

- Interest rates fell.

  Interest rates  →  fell
  (actor)  →  (act)

- The study was funded.

  The study  →  was funded
  (acted upon)  →  (act)

- Dr. Rogers interviewed Gloria.

  Dr. Rogers  →  interviewed  →  Gloria
  (actor)  →  (act)  →  (acted upon)

Also, sometimes the actions in sentences are *intended* for or are *directed to* someone or something. When this is the case, the story will identify a *recipient* (an indirect object) of the action.

- The ethnographer showed the biker his hidden tape recorder.

  The ethnographer → showed → the biker → his hidden
  tape recorder

  (actor)  →  (act)  →  (recipient)  →  (acted upon)

- The biker offered the ethnographer some friendly advice.

    The biker → offered → the ethnographer → some friendly
                                                            advice

    (actor) → (act) → (recipient) → (acted upon)

You might find it helpful to think about the "voice" of the sentence in terms of the *sequencing* of the story. Active-voice sentences introduce the actor first (as the main character or the subject of the sentence), followed by the act and, when it is mentioned, the *acted upon*:

- Knowledge accumulates.

    Knowledge → accumulates
    (actor) → (act)

- Piaget developed.

    Piaget → developed
    (actor) → (act)

- Knowledge accumulates dust.

    Knowledge → accumulates → dust
    (actor) → (act) → (acted upon)

- Piaget developed theories.

    Piaget → developed → theories
    (actor) → (act) → (acted upon)

In passive-voice sentences, the narrative is told in a different order. The *acted upon* is mentioned first, thus becoming the main character of the story (the subject of the sentence). He or she or it is followed by the *act* and (when one is mentioned) the *actor*:

- Adolescent girls were interviewed.

    Adolescent girls → were interviewed
    (acted upon) → (act)

- The piano will be played.

    The piano → will be played
    (acted upon) → (act)

- Adolescent girls were interviewed by Margaret Mead.

  Adolescent girls  →  were interviewed  →  by Margaret Mead
  (acted upon)  →  (act)  →  (actor)

- The piano will be played by David Sudnow.

  The piano  →  will be played  →  by David Sudnow
  (acted upon)  →  (act)  →  (actor)

If the action taken in a passive-voice story is directed to or intended for someone or something, then the recipient of the action may be the first to be mentioned:

- The students were given an exam by the teaching assistant.

  The students → were given → an exam → by the teaching
                                                        assistant
  (recipient)  →  (act)  →  (acted upon)  →  (actor)

## Parallel Relationships

When one part of a sentence is conceptually comparable to one or more others, the parts can be described as being in a parallel relationship with one another:

- Pointing to the constructive nature of perception,
  postmodern social scientists argue
  that "raw" data do not exist, that all data are at best, "parboiled."
                                 this is parallel with this

- The study was funded by government and foundation grants.
                              this is parallel with this

- Influenced by the events of the Great Depression, Keynes
  underestimated the importance of capital accumulation
      and oversold the benefits of spending.
  this is parallel with this

- John Locke believed sensing to be a passive activity; the mind,
  according to Locke, can neither refuse nor blot out transmissions
  from the sense organs.
                         this is parallel with this

> **this** is parallel with **this** and **this**

- Drs. Rogers, Perls, and Ellis, in separate demonstrations of their respective therapeutic approaches, interviewed Gloria, a woman who had agreed to have the three therapy sessions filmed for training purposes.

## Referential Relationships

The anthropologist Robin Dunbar (1996) has suggested that "language evolved to facilitate the bonding of social groups" (p. 123). Evolving hominids, says Dunbar, needed group cohesion to survive, but the elaborate grooming rituals necessary to maintain it took precious time away from other tasks. The appearance of language solved this problem, for it allowed *gossip*—a kind of vocal grooming—to take the place of physical touch. According to Dunbar, "language evolved to allow us to gossip" (p. 79).

Language is not only *the means by which we gossip*, it is, itself, a *gossiper*. Sound strange? Bear with me for a moment. Let's define gossiping as "one person telling another something *about* a third." If you will allow me to stretch this definition so the three participants in the interaction (A gossips to B about C) needn't all be people, I can then point out that some *parts of sentences* (A) gossip to B (readers) *about* other parts of sentences (C). I don't know whether it has anything to do with the evolution of language on the savanna, but gossip is inherent in the structure of language itself.[3]

In making this assertion, I am treating many different types of words and word groups as functionally similar, including (in grammarian terms) adjectives (and articles), adverbs, and pronouns; subject and object complements; appositives and parenthetical expressions; verbal, absolute, and prepositional phrases; and some subordinate or dependent clauses (those used as adjectives or adverbs). All of these parts of sentences tell readers something *about* some other part. You can write well without being able to identify and name an appositive or an absolute phrase, but you should be able to recognize gossip and know how to use it to make your sentences more interesting. Given you already know something about gossip, this shouldn't prove difficult.

---

[3]I'm talking here, of course, about written language, but the same is true of oral language.

    I have named the link between the "gossiper" and the "gossiped about" a *referential relationship*, but this is just a dressed-up word for *gossip connection*. If one part of a sentence says something *about* one or more other parts, that is, if it indicates, describes, or explains (gossips about) the other part(s), then it can be considered referential to the other(s). Here are some of the referential relationships in the following sentences:

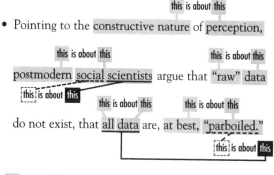

- The study was funded by government and foundation grants.

- Influenced by the events of the Great Depression, Keynes underestimated the importance of capital accumulation and oversold the benefits of spending.

- John Locke believed sensing to be a passive activity; the mind, according to Locke, can neither

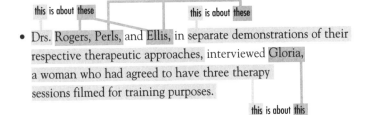

- Drs. Rogers, Perls, and Ellis, in separate demonstrations of their respective therapeutic approaches, interviewed Gloria, a woman who had agreed to have three therapy sessions filmed for training purposes.

**Narrative-Referential Relationships and Parallel-Referential Relationships**

I mentioned earlier that two parts of a sentence can, at times, be in more than one kind of relationship at the same time. In some instances, a string of words may simultaneously tell a story *and* define a referential relationship. In other situations, a cluster of words may be both parallel with *and* referential to another cluster.

Let's begin with an example of a sentence—one I introduced earlier—where the link between the words is both narrative and referential:

- The study was funded.

    The study  →  was funded
    (acted upon)  →  (act)

These words, strung together, tell a story—they create a narrative relationship. However, the word *funded* is also referential to *study*. It provides *gossip* about the study, telling readers that the study was a *funded* study. (Grammarians would call *funded* a subject complement, and because it is a past participle, they might also refer to it as a predicate adjective.) Here are a few more examples of narrative relationships doubling as referential relationships:

- The study is excellent.
    *this is about this*

- The clients felt supported.
    *this is about this*

- The junk bond looked promising.

    *this is about this*

- The coding became a problem.

  this is about this

- The supervisor will be a woman.

  this is about this

In other situations, a word or cluster of words may be both parallel with and referential to another word or cluster. For example:

- The baby, a six-month-old girl, smiled intelligently at the psychologist.

The phrase *a six-month-old girl* is parallel with *the baby*, but it also provides information *about* the baby.

- Locking his office door, Cyril statistically corrected—fudged—the twins' test scores.

Similarly, the word *fudged* is both parallel with and referential to *statistically corrected*: It provides gossip—clarifying information—*about* the "correction."

## Directing the Reader's Eye

When you tell a story to an audience, your gestures, facial expressions, tone of voice, emphases, and pauses all contribute to the telling. And the audience's nonverbal responses, in turn, help you, the storyteller, recognize when they are with you and when they are lost, when you can go forward and when you need to circle back to fill in missing details or clear up confusion. You and the audience keep each other on track, moment by moment.

When you are writing, you don't have the luxury of oral delivery to a live audience. You *do* have other ways, however, of helping ensure your *reading* audience will follow what you are saying. Just as mountain hikers place cairns—little towers of stones—along their trail to mark the path for future trekkers, writers place directional cues throughout their sentences to signal the way for forthcoming readers. As a writer, you have at your fingertips two sorts of cuing devices, two sorts of "literary cairns" that help keep readers from getting lost mid-way through your sentences: *punctuation* and *guiding words*.[4]

Individually and in combination, punctuation marks and guiding words tell readers how the part of the sentence they are presently reading relates to the part(s) they have already read and/or the one they are about to encounter. When these directional signals are coordinated with one another, readers can follow the storied development of a sentence without getting lost. However, when the signals get crossed, that is, when your cues contradict one another or are absent, readers can get mired in ambiguity, confusion, or nonsense.

Each of the various punctuation marks—commas, semicolons, colons, dashes, parentheses, periods, and so on—give readers specific directions for how to relate the different parts of a sentence (or different sentences). In the next chapter, I will be explicating, in detail, which punctuation squiggle does what and which one to use in what circumstances. But first I need to talk about how guiding words, in conjunction with punctuation marks, set up and/or clarify intra-sentence relationships.

## Guiding Words

Guiding words help mark the twists and turns of complicated sentences, directing readers through the complex stories being told. Some words *specify*, *identify*, or *clarify* sentence components; others *connect* them. Some words and word clusters create *suspense* or *anticipation*, preparing readers for upcoming narrative developments. Others direct readers to *return back* (in their minds) to a specific word or phrase earlier in the sentence. A comprehensive cataloging and description of how such guiding words work lies beyond the scope of this book (and probably beyond your tolerance or interest), but I *would* like to offer you a glimpse of how a sentence, in the midst of telling a story, manages to tell readers what to do with their anticipation and their short-term memories.

---

[4]The analogy between cairns and literary clues is somewhat strained. Whereas a hiker's markers are easy to construct and usually simple to spot, a writer's markers are more varied and complex (I don't know of any books devoted to the subtleties of cairn construction), and they are mostly "invisible." That is, readers generally don't pay attention to, and thus don't "see," the embedded clues that keep them from getting lost in the middle of a sentence. Still, both cairns and clues are ways of giving directions, of communicating about a pathway.

## Words that specify, identify, and clarify

Some words within a sentence cue readers about the specificity or familiarity of a character or action in the story; some identify who or what is being talked about; and some clarify what has been discussed or is about to be introduced. Examples of each kind follow:

1. The articles *a*, *an*, and *the* prepare readers to encounter either a specific/familiar person, place, or thing (when *the* is used) or an unspecific/unfamiliar person, place, or thing (when *a* or *an* is used):

• **A** questionnaire was sent to **an** initial sample of 200 households.

The *a* and the *an* signal readers that they haven't yet been introduced to the questionnaire and the sample.

• **The** independent variables were highly correlated with one another.

The *the* indicates that some mention of the independent variables has previously been made.

• I talked to **the** editor of **a** well-respected journal about my manuscript, and she told me that **the** journal has published similar research in the past.

The editor is a specific person, so *the* is an appropriate identification cue. The journal is unspecific when first introduced (hence the *a*) but thereafter is recognizable, so *the* is used the *second* time it is mentioned.

2. Words such as *such, this, these, that, who, whose, those, which, he, she, they, it, his, her, their, its, former,* and *latter* identify who or what is being talked about. A few examples:

• **Such** problems are to be expected when engaging in participant observation.

• However, **this** study focused on the **former** question.

• **She** told **them** not to waste **their** time studying.

• But, of course, **that** is not what she really meant.

• **Those** subjects **who** completed the task ahead of the others were asked to check **their** work.

3. Words such as *first, second, previous,* and *following* clarify what has been discussed or is about to be introduced.

• I chose the participants for three reasons. **First**, they were . . .

• Durkheim proposed that all religions have the **following** elements:

To get a feel for how these kinds of cues work, read the short passage below and then look at the annotated version following it:

> An ethnographer confidently approached a group of bikers, knowing he needed to wait a little while before telling them about his desire to join their gang. He strode up to a large, long-haired fellow, smiled, and thrust out his hand. This was a mistake. The biker sighed.

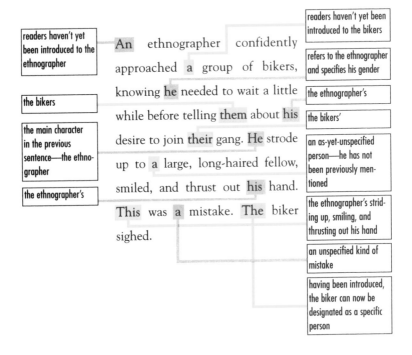

## Words that connect (conjunctions)

By definition, conjunctions make connections. Sometimes by themselves, sometimes in coordination with punctuation marks, they join together different parts of a sentence (or two different sentences). Grammarians distinguish four kinds of conjunctions; you needn't remember the names of them (I'll tell you anyway, in case you are interested), but it will help if you can recognize such connection cues and hear what they do. Here are the most common:

**Coordinating Conjunctions**
*and, but, or, nor, for, yet, so*

**Subordinating Conjunctions**
*after, before, although, though, whether, rather than, because, if, unless, since, when, whereas, while*

**Correlative Conjunctions**
*both . . . and, whether . . . or, either . . . or, neither . . . nor, not only . . . but also, not . . . but*

**Adverbial Conjunctions (or Conjunctive Adverbs)**
*however, also, furthermore, conversely, moreover, nevertheless, similarly, therefore, thus, hence, consequently, indeed, accordingly, further, otherwise*

Different conjunctions define different kinds of links between the sentence parts (or sentences) they join together. Some create simple comparisons (*and, after, before, similarly, both/and, nor, not only / but also*) or contradictions or contrasts (*but, not/but, yet, however, nevertheless, conversely, although, though, whether, otherwise*); others set up choices (*or, either/or, whether/or, neither/nor, whereas, rather than*), conditions (*if, when, while, however, since, unless*), conclusions (*therefore, thus, hence, so, consequently*), elaborations (*after, further, furthermore, also, moreover, indeed*), or explanations (*because, for, hence, accordingly*). A few of these can be found in the paragraph below.

A Pavlovian rat had learned how to salivate on cue, and he enjoyed the rewards of his classical training. Imagine, then, his confusion when some lab assistant placed him in a Skinner box and demanded he make himself useful. He didn't know how to operate the lever, nor did he care to learn; nevertheless, he was interested in eating, so he hallucinated the sound of a buzzer and salivated to that. Although the rat had certainly learned something new, no one in the lab took any notice, for the hallucinations couldn't be empirically measured.

On the following page you will find a repetition of this paragraph; I have highlighted the conjunctions and pointed out the various relationships they create:

| | |
|---|---|
| links the rat's learning and his enjoyment | A Pavlovian rat had learned how to salivate on cue, **and** he enjoyed the |
| compares the rat's not knowing about the lever and his not wanting to learn—an *and* would replace the *nor* if the statements were positive, that is, if the rat knew how to operate the lever and he enjoyed doing so | rewards of his classical training. Imagine, then, his confusion when some lab assistant placed him in a Skinner box **and** demanded he make himself useful. He didn't know how to operate the lever, **nor** |
| sets up a contrast between, on the one hand, his not knowing and not caring about the lever, and, on the other, his interest in eating | did he care to learn; **nevertheless,** he was interested in eating, **so** he hallucinated the sound of a buzzer |
| joins the two actions taken by the rat—the hallucinating and the salivating | **and** salivated to that. **Although** the rat had certainly learned something new, no one in the lab took any notice, **for** the hallucinations couldn't be empirically measured. |

Right-side annotations:

- juxtaposes the two actions taken by the lab assistant
- establishes a logical connection between the rat's interest in eating and his hallucination
- creates a contrast between the rat's new learning and the lab personnel's not noticing
- supplies a logical tie between the people not noticing the rat's hallucinations and their inability to measure them

## Words that create suspense

Because the words of sentences are read *sequentially*, all intra- and inter-sentence relationships (i.e., meanings)[5] are time-dependent. Stories can't begin, unfold, and end without the passage of time, and appended descriptions and comments must always either precede or follow the part of the narrative (or the other descriptions/comments) to which they refer. Thus, during the course of scanning a sentence, readers are continually *expecting* and *remembering*: They are waiting to find out how a description will be phrased or to discover what will happen next, and they are recalling descriptions and happenings they have recently encountered. At certain points in the unfolding of a sentence's story, however, readers' anticipation will be notably heightened or their

[5]As I pointed out in an earlier chapter, meaning within and between sentences depends not only on relationships within the text, but also on relationships between the text and the reader.

memories will be particularly taxed. In this section, I will discuss the times when anticipation develops into suspense; in the next, I will focus on the times when readers' ability to remember is most necessary.

Any film attempting to tell a story requires at least one climactic scene where mysteries or tensions get resolved and loose ends get tied together. Good directors know that for such scenes to be effective, the audience needs to be properly prepared for them. Music and visual effects help to build viewers' anticipation, and they cue the peak of the suspense—the point at which something of critical importance is just about to happen.

The word *suspense* comes from the Latin *pend*, to hang. When an audience is "in suspense," they are "up in the air," not able to predict, but definitely wanting to know, what is going to happen next. As long as the suspense doesn't leave the audience "hanging" so long that they become impatient and bored, it tickles their curiosity, heightening their interest in how the story will turn out.

Although sentences are much smaller narrative structures than films, they too, at times, build suspense prior to the climactic scene of the story, prior to the point where the action in the sentence takes place. Of course, many sentences simply jump in and relate a story without any preamble. Something happens—

- The paper was well written.
- The client started talking.
- I used pseudonyms in the transcripts.
- I used a MANOVA to analyze the data.

—or two or three things happen—

- Postmodern social scientists reject normative guidelines and embrace uncertainty.
- He glanced at the clock and resumed typing his paper.
- The professor turned to the coffee-and-chocolate-stained essay, sighed deeply, and began reading.

—and that's it, end of story. No film could get away with such straightforward simplicity, but sentences don't need to hold their audience's attention nearly so long.

Common to sentences that *do* make use of suspense is a pre-climax word, phrase, or clause[6] that simultaneously provides information and creates uncertainty:

- Unfortunately,
- Unlike their more traditional colleagues,
- To ensure confidentiality of the interviewees,
- The three espressos and two chocolate bars inhaled,
- Whereas many social scientists develop theoretical notions inductively,

Readers reach the height of their suspense as they arrive at the comma at the end of these words/phrases/clauses, just before they encounter the main action of the sentence (see Chapter 4 for a discussion of how commas help to cue the transition from suspense to resolution). At that moment, readers have in hand some information that applies to some or all of the story that follows, but they don't know how it is relevant— that is, what it is *about*—until they read further.

I call these pre-climax preparations *suspense devices* because of the way they pique readers' curiosity and expectancy. Grammarians distinguish four main kinds of suspense-creating word clusters, according to the types of words, phrases, or clauses used. I will acquaint you with the standard grammatical terms as a way of organizing the different referential relationships that can be set up; however, your understanding of how the devices work is more important than your remembering of their formal names. Read the illustrative sentences aloud, and listen for how the suspense is created (by the highlighted word, phrase, or clause), and resolved (by the part of the sentence following the comma).

### Prepositional phrases

Prepositions define the relationship between a thing (a noun, pronoun, or a cluster of words impersonating a noun) and some other word in the sentence. Word clusters beginning with a preposition (and including the thing to which the preposition is attached) are called prepositional

---

[6]A *clause* contains both a subject (the main character of the story the sentence tells) *and* a *predicate* (the action of the story, plus, if mentioned, the person or thing acted upon, the recipient of the action, and any descriptions about them); a *phrase* is a cluster of words containing either a subject *or* a predicate, or neither.

> ### Common Prepositions
> *about, above, according to, across, after, along with, among, apart from, at, because of, before, behind, below, beneath, beside, between, beyond, by, concerning, despite, during, except for, for, from, in, in addition to, in spite of, instead of, into, like, near, next to, of, off, on, over, regarding, since, throughout, to, unlike, up, upon, with, within, without*

phrases. These phrases create suspense when they precede the identification of the main character and his/her/its action in the sentence:

- **Except for some minor typing errors**, the paper was well written.
- **Unlike their more traditional colleagues**, postmodern social scientists reject normative guidelines and embrace uncertainty.
- **Before jazz piano**, David Sudnow studied ethnomethodology.

### Verbals and verbal phrases

Verbals are related to verbs, but rather than carrying the responsibility for the action in sentences, they either impersonate things or describe (say something about) things, actions, or other descriptions. Verbal phrases include the verbal and the words connected to it. Like prepositional phrases, verbals and verbal phrases create suspense when they precede the identification of the main character and his/her/its action in the sentence:

- **Encouraged**, the client started talking.
- **Waking before dawn**, he began writing with his eyes closed.
- **To ensure confidentiality of the interviewees**, I used pseudonyms in the transcripts.

### Absolute phrases

An absolute phrase depicts the ongoing or completed situation of an actor or actors (whether a person, a thing, a place, or an abstraction). When placed at the beginning of a sentence, it creates suspense by offering information (gossip) about the whole of the forthcoming story.

- **The three espressos and two chocolate bars ingested**, he glanced at the clock and resumed typing his paper.

- **Her pen filled with red ink**, the professor turned to the coffee-and-chocolate-stained essay, sighed deeply, and began reading.

### Adverb clauses

If you take a complete story—for example,

- The dependent variables were conceptually (and linearly) related.
- Many social scientists develop theoretical notions inductively.

—and put a subordinating conjunction in front of it (e.g., *after, before, although, though, whether, rather than, because, if, unless, since, when, whereas, while*), the story will no longer be able to stand on its own:

- Because the dependent variables were conceptually (and linearly) related,
- Whereas many social scientists develop theoretical notions inductively,

Called *dependent (adverb) clauses* by grammarians, these word clusters, like the words and phrases discussed above, create suspense when they precede the identification of the main character and his/her/its action in a sentence:

- **Because the dependent variables were conceptually (and linearly) related**, I used a MANOVA to analyze the data.
- **Whereas many social scientists develop theoretical notions inductively**, Bateson derived his abductively.

Most films build and resolve suspense a number of times throughout the course of the story they tell—

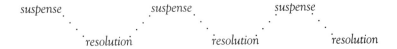

—and sometimes, if the film is more character study than murder mystery, the story may proceed for a long time before any suspense is introduced. Action- or horror-films, in contrast, often begin with a bang and then pull viewers closer and closer to the edges of their seats by piling new suspense onto old:

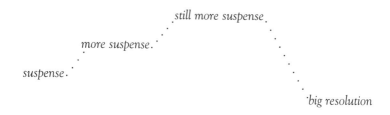

Sentence patterns can follow similar trajectories. For example, a sentence might introduce and resolve suspense more than once in the course of the story it is telling:

> **suspense**                                                    **resolution**
> - To ensure confidentiality of the interviewees, I used pseudonyms in the transcripts, and as an extra precaution, I also erased the tapes.
>                                                        **suspense**          **resolution**

Alternatively, a sentence may delay the introduction of suspense until part of the story has already been told:

> **suspenseless story**
> - The professor turned to the coffee-and-chocolate-stained essay, but, before she could begin reading it, her stomach started growling.
>                   **suspense**                                    **resolution**

Then again, a sentence might build suspense before offering any resolution:

> **suspense**
> - Except for some minor typing errors, and despite the poor choice of topic, the paper was well written.
>             **suspense**                              **resolution**

> **suspense**                              **suspence**
> - Waking before dawn, tugged by his need to finish the chapter, but not yet ready to let go of the dream he had been having, he began writing with his eyes closed.          **suspence**
>             **resolution**

**Words that trigger recall**

Just as *suspense devices* direct readers' attention *forward*, heightening expectancy and anticipation, *recall devices* direct readers' attention *backward*, intensifying associations with earlier-read words or word clusters. Moment by moment, readers place the word or word cluster they are presently scanning within the immediate context of the earlier words in the sentence (and the previous sentence or two). Without short-term memory, readers could not follow the unfolding of the sentence's story.

Some sentences require a minimal amount of remembering. A narrative is laid out, one word following the next—

- John Stuart Mill was held intellectually captive for many years.
- Charles Darwin's grandfather proposed a theory about the transmutation of living forms.
- Kübler-Ross's five stages of dying have become part of our common cultural currency.

—or an appended description is placed just after that which it describes:

this requires readers to remember this

- John Stuart Mill, an advocate of personal liberty, was held intellectually captive for many years by his dictatorial father.

this requires readers to remember this

this requires readers to remember this

- Charles Darwin's grandfather, Erasmus Darwin, proposed, long before Charles was born, a theory about the transmutation of living forms.

this requires readers to remember this

these require readers to remember this

- Kübler-Ross's five stages of dying—denial, anger, bargaining, depression, acceptance—have become part of our common cultural currency.

Many sentences, however, require readers to remember for longer stretches of time or to hold multiple relationships in mind simultaneously. For example, sentences with *personal* and/or *reflexive pronouns* require readers to remember back to previously identified persons, places, or things, and sentences with conjunctions and/or punctuation marks require readers to sort out which components are being related and how the relationship between them is to be understood.

### Sentences with personal and reflexive pronouns

Some actors and stunt doubles work in films as "stand-ins" for the stars, performing dangerous stunts or waiting in position on the set while the lighting and camera crews get everything prepared for the shooting of a scene. The stars remain in their trailers at such times, staying "fresh" until everything is safe and ready. Some words similarly work as "stand-ins" for the "stars" of a sentence. After someone or something appears for the first time in a story, another word—a *personal or reflexive pronoun*—may take his, her, or its place for a while, allowing the "starring word" to "stay fresh" in the mind of the readers.

---

**Personal and Reflexive Pronouns**

*I, me, you, we, us, he, him, she, her, they, them, it, my, mine, your, yours, our, ours, his, her, hers, their, theirs, its, myself, yourself, ourselves, himself, herself, themselves, itself*

---

Pronouns cue readers to recall "starring" words found earlier in the sentence or text:

- John Stuart Mill, an advocate of personal liberty, was held

  this requires readers to remember this

  intellectually captive for many years by his dictatorial father.

- The professor turned to the coffee-and-chocolate-stained essay, but before she could

  this cues readers to recall this      this cues readers to recall this

  begin reading it, her stomach started growling.

  this cues readers to recall this

this cues readers to recall the author (whose name last appeared on the title page of the paper)

• I asked the girl's father if he had talked to her about her having

these cue readers to recall the father          these cue readers to recall the girl

stolen his watch; he said that he had kept himself from

this cues readers to recall the daughter       these cue readers to recall the father

confronting her about it; and he and his wife had agreed that

this cues readers to recall the stealing

they should wait until after her birthday.

this cues readers to recall the father and his wife      this cues readers to recall the daughter

### Sentences with retrace cues

When readers encounter a conjunction and/or a punctuation mark partway through a sentence, they know they are being invited to consider a relationship of some kind—a connection between some or all of the sentence they have read up to that point and some or all of what is to follow. If they have just gotten to the end of a *suspense device* (a word, phrase, or clause), they know that what they have just read will be about some or all of what *follows*. But if the sentence has thus far been suspenseless—

• The study is excellent;
• The interviewer speaks Spanish and
• The students felt supported, and
• The junk bond looked promising,
• Some conflict theorists claim that conflict is necessary for constructive social change,
• The writing went well,

—then readers often don't know, at that moment, the scope or nature of the relationship being created. Only after reading *the first word or two following the conjunction and/or punctuation mark* do they discover what parts of the sentence are to be included in the relationship and what type of relationship is being established. I call these first few words *retrace cues* because they tell readers precisely how far they need to *go back* in the sentence to locate and define the other component(s) in the relationship.[7]

To retrace means "to go back over," or to recall in memory, steps previously taken. Retrace cues tell readers to hold in mind an earlier part (or earlier parts) of a sentence so they will know how to approach and make sense of the part they are about to read. All retrace cues are *ad hoc* recall devices: They are *inducted into service* by virtue of their placement in the sentence (i.e., following a conjunction and/or a punctuation mark).

Let's take the fifth of the suspenseless sentences above and extend it. I have highlighted the retrace cue—the word following the punctuation mark:

- Some conflict theorists claim that conflict is necessary for constructive social change, for the resolution of differences.

The retrace cue (*for*) directs readers to do four things:

a. Juxtapose the part of the sentence beginning with the retrace cue (*for the resolution of differences*) with the earlier part of the sentence starting with the *same word* (*for constructive social change*):

    → for constructive social change
    → for the resolution of differences

b. Consider the two parts parallel (i.e., conceptually comparable) to one another.

c. Read the part of the sentence preceding these two parallel phrases (*Some conflict theorists claim that conflict is necessary*) as a stem for each of them:

    - Some conflict theorists claim that conflict is necessary
        → for constructive social change[,]
        → for the resolution of differences

d. Read the part of the sentence beginning with the retrace cue (*for the resolution of differences*) as a *continuation* of the stem:

    - Some conflict theorists claim that conflict is necessary . . . for the resolution of differences.

[7]Retrace cues are still necessary after a suspense phrase-and-comma, if only to confirm the referential relationship that the suspense phrase is setting up. See below.

Note that the retrace cue retroactively, and simultaneously, defines both the stem and the parallel branches of the sentence:

- Some conflict theorists claim that conflict is necessary

  ┌─▶ **for** constructive social change[,]

  └──**for** the resolution of differences

In this instance, the retrace cue takes readers back to an *identical* word—a *twin word*—earlier in the sentence. Note, though, that not all twins are identical. Thus, a retrace cue can also return readers to an earlier occurrence of a *non-identical* twin word—to a twin that is the *same kind* of word as the retrace cue; to a twin word for which the retrace cue is a *substitute*; or to a twin word for which the retrace cue is a *complement*. I will provide an example of each by successively changing the ending of the sentence (the conjunction or punctuation mark is highlighted in black; the retrace cue is in green; the earlier twin words are underlined):

- Some conflict theorists claim that conflict is necessary for **constructive** social change **and** productive interpersonal relationships.

- Some conflict theorists claim that **conflict** is necessary for constructive social change **because** it helps identify maladjustment.

- **Some conflict theorists** claim that conflict is necessary for constructive social change**;** others argue that social change gives rise to conflict.

☞ **Taking readers back to a twin word of the *same kind* earlier in the sentence**

- Some conflict theorists claim that conflict is necessary for **constructive** social change **and** productive interpersonal relationships.

In this sentence, the retrace cue (*productive*) follows a conjunction (*and*) rather than a punctuation mark, but the implicit directions to readers (for how to read the sentence) are the same. The retrace cue tells readers to juxtapose, and consider parallel, the part of the sentence beginning with the retrace cue (*productive interpersonal relationships*) with the earlier part of the sentence starting with the *same kind of word*—in this instance, with another adjective (_constructive_ social change).

- Some conflict theorists claim that conflict is necessary for
  → constructive social change [and]
  → productive interpersonal relationships

The retrace cue also directs readers to consider the phrase beginning with the retrace cue as a continuation of the stem:

- Some conflict theorists claim that conflict is necessary for . . . productive interpersonal relationships.

☞ **Taking readers back to a twin word for which the retrace cue is a _substitute_**

- Some conflict theorists claim that **conflict** is necessary for constructive social change **because** it helps identify maladjustment.

The retrace cue (the word following the conjunction, _because_) tells readers to juxtapose the part of the sentence it begins (_it helps identify maladjustment_) with the earlier part of the sentence beginning with the word for which it is a _substitute_ (_conflict is necessary for constructive social change_).

- Some conflict theorists claim that
  → conflict is necessary for constructive social change
          [because]
  → it helps identify maladjustment

Also, the part of the sentence beginning with the retrace cue (_it helps identify maladjustment_) can, again, be read as _a continuation_ of the stem:

- Some conflict theorists claim that . . . it helps identify maladjustment.

☞ **Taking readers back to a twin word for which the retrace cue is a _complement_[8]**

- **Some conflict theorists** claim that conflict is necessary for constructive social change; others argue that social change gives rise to conflict.

[8]Any _complementary_ retrace cue will also necessarily be the _same kind_ of word as the one to which it returns readers. Also, note that complements (e.g., self/other, teacher/student) are not compliments (e.g., "my, what a nice theory of conflict").

The retrace cue follows a semicolon this time, and because it happens to be a complement for the words at the beginning of the sentence, no stem precedes the two parallel phrases:

→ Some conflict theorists claim that conflict is necessary for constructive social change[;]

→ others argue that social change gives rise to conflict

Let's go back now to the sentences I began on page 102 and provide endings for them. Notice how each retrace cue pairs up with its earlier twin, thereby telling readers how to make sense of the intra-sentence relationship.

- **The study** is excellent**; it** should be published.
  - → The study is excellent[;]
  - → it should be published

- The interviewer **speaks** Spanish **and** understands French.
  - The interviewer
    - → speaks Spanish [and]
    - → understands French

- **The students** felt supported**, and** the teacher felt respected.
  - → The students felt supported[, and]
  - → the teacher felt respected

- The junk bond looked **promising,** too promising.
  - The junk bond looked
    - → promising[,]
    - → too promising

- **The writing went well**, which surprised me.
  - The writing went well[,]
    - → which surprised me

The retrace cue in this last example is a special case. It doesn't take readers back to a twin word earlier in the sentence, and it doesn't set up a parallel relationship between the phrase it begins (*which surprised me*) and some part of the sentence prior to the comma. Rather, it creates a *referential* relationship: The phrase *which surprised me* is *about* the clause *The writing went well*.

Grammarians refer to the word *which* (as well as to *that, what, who, whose, whom, whoever, whomever*) as a *relative pronoun*. Relative pronouns create referential, rather than parallel relationships, even when they are serving as retrace cues:

- The methodologist, who had studied with Garfinkle, offered many useful suggestions.

  this is about this

- The methodologist, whose expertise included ethnomethodology, offered many useful suggestions.

  this is about this

- Milton Erickson, whom I never met, significantly influenced the practice of brief therapy.

  this is about this

- The blind reviewers, whoever they were, knew what they were talking about.

  this is about this

Note, however, that a post-comma relative pronoun will return readers to a twin relative pronoun earlier in the sentence if one is there to go back to.

- The tape recorder **that** I bought for my interviews, that I desperately needed for my interviews, quit working at the worst possible time.
  - The tape recorder
    - → that I bought for my interviews[,]
    - → that I desperately needed for my interviews[,]

      quit working at the worst possible time.

The two clauses (*that I bought for my interviews*; *that I desperately needed for my interviews*) are parallel with one another and referential to the stem (*The tape recorder*).

# The Story Went Thataway

Guiding words specify, identify, and clarify; they make connections; they create suspense; and they trigger readers' recall. If you keep in mind how they work while you compose your sentences, you can more purposefully provide direction for your readers (see Chapter 6, pp. 171–194 for a detailed illustration). I will be talking about guiding words throughout the next chapter to help explain how punctuation works, but, before we go on, look at the paragraph below. Read it a few times and see if you can recognize how the guiding words keep you from getting lost.

> The boxer landed a left hook to his opponent's cheek, and the crowd leapt to its feet. The sociologist watched and listened from the third row, and she speculated aloud about the societal needs for such violence. Her date for the evening rudely told her to quit analyzing, to enjoy the spectacle for what it was. The sociologist responded with a few words about conflict theory, went on to explain some basic functionalist theory, emptied her beer glass onto the startled man's head, and left alone for a pleasurable night at the theater.

Here is the same paragraph with many of the guiding words highlighted and explained:

A specific boxer.

A non-specific left hook.

Comma & conjunction: juxtaposes the boxer's action and the crowd's response.

A specific crowd—the one watching the match.

Retrace cue: helps define a parallel relationship between the actions of the boxer and those of the crowd.

Suspense device: creates anticipation about what the sociologist will do while she watches and listens. This phrase is referential to the sociologist (in the guise of the pronoun she) and her speculation.

Recall device: a pronoun substituting for the sociologist.

Retrace cue: continues to define The sociologist as the stem. Also establishes emptied her beer glass . . . as the third in a list of parallel actions.

Comma & conjunction: alerts readers that what follows will be the last item of the list.

The boxer landed a left hook to his opponent's cheek, and the crowd leapt to its feet. **As the sociologist watched and listened from the third row**, she speculated aloud about societal needs for such violence. Her date for the evening rudely told her to quit analyzing, to enjoy the spectacle for what it was. The sociologist responded with a few words about conflict theory, went on to explain some basic functionalist theory, emptied her beer glass onto the startled man's head, and left alone for a pleasurable night at the theater.

Recall device: a pronoun referring to the boxer.

Recall device: a pronoun replacing the crowd's.

Conjunction: juxtaposes the watching and the listening.

Retrace cue: defines The sociologist as the stem and watched as the parallel word.

Recall device: refers back to the boxer's left hook.

Recall devices: pronouns substituting for the sociologist.

Retrace cue: defines the phrase that it begins (to enjoy the spectacle . . .) as parallel with to quit analyzing; it also establishes Her date for the evening rudely told her as the stem for both.

Recall device: a pronoun substituting for the spectacle.

Retrace cue: defines The sociologist as the stem and responded with a few words . . . as a parallel phrase.

Retrace cue: maintains The sociologist as the stem and defines left alone for a pleasurable night as conceptually comparable to the three earlier-named actions.

How fortunate that readers don't require explicit directions to negotiate their way through sentences. If all orienting signals needed to be spelled out, it would take forever to read (and write!) the simplest of papers.

# 4
# How Punctuation Works

*If you are getting your commas, semi-colons, and full-stops [i.e., periods] wrong, it means that you are not getting your thoughts right, and your mind is muddled.*

—The Archbishop of York[1]

*All I'm trying to say is that muddle is something to get angry about.*

—Gregory Bateson

As I explained in Chapter 3, every sentence you write tells a story, and the more complex the story, the more you need to provide cues for how to follow it. Without such directional help—provided by *punctuation marks* and *guiding words*—readers would quickly get in a muddle, losing track of who is who, what is what, who is doing what to whom, what is being done by whom, and so on. When the directions provided by punctuation marks and guiding words are clear and unambiguous, readers can more easily follow your line of thought, smoothly negotiating the pathways of even your more complicated sentences. If, however, your directions for readers are missing, misplaced, or contradictory, readers will stumble or get lost.

In the previous chapter, I mapped out, in slow-motion detail, how guiding words help readers follow a sentence's story line and keep track

[1]The comments of the archbishop, a Dr. Temple, appeared in a 1938 newspaper article (see Partridge, 1994, p. 259).

of any parallel and/or referential relationships augmenting the narrative. In this chapter, I turn my attention to punctuation marks, explaining how they, in coordination with guiding words, participate in telling readers what to do: what to anticipate, what to remember, what parts of the sentence to compare, and how to understand the resulting relationship(s).

Punctuation conventions have evolved over the years. Until the 18th century, writers used punctuation marks mostly as a way of indicating how to read a text aloud—such as where to take pauses for a breath. It is more common now for writers to consider grammar rather than oration when making their punctuation choices (see McArthur, 1992, pp. 824-826), and this shift has led to greater "inter-writer reliability." However, variations still exist, particularly between popular and scientific writers.

As a writer, my goal is to make it easy for readers to find their way through my sentences. If they are going to slow down or pause or go back over a passage, I want this to be because they are reflecting on my ideas or appreciating the way I have described or explained something; I don't want them scratching their heads in bewilderment, trying to get their bearings. In this chapter, I describe how to keep your readers oriented and stumble-free. My explanations may differ somewhat from those of other advice-givers, but if you follow my suggestions, your placement choices will be consistent, and most of your professors, colleagues, and/or copyeditors (the fine-tooth-comb folks who clean up manuscripts prior to publication) will consider them correct.

## Commas

*All morning I worked on the proof of one of my poems, and*
*I took out a comma; in the afternoon I put it back.*
                                                    —Oscar Wilde

Some writers still insert commas where they think readers will need to pause and take a breath. I suggest you not follow this practice—just think what would happen to your comma-placement choices if you (or Katherine, your imaginary reader) were to take up marathon running or develop a heart condition. More seriously, I suggest that as you compose your sentences, you think not of pauses but of the intra-sentence *relationships* you are setting up. Guiding words sometimes can (and should) act alone, telling readers what sentence components to juxtapose and what to make of (how to interpret) the resulting relationship. But when guiding words can't provide readers with all the necessary directional cues for how to read a sentence, commas (and other punctuation marks) become essential for preventing ambiguity or misunderstanding.

Now, before I start ladling out the advice, let me tell you a quick story about a time when I was about ten years old. I was in our family's living room making light of a serious situation, and my father, an accomplished punster whom I emulated to the best of my ability, was admonishing me to be more discriminating in my use of humor. "Douglas," he sternly told me, "not *everything* is funny." I, predictably, laughed off his counsel, thereby demonstrating how badly I needed it. I have since developed some discretion in my use of humor (or do you think various passages in this book belie my claim?), and I have gone on to offer others a more generalized version of the advice he gave me that day: "Always consider the context."[2] Sometimes a pun is best not cracked, sometimes an opinion is best not voiced, and sometimes a comma is best not inserted. I suppose this is as good a place as any to start—with a suggestion about when *not* to use a comma.

#### ➤ Don't interrupt the unfolding of a story unless you have something to say

Narrative relationships must remain inviolable. Don't sever the connections between the primary components of a sentence's story; otherwise, you will disrupt the flow of the plot. Thus, don't place a comma between the actor and the act, the act and the acted upon, the act and the recipient of the action, or the acted upon and the recipient of the action. (Or, as the grammarians would put it, between a subject and a verb, a verb and a direct object, a verb and an indirect object, or a direct and indirect object.)

   ✓  The ethnographer gave the biker the tape recorder.

     ✗  The ethnographer, gave the biker the tape recorder.

     ✗  The ethnographer gave, the tape recorder to the biker.

     ✗  The ethnographer gave, the biker the tape recorder.

---

[2] The irony of having a *general* rule about the *specificity* of context has not escaped my notice. Maybe everything *is* funny after all.

✗   The ethnographer gave the tape recorder, to the biker.

✗   The ethnographer gave the biker, the tape recorder.

You *can*, however, interrupt the narrative *if you have something to say*— that is, if you provide explanatory or descriptive information (gossip) about the actor(s), the act, the acted upon, or the recipient(s) of the action.

✓   The ethnographer, **looking ashen,** gave the biker the tape recorder.

✓   The ethnographer gave, **or, more accurately,** *surrendered,* the tape recorder to the biker.

✓   The ethnographer gave, **alas,** the biker the tape recorder.

✓   The ethnographer gave the tape recorder, **a Sony TCM-80V,** to the biker.

✓   The ethnographer gave the biker, **Carl,** the tape recorder.

**•◦   Differentiate *essential* from *non-essential* gossip, and punctuate accordingly**

All gossip is potentially interesting, but certain gossip is essential. Let me explain. If the descriptive information you provide in a sentence is necessary for readers to distinguish someone or something from someone or something else—that is, if it clarifies the *identity* of someone or something—then the information, the gossip, is *essential.* (Grammarians call an essential piece of gossip a *restrictive element.*) Don't set off essential gossip with commas—it is part of who or what the someone or something *is.*

- The woman reading a novel ordered a second cappuccino.

- The bill still in committee won't come to the floor for another few weeks.

- The student who had read David Harvey once again challenged the professor's assumptions about urbanization.

The absence of commas in these sentences allows the gossip to differentiate the person or thing being discussed from someone or something else—perhaps from someone who *isn't* reading a novel, from a bill that *isn't* still in committee, from one or more students who *hadn't* read David Harvey.

- The woman reading a novel ordered a second cappuccino whereas the man reading poetry asked for mint tea.
- The bill still in committee won't come to the floor for another few weeks, but the one that has just come out should be voted on this afternoon.
- The student who had read David Harvey once again challenged the professor's assumptions about urbanization; the others in the class rolled their eyes and yawned.

If a piece of gossip enhances the reader's understanding of someone or something in a sentence, but the identity of the someone or something *is not in question*—that is, if it has already been established or is clear from the context—then you can consider the gossip *non-essential*. Non-essential gossip (nonrestrictive elements) must be parenthetically enclosed in commas, parentheses, or dashes. (I will discuss using parentheses and dashes below, under their own headings.)

- The woman, reading a novel, ordered a second cappuccino.

The commas on either side of the gossip establish it as an interesting, non-essential bit of information about the woman. The commas tell readers, "You already know who the woman is, so that's settled, but here is something that might pique your interest: She happened to be reading a novel."

- The bill, still in committee, won't come to the floor for another few weeks.

Only one bill, previously identified, is being talked about. The phrase *still in committee* augments readers' understanding of the status of the bill; it doesn't isolate and define the bill in contradistinction to others.

- The student, who had read David Harvey, once again challenged the professor's assumptions about urbanization.

The gossip in this sentence augments readers' knowledge about the student. By enclosing it in commas, the writer is saying to readers: "I know you know who the student is; I should, however, fill you in on something: He had read David Harvey."

Let me give you another couple of illustrations with which to test your discernment.

- As the social worker began talking, the daughter who had been abused shot her father an angry glance.
- As the social worker began talking, the daughter, who had been abused, shot her father an angry glance.

The first example implies that *more than one daughter* was in the room with the father and social worker—the daughter who had been abused was the one who shot the angry glance.

> ✓ As the social worker began talking, the daughter who had been abused shot her father an angry glance. Her sister wondered if the social worker had noticed.

The second example implies that *only one* daughter was in the room with the father and social worker.

> ✓ As the social worker began talking, the daughter, who had been abused, shot her father an angry glance. She wished her sister were there.

The fact that the daughter had been abused is important information, but because she alone was in the room with the adults, readers can still distinguish who she is without the added description.

- The students who asked the most difficult questions were obviously better prepared.
- The students, who asked the most difficult questions, were obviously better prepared.

The first sentence of this pair tells readers that the less-prepared students in the room asked easier questions than the better-prepared students.

> ✓ The students who asked the most difficult questions were obviously better prepared. The students who asked the easier questions probably hadn't read the material as closely.

The second illustrative sentence says that people other than students were in the room (perhaps faculty members, professionals, or people from the community), and they demonstrated their lack of preparation by asking easier questions.

&#10003;  The students, who asked the most difficult questions, were
obviously better prepared. The faculty members seemed not
to have read the material as closely.

In the first example, some number of students (within a larger group of
students) asked the most difficult questions; in the second, all of the
students (within a larger group made up of students and non-students)
asked the most difficult questions.

**➠ Reserve your *whiches* for non-essential gossip**

As an undergraduate in Canada, I cultivated the habit, more common
among British than American writers, of using *which* at the beginning
of phrases or clauses providing essential gossip (i.e., at the beginning of
restrictive elements).

- The journal which finally accepted her manuscript for publication has an excellent reputation in the field.
- Data-gathering which relies on participant observation and in-
depth interviews has been criticized for being "more journalistic
than scientific."

I thought my *whiches* made my writing sound more cultured, more academic, more, well, more British, and this held some allure. But had I
read Fowler's *Modern English Usage*, a most *British* English style manual,
I would have quickly squelched my pretensions. He points out that
writers reaching for "literary" sophistication tend to substitute their
*whiches* for their *thats*, but that their efforts are based on a misunderstanding of the differences between speech and writing. He goes on:

> The two kinds of relative clause, to one of which *that* and
> to the other of which *which* is appropriate, are the defining
> and the non-defining; and if writers would agree to regard
> *that* as the defining relative pronoun, and *which* as the non-
> defining, there would be much gained both in lucidity and
> in ease. (Fowler, 1965, pp. 625-626)

Of course, before giving up my *whiching* habit, I would have had to have
understood what Fowler was saying. In case you find yourself as challenged today as I would have been then, allow me to translate his jargon into mine: Use *which* for *non-essential* (non-identifying) *gossip*; use
*that* for *essential* (identifying) *gossip*.

✗   The journal which finally accepted her manuscript for publication
has an excellent reputation in the field.

   ✓   The journal that finally accepted her manuscript for publication has an excellent reputation in the field.

   ✓   The paper, which builds on Gilligan's criticisms of Kohlberg's
theory of moral development, will be the lead article.

The gossip in the first correct sentence—*that finally accepted her manuscript*—distinguishes the journal that accepted the paper from those
that didn't.

   ✓   The journal that finally accepted her manuscript for publication
has an excellent reputation in the field.

The parenthetical gossip in the second correct sentence—*which builds
on Gilligan's criticisms of Kohlberg's theory of moral development*—provides
interesting information, but it doesn't identify the paper in contradistinction to others.

   ✓   The paper, which builds on Gilligan's criticisms of Kohlberg's
theory of moral development, will be the lead article.

Let's take another look at the other illustrative sentence:

✗   Data-gathering which relies on participant observation and in-
depth interviews has been criticized for being "more journalistic than scientific."

   ✓   Data-gathering that relies on participant observation and in-
depth interviews has been criticized for being "more journalistic than scientific."

   ✓   The criticism, which some qualitative researchers would take
as a compliment, is based on the assumption that objectivity
and truth are synonymous.

The gossip in the first correct sentence—*that relies on participant observation and in-depth interviews*—identifies a *particular kind* of data-gathering.

   ✓   Data-gathering that relies on participant observation and in-
depth interviews has been criticized for being "more journalistic than scientific."

The parenthetical gossip in the second correct sentence—*which some
qualitative researchers would take as a compliment*—enhances readers'
understanding of the criticism, but it doesn't define or distinguish it relative to other criticism.

✓ The criticism, which some qualitative researchers would take as a compliment, is based on the assumption that objectivity and truth are synonymous.

**➣ Remember to insert the second of paired commas**

Paired commas parenthetically enclose non-essential gossip—that is, they impersonate parentheses, marking the beginning and end of a piece of non-identifying descriptive or explanatory information.

$$[. . . , . . . , . . .] = [. . . (. . .) . . .]$$

✓ The son, a 14-year-old with long hair and tattoos, looked at me with a penetrating glare and began to snicker.
✓ My supervisor, who had had years of training in Milan, tended to speak in circles, and he kept muttering something about hypotheses.

When readers encounter the first comma of the pair, they are cued to begin a detour away from the narrative pathway; when they reach the second comma, they know that the detour is over, that it is time to return to the main thoroughfare of the story being told.

✓ My computer, which had worked well for years, decided to fizzle the night before my qualifying exam was due.
✓ Symbolic interactionism, stemming from the work of George Herbert Mead, holds that meaning depends on social relationships.

If you forget to insert the second comma of the pair, you force your readers to grope around and discover for themselves where the narrative picks up again. In the process they may get lost or, at the very least, irritated by your leaving them in the lurch.

✗  The son, a 14-year-old with long hair and tattoos looked at me
   with a penetrating glare and began to snicker.

✗  My supervisor, who had had years of training in Milan tended
   to speak in circles, and he kept muttering something about
   hypotheses.

✗  My computer, which had worked fine for years decided to fizzle
   the night before my qualifying exam was due.

✗  Symbolic interactionism, stemming from the work of George
   Herbert Mead holds that meaning depends on social relationships.

•◦ **Use a coordinating conjunction *with a comma* to connect two
   complete stories**

If you wish to link two complete stories (independent clauses), you can
use a semicolon (see page 137), or you can use a comma together with
a coordinating conjunction (*and, but, or, nor, for, yet, so*), but you can't
use only a comma or only a conjunction—neither is capable of creating such a connection on its own.

✓  Piaget believed that infants and children pass through a series
   of invariable *cognitive* stages, **and** Kübler-Ross believed that
   dying people pass through a series of invariable *emotional*
   stages.

   ✗  Piaget believed that infants and children pass through a
      series of invariable *cognitive* stages **and** Kübler-Ross believed
      that dying people pass through a series of invariable *emo-
      tional* stages.

   ✗  Piaget believed that infants and children pass through a
      series of invariable *cognitive* stages, Kübler-Ross believed
      that dying people pass through a series of invariable *emo-
      tional* stages.

When readers arrive at a comma-conjunction combination at the end of
a complete story, they are signaled to prepare for a second complete story.

   →  Piaget believed that infants and children pass through a
      series of invariable *cognitive* stages[**, and**]
   →  Kübler-Ross believed that dying people pass through a
      series of invariable *emotional* stages.

Immediately following the comma-and-conjunction, readers find a *retrace cue* (see Chapter 3), a recall device that provides a second directional signal for how to follow the narrative line of the sentence.

Commas and/or conjunctions set up relationships within sentences; retrace cues define the starting points of the parts related. When readers encounter a retrace cue after a coordinating conjunction or comma-conjunction combination, they are taken back (in their memory) to an earlier *twin* word in the sentence, a word to which the retrace cue is *identical*, *similar*, or *complementary*, or for which it is a *substitute*. (Each is illustrated in Chapter 3.)

In this case, the retrace cue returns readers to *Piaget*, a twin that is the same kind of word as (i.e., similar to) *Kübler-Ross*.

✓ <u>Piaget</u> believed that infants and children pass through a series of invariable *cognitive* stages **, and** Kübler-Ross believed that dying people pass through a series of invariable *emotional* stages.

Both the comma-and-conjunction and the retrace cue give readers the same message: "Connect the Piaget story with the Kübler-Ross story, and consider them parallel with one another."

Here is another example:

✓ The biker rewound the cassette tape, for he wanted to hear what the ethnographer had recorded.

The comma-and-conjunction tells readers to juxtapose two complete stories and treat them as structurally parallel; the retrace cue (he), a pronoun, defines the boundaries of the two parallel components by taking readers back to a twin word (biker) for which it is a substitute:

✓ <u>The biker</u> rewound the cassette tape **, for** he wanted to hear what the ethnographer had recorded.

→ The biker rewound the cassette tape[, for]

→ he wanted to hear what the ethnographer had recorded

As in the previous example, the punctuation (the comma) and the guiding words (the coordinating conjunction and the retrace cue) are well coordinated, so readers are given clear directions for proceeding.

**•➤ Use a coordinating conjunction *without a comma* to join sentence components that are not complete stories**

A coordinating conjunction (*and, but, or, nor, for, yet, so*) *not* preceded by a comma establishes a parallel relationship between words or word clusters that don't, in and of themselves, tell a story.

✓  The ethnographer looked confident but felt like crying.

The conjunction (*but*) signals readers to prepare to encounter the second half of a parallel relationship, and the retrace cue (*felt*) links back to the twin word *looked*. This establishes *The ethnographer* as the stem and *looked confident* and *felt like crying* as parallel actions.

✓  The ethnographer <u>looked</u> confident **but** felt like crying.
- The ethnographer
  → looked confident [but]
  → felt like crying.

Now, let's see what would happen if you were to place a comma before the coordinating conjunction.

✗  <u>The ethnographer</u> looked confident**, but** felt like crying.

As you know from the discussion above, a comma-conjunction combination at the end of a complete story signals readers to expect a second complete story, parallel to the first, to follow.

→ The ethnographer looked confident[, but]
→ felt like crying.

Of course, the phrase *felt like crying* isn't parallel to *The ethnographer looked confident*, so readers may be momentarily confused. Conflicting signals make for difficult reading.

The conjunctions in the following example establish two sets of parallel relationships.

✓  The historian and the geographer argued about time and space.

The signals provided by the conjunctions and the two retrace cues (*the geographer* and *space*) coordinate well with each other.

✓  <u>The historian</u> **and** the geographer argued about <u>time</u> **and** space.
  → The historian [and]
  → the geographer

                argued about

                            → time [and]
                            → space.

Look, though, at what happens when commas are inappropriately inserted:

✗  The historian, and the geographer argued about time, and space.

The contradictory signals sent by the comma-conjunctions and the retrace cues render the sentence incomprehensible.

Here is another illustration:

✓  The postmodern anthropologist couldn't decide whether to deconstruct *The Savage Mind* or to compose an ironic poem.

The conjunction (*or*) tells readers to connect and consider parallel two words or word clusters; the retrace cue (*to*), signaling back to an identical twin word earlier in the sentence, designates what the two phrases will be.

✓  The postmodern anthropologist couldn't decide whether <u>to</u> deconstruct *The Savage Mind* `or` to compose an ironic poem.

  • The postmodern anthropologist couldn't decide whether
    → to deconstruct *The Savage Mind* [or]
    → to compose an ironic poem.

However, confusion ensues if a comma is inserted before the *or*:

✗  The postmodern anthropologist couldn't decide whether to deconstruct *The Savage Mind*, or to compose an ironic poem.

The comma-conjunction instructs readers to put the phrase *to compose an ironic poem* in a parallel relationship with the earlier complete story, but, of course, this doesn't make sense.

    → The postmodern anthropologist couldn't decide whether
      to deconstruct *The Savage Mind*[, or]
    → to compose an ironic poem.

Here is a final example:

✗  A good hypothesis transforms a research question into a declarative statement, and predicts a specific relationship between variables.

The comma-and-conjunction prepares readers for a retrace cue that will be a twin of *A good hypothesis* (such as the pronoun). Instead, they find a word (*predicts*) that is parallel with and takes them back to *transforms*.

The directional signals clash, and readers are caught in the cross-fire.

> → A good hypothesis transforms a research question into a declarative statement[, and]
> → predicts a specific relationship between variables.

You have two simple solutions available: You can put in a pronoun or take out the comma. Either way, the signals from the punctuation (or its absence), the conjunction, and the retrace cue will then accord with one another.

> ✓ <u>A good hypothesis</u> transforms a research question into a declarative statement, and it predicts a specific relationship between variables.
>
>> → A good hypothesis transforms a research question into a declarative statement[, and]
>> → it predicts a specific relationship between variables.

> ✓ A good hypothesis <u>transforms</u> a research question into a declarative statement and predicts a specific relationship between variables.
>
>> • A good hypothesis
>>> → transforms a research problem into a declarative statement [and]
>>> → predicts a specific relationship between variables.

### •• Place commas at the end of all suspense devices

Suspense devices (see Chapter 3 for a thorough discussion) build anticipation, heightening readers' curiosity about the story to follow.

> ✓ As Hitler invaded Poland,
> ✓ Her contributions finally recognized,
> ✓ Within the next six months,
> ✓ Furious,
> ✓ Lifting the tape recorder to his ear,
> ✓ To compete culturally with the U.S.,
> ✓ Had the World Wide Web not been created,
> ✓ Unless you have read Turner (1986),

The commas at the end of these statements cue readers that the suspense has been fully articulated and is about to be resolved.

Some authors don't use a comma to indicate the transition between suspense and story if the words themselves provide enough direction.

✓ Before Watergate the country was less cynical, more smugly innocent.

✓ Although not traditional my method is certainly not avant-garde.

However, I recommend you get in the habit of always marking the shift between suspense and resolution. Even if some readers find your commas unnecessary, your including them will never be wrong, and you will often help prevent misreading (or the necessity of rereading).

✓ Before Watergate, the country was less cynical, more smugly innocent.

✓ Although not traditional, my method is certainly not avant-garde.

✓ Before her talk, she felt nervous and irritable. After, she was able to relax.

✓ After she was able to relax, she started to enjoy herself.

This habit will also help you avoid writing sentences that inadvertently leave readers completely up in the air.

✗ Whereas the European witch hunts of the 15th, 16th, and 17th centuries were organized and carried out by men.

If you search for a place to insert a comma, you will discover that the end of the suspense coincides with the end of the sentence, and that means you have a problem—you can't end a sentence until you have *resolved* the suspense.

✓ Whereas the European witch hunts of the 15th, 16th, and 17th centuries were organized and carried out by men, the victims were almost exclusively women.

### ↝ Make sure your suspense devices imprint to their real mother

As the ethologist Konrad Lorenz discovered, newly hatched greylag goslings attach themselves (imprint) to the first moving object they see. That object becomes "mother," even if "she" happens to be a male scientist. Once the baby birds have imprinted, they follow their "mother" everywhere.[3]

---

[3] Carroll Ballard's 1996 film *Fly Away Home* (starring Anna Paquin and Jeff Daniels) depicts some of the consequences of this programmed behavior—a young girl becomes "mother" to a gaggle of goslings.

Suspense devices lack the fuzzy down of baby geese, but many of them imprint in the same way. Save for adverb clauses and absolute phrases (see Chapter 3), suspense devices attach themselves to whatever they see first—to whatever is placed directly after them in the sentence. As with goslings, this hard-wired behavior usually works out for the best, but if something disrupts the process, that is, if the first thing following the suspense device is not the real mother, the results can be as hilarious as little geese happily waddling after a big, featherless, wingless, beakless ethologist. Let's take a look at a few examples. Grammarians call the following errors *dangling modifiers*, but I think of them as *waddling suspenselings*.

✗ While waiting for the questionnaires to be returned, the literature review was rewritten.

Can't you just see the literature review in the corner of the window, looking out over the stormy sea, waiting for the questionnaires to come back? The *researcher*, not the literature review, was waiting for the questionnaires to come back.

✓ While waiting for the questionnaires to be returned, I rewrote the literature review.

✗ Following Lakoff (1987), readers will be provided with an understanding of how "the classical theory of categorization is as wrong for language as it is for the rest of the mind" (p. 182).

The *author of the sentence* is the one doing the following.

✓ Following Lakoff (1987), I assume that "the classical theory of categorization is as wrong for language as it is for the rest of the mind" (p. 182).

✗ Never having been married, the therapist's suggestions to the couple were perceived as naive.

I'm not sure whether marriage laws will ever relax to the point where they will allow legal unions between consenting suggestions. The *therapist* was the one who hadn't been married.

✓ Never having been married, the therapist offered suggestions that the couple perceived as naive.

✗ Focusing on the positive changes he had initiated over the previous three years, the audience was given a predictable re-election speech.

How fortunate for the political candidate making his speech—how often does the audience focus on positive changes? Of course, the sentence meant to say that the focusing was the *candidate's*.

✓ Focusing on the positive changes he had initiated over the previous three years, the candidate gave the audience a predictable re-election speech.

✗ To improve reliability, the questionnaire was lengthened by fifteen items.

Perhaps after some new breakthroughs in AI (artificial intelligence), researchers will be able to sit back and let their data-gathering instruments find ways to improve their own reliability. Until then, we have to do it ourselves.

✓ To improve reliability, I added fifteen items to the questionnaire.

✗ As a means of organizing our thoughts to reach understanding, Wolcott (1994) proposed that "research is . . . not an end in itself" (p. 37).

I can think of a number of apt descriptions of Wolcott, but "a means of organizing our thoughts to reach understanding" is not one of them.

✓ As a means of organizing our thoughts to reach understanding, research is an important tool; however, it "is not an end in itself" (Wolcott, 1994, p. 37).

✗ As a geographer, examining Los Angeles can illuminate "a paradigmatic window through which to see the last half of the twentieth century" (Soja, 1989, p. 221).

All the geographers I know are people; I've never met one who was an examining.

✓ As a geographer, I agree with Soja's (1989) description of Los Angeles as "a paradigmatic window through which to see the last half of the twentieth century" (p. 221).

✗ Although obviously an imposter, the biker didn't know he was a social scientist.

According to George Kelly (1955), we all attempt to predict and control our experience, and this makes us all quasi-scientists, even if we haven't received any formal scientific training. This sentence suggests that the biker, revealed as an imposter, hadn't been reading his Kelly;

otherwise, he would have known very well that he, along with everyone else, is a social scientist. But, of course, the sentence has nothing to do with the ideas of George Kelly; rather, it is about (or, at least, *wants* to be about) the biker not having known that the imposter in front of him was an ethnographer, a social scientist. Two straightforward solutions present themselves:

✓ Although the ethnographer was obviously an imposter, the biker didn't know he was a social scientist.

✓ Although obviously an imposter, the ethnographer had not yet revealed he was a social scientist.

In the first five illustrations above, I was able to reattach the waddling suspenselings to their true mothers (i.e., to the actor of the story—the subject of the sentence) by changing passive voice constructions to active voice (see Chapter 3). ~~If passive-voice sentences are avoided in favor of active-voice sentences~~, If you favor active- over passive-voice sentences, you will cut down on the number of words it takes to say what needs saying, and you will decrease the chances of some mis-imprinted suspense phrase unintentionally amusing your readers.

➡ **Place commas between parallel items in a list**

Commas tell readers to compare successive items in a list and to consider each one parallel with the others.

✓ Rousseau, Hegel, and Marx each espoused anti-positivist views.

→ Rousseau[,]

→ Hegel[, and]

→ Marx

each espoused anti-positivist views.

✓ Rosenhan and his confederates pretended they heard voices, used this symptom as a pretext for gaining admission to a variety of psychiatric hospitals, acted normal once they were admitted, and waited for someone to notice they were sane.

• Rosenhan and his confederates

→ pretended they heard voices[,]

→ used this symptom as a pretext for gaining admission to a variety of psychiatric hospitals[,]

→ acted normal once they were admitted[, and]

→ waited for someone to notice they were sane.

✓ Octavio Paz considers Levi-Strauss's writings to have a threefold importance: anthropological, philosophical, and aesthetic.

- Octavio Paz considers Levi-Strauss's writings to have a threefold importance:
  → anthropological[,]
  → philosophical[, and]
  → aesthetic.

✓ Norbert Weiner coined the word *cybernetics*, Jacques Derrida invented the term *différance*, and Clifford Geertz introduced the phrase *thick description*.

  → Norbert Weiner coined the word *cybernetics*[,]
  → Jacques Derrida invented the term *différance*[, and]
  → Clifford Geertz introduced the phrase *thick description*.

**➥ Include a comma between the last two items in a list**

Journalists typically leave out the comma between the second-to-last and the last item in a list.

- The film won four Academy Awards: Best Cinematography, Best Editing, Best Costumes and Best Musical Score.

After you land a job at *The Times*, *The Post*, or *The Herald*, you can start dropping that last comma, but until then, follow the convention in academia and the professional disciplines: Insert the final comma (as I did earlier in this sentence). Without the last comma to provide clear directional guidance, readers may have trouble distinguishing components in the list.

✗ The film won Academy Awards for Cinematography, Editing, Costumes and Musical Score.

In the earlier version of this sentence, the mentioning of *four* awards and the repetition of the word *best* helped prevent misreading, despite the absence of the final comma. Scanning *this* sentence, however, readers might initially think the Academy, in an effort to shorten the length of their yearly extravaganza, had come up with a new joint-category Oscar: "Costumes and Musical Score."

✗ The film won Academy Awards for Cinematography, Editing, Costumes and Musical Score.

- The film won Academy Awards for
  - → Cinematography[,]
  - → Editing[,]
  - → Costumes and Musical Score.

A final comma sets readers straight.

- ✓ The film won Academy Awards for Cinematography, Editing, Costumes, and Musical Score.
  - The film won Academy Awards for
    - → Cinematography[,]
    - → Editing[,]
    - → Costumes[, and]
    - → Musical Score.

## ⚫➤ Don't place a comma after the last item of a list

Once you get started placing commas after list items, don't get carried away. Resist the urge to put a comma after the last item.

- ✗ Victor Frankl considered spirituality, freedom, and responsibility, the three most distinctive human qualities.

Putting a comma after *responsibility* interrupts the narrative flow of the sentence; leaving it out allows the story to unfold.

- ✓ Victor Frankl considered spirituality, freedom, and responsibility the three most distinctive human qualities.
  - Victor Frankl considered
    - → spirituality[,]
    - → freedom[, and]
    - → responsibility[ ]
      the three most distinctive human qualities.

Of course, if the end of a list coincides with the end of a suspense phrase, you will need to insert a comma, but the insertion will have nothing to do with the list itself. Here is a sentence with two lists, each a part of a suspense phrase:

- ✓ Before Mikhail Gorbachev, Lech Walesa, and Vaclav Havel, before the rusting of the Iron Curtain, the fall of the Berlin Wall, and the thawing of the Cold War, Americans viewed Eastern Europeans with suspicion and fear.
  - → Before Mikhail Gorbachev, Lech Walesa, and Vaclav Havel[,]

→ before the rusting of the Iron Curtain, the fall of the Berlin Wall, and the thawing of the Cold War[,]
  
  Americans viewed Eastern Europeans with suspicion and fear.

You will also need to insert a comma after the last item of a list if the sentence needs a comma-and-conjunction to join two complete stories, but, again, the comma will have nothing to do with the list per se.

✓ The biker listened to the tape, to his friends' angry shouting, and to the pleading of the incompetent imposter, **and** he mulled over his various options.

→ The biker listened
  → to the tape[,]
  → to his friends' angry shouting[, and]
  → to the pleading of the incompetent imposter[, and]
→ he mulled over his various options.

•◆ **Be sure each list item is structurally parallel with the others**
After you have composed a list-containing sentence, check that the list items are all parallel.

✓ Lab researchers strive to increase between-group variance, decrease within-group variance, and control extraneous variables.

You can do this easily by first confirming that your retrace cues—in this case, *decrease* and *control*—are each twins of the word they recall (*increase*).

✓ Lab researchers strive to <u>increase</u> between-group variance, decrease within-group variance, and control extraneous variables.

• Lab researchers strive to
  → increase between-group variance[,]
  → decrease within-group variance[, and]
  → control extraneous variables

The second step involves connecting each list item to the non-list part of the sentence—in this case, the stem, *Lab researchers strive to*—and confirming that the result is a complete story:

✓ Lab researchers strive to increase between-group variance.

✓ Lab researchers strive to decrease within-group variance.

✓ Lab researchers strive to control extraneous variables.

If both checks check out, you know that the parallel structure of your sentence is in good shape.

Let's take a look at a muddled version of the lab-researcher sentence and use this two-step procedure to isolate the problem and find a solution.

✗ Lab researchers strive to increase between-group variance, decrease within-group variance, and they do their best to control extraneous variables.

- Lab researchers strive to
  → increase between-group variance[,]
  → decrease within-group variance[, and]
  → they do their best to control extraneous variables.

When combined with the stem, the first two list items each create a complete sentence.

✓ Lab researchers strive to increase between-group variance.

✓ Lab researchers strive to decrease within-group variance.

But when the third item is combined with the stem, nonsense ensues:

✗ Lab researchers strive to they do their best to control extraneous variables.

Sometimes the simplest solution is simple deletion.

✓ Lab researchers strive to increase between-group variance.

✓ Lab researchers strive to decrease within-group variance.

✓ Lab researchers strive to ~~they do their best to~~ control extraneous variables.

Now all stem-plus-list item stories are complete.

✓ Lab researchers strive to **increase** between-group variance, **decrease** within-group variance, and **control** extraneous variables.

Here is a solution that dismantles the list and preserves the final clause of the muddled sentence:

✓ Lab researchers strive to increase between-group variance and decrease within-group variance, and they do their best to control extraneous variables.

If you replace the comma between the first two parallel phrases with a conjunction (*and*), you will create a sentence with two sets of parallel phrases—one between the phrases beginning with *increase* and *decrease*, and the other between the final clause (*they do their best . . .*) and the rest of the sentence.

> ✓ <u>Lab researchers</u> strive to <u>increase</u> between-group variance **and** decrease within-group variance, **and** they do their best to control extraneous variables.
>
> → Lab researchers strive to
> > → increase between-group variance [and]
> > → decrease within-group variance[, and]
> → they do their best to control extraneous variables.

I prefer the first version, but this one is grammatically correct.

## ➴ Place a comma between two or more interchangeable descriptions

If you wish to use more than one adjective to describe someone or something, and if the order of your descriptions (i.e., the adjectives) can be switched without the result sounding wrong or ridiculous, then *insert a comma* between them. If you *can't* reverse the order of the descriptions without creating nonsense, then *don't insert a comma* between them.

- The postmodern social scientist was notorious for repudiating conventional, restrictive notions of linear time and space, for rejecting representation and formulaic thinking. Imagine, then, how guilty and frightened he felt getting out the recipe for his favorite eggplant casserole. What if a savvy, unfriendly graduate student saw him obediently following the step-by-step procedures? He drew the dark, heavy blinds across the kitchen window, and, reading the recipe through, allowed himself the illicit pleasure of picturing the finished dish.

Let's assume you have just written this paragraph, but you aren't sure whether your multiple-adjective comma placement is correct. The reverse-order test can help you check.

- The postmodern social scientist

Do you need a comma between *postmodern* and *social*?

- The postmodern, social scientist

If you do, then *postmodern* and *social* should be reversible.

    ✗  A social, postmodern scientist

A postmodern scientist who goes to lots of parties is different from a postmodern scientist who studies social phenomena, so, no, the descriptors are *not* reversible. You were correct: *No comma* should be inserted between *postmodern* and *social.*

    How about the next one?

- conventional, restrictive notions

Is the comma necessary? See what happens if you reverse the order of the descriptors.

    ✓  restrictive, conventional notions

This makes just as much sense as the way you originally wrote it. If you can change the order with no loss of meaning, then you need a comma.

    Let's go on:

- favorite eggplant casserole

Comma or no?

- favorite, eggplant casserole

If you insert a comma, then the two adjectives must be interchangeable:

- eggplant, favorite casserole

The word *favorite* describes the *eggplant* casserole, but *eggplant* can't describe *favorite casserole.* Only the original order works; therefore, *don't* insert a comma.

    In the next example, you have a comma between the first two adjectives and no comma between the second and third.

- a savvy, unfriendly graduate student

Let's check the first two adjectives first. Can you reverse the order?

    ✓  an unfriendly, savvy graduate student

This makes just as much sense as the original, so the comma is appropriate. Do you also need a comma, however, between the second and third adjectives?

- a savvy, unfriendly, graduate student

You would only put a comma between *unfriendly* and *graduate* if you could reverse their order without creating nonsense.

- a savvy, graduate, unfriendly student

No, this sounds confused. The word *graduate* needs to stay attached to *student*, so you *should not* place a comma between it (*graduate*) and the descriptor preceding it.

The last example is easier to figure out.

- the dark, heavy blinds

You can have *heavy*, *dark* blinds just as easily as *dark*, *heavy* ones, so the comma is appropriate and necessary.

**➥ If you can slide smoothly into a quotation, don't interrupt the transition with a comma**

The quotation in the following illustration requires no comma to set it off.

> ✓ Benedict (1934/1989) considered anyone believing in "racial purity" to be "the victim of a mythology" (p. 15).

If you *were* to insert a comma, you would create a muddle:

> ✗ Benedict (1934/1989) considered anyone believing in "racial purity" to be, "the victim of a mythology" (p. 15).

The comma in the following example is correct, but some readers would consider the introduction to the quote clumsy:

> ✓ Benedict (1934/1989) said, "The racial purist is the victim of a mythology" (p. 15).

Let's go back to the first example for a moment.

> ✓ Benedict (1934/1989) considered anyone believing in "racial purity" to be "the victim of a mythology" (p. 15).

If you were to add another sentence or two to it, you would need to insert a clarifying parenthetical insertion set off by commas.

> ✓ Benedict (1934/1989) considered anyone believing in "racial purity" to be "the victim of a mythology" (p. 15). "Heredity," she said, "is an affair of family lines. Beyond that it is mythology" (p. 15).

Notice that the first parenthetical comma is placed *inside* the double quotation mark. In general, put commas and periods inside quotation marks; put semicolons, colons, and dashes outside.

The quotations in the following two examples are introduced by suspense phrases, so commas are necessary.

> ✓ According to Benedict (1934/1989), "The racial purist is the victim of a mythology. . . . Heredity is an affair of family lines. Beyond that it is mythology" (p. 15).

✓ For Benedict (1934/1989), "The racial purist is the victim of a mythology. . . . Heredity is an affair of family lines. Beyond that it is mythology" (p. 15).

**•• Use commas to eliminate redundancy and highlight differences**
When precisely parallel stories are juxtaposed with one or more semicolons, you can use commas to eliminate words common to each of the stories. Such streamlined comparisons accentuate the contrast between the clauses.

• The teacher read the assigned readings the night before class; the students read the assigned readings the morning of the test.

> [,] = [read the assigned readings]

✓ The teacher read the assigned readings the night before class; the students, the morning of the test.

When you use a comma in this way, you turn it into the punctuation equivalent of a pronoun: It takes the place of something mentioned earlier in the sentence.

• The biker looked furious; the ethnographer looked frightened.

> [,] = [looked]

✓ The biker looked furious; the ethnographer, frightened.

• Two methodologists consulted on her analysis. One insisted she use stepwise regression; the other insisted she use standard regression.

> [,] = [insisted she use]

✓ Two methodologists consulted on her analysis. One insisted she use stepwise regression; the other, standard regression.

Double check that your juxtaposed stories are parallel. If they aren't, your redundancy-eliminating efforts will generate confusion rather than clarity.

✗   The first researcher talked to her rats constantly; the second, sporadically did.

To unmuddle the second half of the sentence, go back to the uncondensed version.

> [,] = [researcher talked to her rats]

- The first researcher talked to her rats constantly; the second [researcher talked to her rats] sporadically did.

Now fix the problem—

✓   The first researcher talked to her rats constantly; the second [researcher talked to her rats] sporadically.

—and recondense it:

> [,] = [researcher talked to her rats]

✓   The first researcher talked to her rats constantly; the second, sporadically.

## Semicolons

The semicolon is excellent for making pithy comparisons or for juxtaposing complex mini-stories. Some composition writers have described it as a halfway point between a comma and a colon. I find this notion misleading—rather like characterizing a zebra as a halfway point between a horse and a tiger. Semicolons, like zebras, have unique properties unto themselves.

### ➻ Use semicolons to connect two complete stories

You can always juxtapose two or more complete stories (independent clauses) simply by placing them side by side (or, more accurately, end to end) as stand-alone sentences.

✓   Herb, a symbolic interactionist, and Pete, a social exchange theorist, ordered a second pitcher of beer. Their conversation loosened up a little more. Herb silently worried whether their dialogue was generating enough meaning. Pete privately questioned the emotional and intellectual costs of participating.

However, if you want to connect the stories more closely—for reasons of rhythm or meaning—you can link them with either a comma-and-conjunction (see pp. 120-121) or a semicolon.

> [;] = [,] + [coordinating conjunction]

✓ Herb, a symbolic interactionist, and Pete, a social exchange theorist, ordered a second pitcher of beer**, and** their conversation loosened up a little more. Herb silently worried whether their dialogue was generating enough meaning; Pete privately questioned the emotional and intellectual costs of participating.

As connectors of complete stories, a semicolon and a comma-and-conjunction are comparable; however, their *technical* similarity does not amount to *aesthetic* equivalence, and they don't always produce the same *semantic* result. My use of them in the second version of the Herb-and-Pete paragraph highlights their respective strengths. The comma-and-conjunction eliminates the choppiness of the second sentence in the original version, and it ties together the *loosening of the conversation* and the *drinking of the beer*. The semicolon joining the third and fourth sentences highlights the complementarity of Herb and Pete's personal thoughts.

Semicolons offer immediacy of comparison. Acting like they just gulped down too many espressos, semicolons say to readers, *"You've read the first of the two sides of the sentence? Good, now, quick, take a look at the other side. See the difference? See the similarity? Treat the two sides like equals."*

✓ Hannah Arendt observed the banality of evil in the trial of Adolf Eichmann; Stanley Milgram found it in his laboratory (Ross & Nisbett, 1991).
   → Hannah Arendt observed the banality of evil in the trial of Adolf Eichmann[;]
   → Stanley Milgram found it in his laboratory.
✓ The economist said "time is money"; the political scientist countered with "money is power."
   → The economist said "time is money"[;]
   → the political scientist countered with "money is power."

✓ The biker mistook the ethnographer for an undercover cop; the ethnographer misjudged the biker as the leader of the gang.

    → The biker mistook the ethnographer for an undercover cop[;]

    → the ethnographer misjudged the biker as the leader of the gang.

#### •◦ Make sure *each side* of the semicolon is a complete story

You can't use a semicolon to attach complete and incomplete stories.

✗ Ernst von Glasersfeld classifies himself as a radical constructivist; not a social constructionist.

    → Ernst von Glasersfeld classifies himself as a radical constructivist[;]

    → [not] a social constructionist.

The phrase *a social constructionist* is not a complete story and is not parallel with the part of the sentence preceding the semicolon. You can solve the problem by replacing the semicolon with a comma or by rewriting the part of the sentence following the semicolon.

✓ Ernst von Glasersfeld classifies himself as a radical constructivist, not a social constructionist.

    • Ernst von Glasersfeld classifies himself as

        → a radical constructivist[,]

        → [not] a social constructionist.

✓ Ernst von Glasersfeld classifies himself as a radical constructivist; he is not a social constructionist.

    → Ernst von Glasersfeld classifies himself as a radical constructivist[;]

    → he is not a social constructionist.

#### •◦ Place semicolons between complex list items

When you have complexity *within* list items (elaborate phrasing, internal punctuation), you need to use semicolons *between* them to help keep your comparisons clear.

✓ The economist, an efficiency expert, said "time is money"; the political scientist, not to be outdone, countered with "money is power"; the systems theorist, ruining the fun, said "power is an inappropriate metaphor for social relationships."

✓ The history of psychology is replete with examples of reductionistic thought; I will offer three. Wilhelm Wundt considered "will" and "intelligence" to be transformations of elementary physiological phenomena (Mancias, 1986, p. 62); Charles Spearman believed there to be a single *g*, or "general intelligence," underlying all cognitive activity (Gould, 1981); and Clark Hull came to the conclusion that "a moderate number of ordinary equations" could quantitatively express the primary laws of psychology (Watson & Evans, 1991, p. 485).

**•◦ Place semicolons in front of mid-sentence stories beginning with adverbial conjunctions**

Adverbial conjunctions (or conjunctive adverbs) help create *semantic* connections between different parts of sentences (see Chapter 3).

> *however, also, furthermore, conversely, moreover,*
> *nevertheless, similarly, therefore, thus, hence,*
> *consequently, indeed, accordingly, further, otherwise*

However, unlike *coordinating* conjunctions (*and, but, or, nor, for, yet, so*), adverbial conjunctions don't help forge *grammatical* connections. This means you can't link two complete stories with a comma and an adverbial conjunction.

✗ Many social scientists have looked to biology for the causes of human behavior, however "the biological substrate . . . is not a cause of action but, at most, a *constraint* upon it or a *condition* for it" (Bruner, 1990, pp. 20-21).

✗ Yeatman (1990) argues that sociology is biased against the feminist agenda, indeed she believes that "the fundamental theoretical structures of sociology are masculinist" (p. 284).

✗ The ethnographer couldn't understand why Carl was so upset by the high-quality recording of the bikers' voices, moreover he was confused by the argument that had broken out between Carl and the others.

When an adverbial conjunction marks the beginning of a new story, put a semicolon (or a period) in front of it and a comma behind it.

✓ Many social scientists have looked to biology for the causes of human behavior; however, "the biological substrate . . . is not a cause of action but, at most, a *constraint* upon it or a *condition* for it" (Bruner, 1990, pp. 20-21).

✓ Yeatman (1990) argues that sociology is biased against the feminist agenda; indeed, she believes that "the fundamental theoretical structures of sociology are masculinist" (p. 284).

✓ The ethnographer couldn't understand why Carl was so upset by the high-quality recording of the bikers' voices; moreover, he was confused by the argument that had broken out between Carl and the others.

✓ Intelligence test scores are *ordinal* measurements; nevertheless, most researchers treat them as *interval* measurements.

If you don't use the adverbial conjunction to *begin* a story, then enclose it in commas:

✓ Yeatman (1990) argues that sociology is biased against the feminist agenda; she believes, indeed, that "the fundamental theoretical structures of sociology are masculinist" (p. 284).

✓ The ethnographer couldn't understand why Carl was so upset by the high-quality recording of the bikers' voices; he was confused, moreover, by the argument that had broken out between Carl and the others.

✓ Intelligence test scores are *ordinal* measurements; most researchers, nevertheless, treat them as *interval* measurements.

## Colons

A colon tells readers to "expect an explanation, elucidation, or elaboration of what you just read." It is, thus, the punctuation equivalent of a suspense device: It creates anticipation for what is to follow. Also like a suspense device, a colon creates a referential relationship; however, the referentiality points in the opposite direction. A suspense phrase or clause is about someone or something *later* in the sentence.

                                    this is about this

• Frightened by the angry bikers, the ethnographer tried to kick-start his blue Suzuki.

The statement following a colon is about someone or something *earlier* in the sentence.

- Think "wit" and "economics" simultaneously, and one name comes immediately to mind: John Kenneth Galbraith.

this is about this

## ⊸ Use colons to create anticipation

When readers encounter a colon, they look forward to being given a "punch line" of some sort. Thus, the statement following the colon should satisfy their expectation, providing a conclusion, a completion of an idea.

> ✓ In 1979, the anthropologist William Arens fired up a controversy that has since continued to boil. Having combed the classic anthropological literature for descriptions of cannibalism, he came to an unsettling conclusion: No extant account is trustworthy (see Osborne, 1997).

You will disappoint your readers if your post-colon statement isn't quickly conclusive. Don't promise something you can't deliver, and don't let the impact of your "punch line" dribble away.

> ✗ In 1979, the anthropologist William Arens fired up a controversy that has since continued to boil: Having combed the classic anthropological literature for descriptions of cannibalism, he came to the unsettling conclusion that none of the extant accounts were trustworthy (see Osborne, 1997).

Conversely, don't offer a snappy conclusive statement without having first signaled your readers to expect it.

> ✗ In 1979, the anthropologist William Arens fired up a controversy that has since continued to boil. Having combed the classic anthropological literature for descriptions of cannibalism, he came to an unsettling conclusion. No extant account is trustworthy (see Osborne, 1997).

If you compare across different style manuals, you will find some minor disagreements on how and when colons should be used. The next two suggestions accord with those of the APA *Manual*.

## ⊸ Capitalize the first letter of post-colon complete stories

Capitalize the first word following a colon if the word begins a complete story (an independent clause).

✓ Kennedy knew something in 1961 that subsequent presidents have forgotten or disregarded: "The United States is neither omnipotent nor omniscient— . . . there cannot be an American solution to every world problem" (quoted in Schlesinger, 1968, p. 142).

✓ The Milgram experiments underscore how difficult it is for most people to enact the credo teenagers so easily proclaim: "Question authority!"

If the part of the sentence following a colon does not form a complete sentence, however, leave the first letter of the first word in lower case.

✗ The holy grail of modernist science—truth—has two handles: Prediction and control.

   ✓ The holy grail of modernist science—truth—has two handles: prediction and control.

**➻ Place colons only at the end of complete stories**

Some style manuals take the position that as long as you have a complete story (an independent clause) on the right side of a colon, you don't need one on the left.

• Responsibility as it is commonly understood today is more time- and culture-bound than many of us assume. As Connolly (1991) recognized: "In other times and places [responsibility] . . . was not so agent-centered as it is today: the primary human locus of responsibility was often the family or the clan rather than the individual" (p. 95).[4]

However, the APA *Manual* stipulates that the section of the sentence preceding the colon must be "grammatically complete" (1994, p. 64). If you are following APA guidelines, you would then need to either exchange the colon for a comma—

   ✓ Responsibility as it is commonly understood today is more time- and culture-bound than many of us assume. As Connolly (1991) recognized, "In other times and places [responsibility]. . . was not so agent-centered as it is today: the primary human locus of responsibility was often the family or the clan rather than the individual" (p. 95).

[4]Notice that Connolly didn't capitalize the first word following the colon: ". . . as it is today: the primary . . . ." If the book had been prepared following APA conventions (many are not), the *t* of the *the* would have been uppercase: *The*.

—or rewrite the passage:

> ✓ Responsibility as it is commonly understood today is more time- and culture-bound than many of us assume : "In other times and places [responsibility] . . . was not so agent-centered as it is today: the primary human locus of responsibility was often the family or the clan rather than the individual" (Connolly, 1991, p. 95).

**•◆ Use colons to eliminate clumsy introductions to quotations**

If you don't need to repeat or highlight the author of a quotation, colons can help you stay away from clumsy or unnecessary introductory phrases, such as *she said, he stated,* and so on. The two examples below marked ✗ aren't wrong, only less elegant than the checked (✓) versions.

> ✓ All musical expression involves the audience in some significant way; however, jazz stands out from the rest : "The jazz performance, perhaps more than any other kind of artistic event, allows the audience to confront the creative act" (Gioia, 1988, p. 101).

> ✗ All musical expression involves the audience in some significant way; however, jazz stands out from the rest. Gioia (1988) explained, "The jazz performance, perhaps more than any other kind of artistic event, allows the audience to confront the creative act" (p. 101).

> ✓ If the ethnographer had been adequately familiar with the work of Talcott Parsons, he would have known immediately why the biker was so furious : "The normal reaction of a well-integrated individual to an infraction of an institutional rule is one of moral indignation" (Parsons, 1954, p. 60).

> ✗ If the ethnographer had been adequately familiar with the work of Talcott Parsons, he would have known immediately why the biker was so furious. Parsons (1954) stated, "The normal reaction of a well-integrated individual to an infraction of an institutional rule is one of moral indignation" (p. 60).

**•◆ Use colons to set up lists**

Colons prepare readers for the imminent arrival of a series of parallel items.

✓ The workshop will cover three main areas: (a) the management of pain, (b) the pain of management, and (c) the relief of both.
- The workshop will cover three main areas[:]
    - → the management of pain[,]
    - → the pain of management[, and]
    - → the relief of both.

✓ To help explain why battered women stay in abusive relationships, Walker (1979) advanced a "cycle theory of violence." The battering cycle, she found, involves three distinct phases: the tension-building phase; the explosion or acute battering incident; and the calm, loving respite.
- The battering cycle, she found, involves three distinct phases[:]
    - → the tension-building phase[;]
    - → the explosion or acute battering incident[; and]
    - → the calm, loving respite.

Remember that your introduction to the list must be a complete story (an independent clause):

✗ The battering cycle, she found, involves three distinct phases. They are: the tension-building phase; the explosion or acute battering incident; and the calm, loving respite.

## Exclamation Points

*Any writer of prose should be compelled, by law if necessary, to submit professional credentials and undergo a waiting period of seven days before placing an exclamation point at the end of a sentence.*

—Lewis Thomas

*Consider prose without the [exclamation point]: Whew, that's a relief. White whale off the starboard bow. Stop, thief. Help, I'm drowning. Hold that line. Storm the Bastille. . . . Don't these sentences, denuded of their [exclamation point], seem flat, listless and missing something?*

*You bet! (No. That's an example of abusing the [exclamation point] to add unwarranted enthusiasm.)*

—William Safire

An exclamation point at the end of a sentence signals readers to "hear" what they have just read as if it had been spoken at a heightened volume. If you are a therapist, say, writing a case study of your work with a vociferous couple, you will find exclamation points indispensable.

✓ The woman then turned to her husband and voiced her considerable frustration: "Stop telling me what to do, Hank! I'm sick of it! You treat me like your goddamn daughter! I'm a woman! Got it? Your wife, not your goddamn daughter!"

Without exclamation marks, the woman's protestations would read as if they were being mumbled by someone feeling defeated or exhausted.

✗ The woman then turned to her husband and voiced her considerable frustration: "Stop telling me what to do, Hank. I'm sick of it. You treat me like your goddamn daughter. I'm a woman. Got it? Your wife, not your goddamn daughter."

If you *do* find occasions to use them, limit yourself to one per sentence.

✗ The woman then turned to her husband and voiced her considerable frustration: "Stop telling me what to do, Hank!!! I'm sick of it!!! You treat me like your goddamn daughter!!! I'm a woman!!! Got it? Your wife, not your goddamn daughter!!!!!"

Reading through the journals in your discipline, you won't encounter many exclamation marks. This is not to say that the authors of the articles aren't passionate people, but the nature of the prose invites a calm, measured tone. You may be enthusiastic about your work, but, as a general rule, you don't want to let your readers know you are bouncing up and down in your writing chair.

✗ I removed the effects of multicollinearity by calculating semi-partial correlations, thereby removing intercorrelations among the independent variables!

✗ Developmental theorists must account for both continuous and discontinuous change!

✗ $p < .05$!

Sometimes popular writers use an exclamation point within parentheses to communicate ironic detachment—as if, with raised eyebrows, they were saying, "Can you believe this!?" or "O my Gawd!" or "Arrrgghh!"

✓ If George Bush had died in office and Dan Quayle had taken over as president (!), scores of want-ads for political satirists would have appeared in newspapers around the world.

However, if there were a Miss Manners of the social sciences, she would tell you that such sniping has no place in our field.

   **✗**  Glaser and Strauss (1967) originally collaborated **(!)** on a "grounded theory" method for analyzing qualitative research data.

      **✓**  Glaser and Strauss (1967) originally collaborated on a "grounded theory" method for analyzing qualitative research data; however, they subsequently evolved divergent interpretations of the approach (see Glaser, 1992, for his point-by-point critique of Strauss & Corbin, 1990).

## Parentheses

If an exclamation mark tells readers to raise the imaginary volume of a written statement, parentheses tell them to lower it. Of the three punctuation marks that can parenthetically enclose information (parentheses, commas, dashes), parentheses are the most apologetic about interrupting the flow of the sentence. They signal readers to "treat the information inside us as if it were whispered gossip, a murmured aside about something or someone elsewhere in the sentence." Dashes never apologize about the gossip they enclose: They *highlight* it (see pages 150-152). Commas strike a middle ground, neither whispering nor proclaiming.

**➡️ Avoid giving incidental gossip unwarranted prominence**
If you were writing a paper, say, about the influence of psychoanalysis on the arts, the following sentence would probably fit well:

      **✓**  Freud once said (in an interview with Giovanni Papini) he considered himself more artist than scientist (Hillman, 1983, p. 3).

The detail about the interview provides a little context for Freud's statement, and its placement in parentheses tells readers that the information is incidental to the story being told about Freud.

Now let's see what happens if you were to trade in the parentheses for commas.

      **✓**  Freud once said**,** in an interview with Giovanni Papini**,** he considered himself more artist than scientist (Hillman, 1983, p. 3).

This version gives a little more prominence to the Papini information—a shade more than it deserves, perhaps, given the focus of the paper. Still, the comma-enclosed gossip probably won't distract readers, and it doesn't detract from the main focus of the sentence. Look, though, at the effect of trading up from commas to dashes:

> ✗    Freud once said—in an interview with Giovanni Papini—he
>      considered himself more artist than scientist (Hillman, 1983,
>      p. 3).

This version would be appropriate if Papini were better known or if the interview had been conducted by a prominent figure—Carl Jung, perhaps, or T. S. Eliot or John Dewey. But, in this case, the dashes give the Papini gossip an air of importance it doesn't deserve.

How often have you seen a newspaper or a television station hype a news story beyond appropriate limits? And have you ever had to endure listening to a singer whose self-esteem painfully outstripped his or her ability to carry a tune? If you have, you know well the problem of unwarranted prominence. Avoid using dashes to enclose information belonging in parentheses and you will contribute much to the aesthetic and semantic quality of your work.

### ➠ Never slam on your brakes while flooring the gas pedal

Let's take a look at another sentence, one for which parentheses would be utterly inappropriate:

> ✗    James Hillman (philosopher-poet of the soul) considers psycho-
>      analysis to be "a work of imaginative tellings in the realm of
>      poiesis" (Hillman, 1983, pp. 3-4).

The high-minded (and probably over-written) phrase *philosopher-poet of the soul* is meant to grab readers' attention. Putting it inside of parentheses would be like slamming on your brakes while flooring the gas pedal, or wearing neon clothes under a dark overcoat. The phrase cries out for dashes, though it might settle for commas.

> ✓    James Hillman—philosopher-poet of the soul—considers psy-
>      choanalysis to be "a work of imaginative tellings in the realm of
>      *poiesis*" (Hillman, 1983, pp. 3-4).

> ✓    James Hillman, philosopher-poet of the soul, considers psycho-
>      analysis to be "a work of imaginative tellings in the realm of
>      *poiesis*" (Hillman, 1983, pp. 3-4).

# Square Brackets

Because quotations are always torn from their original context, they don't always fit perfectly into their new surroundings (i.e., your paper). Square brackets give you the ability to make necessary editorial alterations in the quote—changing tenses or punctuation, clarifying to whom or what a pronoun refers, pointing out errors in the original, and so on—and to alert readers that you have done so (see also Chapter 2, pp. 66–67).

✓ R. D. Laing (1969) used quotations from a recovering patient, Joan, to illustrate some of his ideas about schizophrenia: "Joan [said], 'We schizophrenics say and do a lot of stuff that is unimportant, and then we mix important things in with all this to see if the doctor cares enough to see them and feel them'"(p. 164).

In this example, I changed Laing's present-tense *says* to the past tense *said*. In the next, I inserted a colon to help the passage read more smoothly.

✓ Turner and Fine (1995) put it this way: "As supervisors we are in a seemingly contradictory position[:] having the power to make evaluation judgments but recognizing that these are based on partial and subjective knowledges" (p. 58).

The square-bracket insertion in the following illustration helps readers be clear it was Talcott Parsons, not his friend, who found German formality disagreeable.

✓ As an official exchange student in Germany, Parsons met formally with the rector of the university where he was studying. Following the meeting, a friend of Parsons's asked him if he had correctly addressed the man as *Euer Magnifizenz*. "The idea [for Parsons] of addressing a rather seedy-looking elderly professor as 'Your Magnificence' seemed more than a little ridiculous" (Parsons, 1954, p. 112), so he called him *Herr Professor*.

And, below, the inclusion of *sic* in square brackets clarifies that the typographical error was in the original source:

✓ "Such ideomotor and ideosensory processes were early recognized as the basis of many hypnotic phenomena, . . . and they can be easily measured today with pschophysiootical isruments [*sic*]" (Erickson, Rossi, & Rossi, 1976, p. 22).

# Dashes

*Somehow this invaluable tool is widely regarded as not quite proper—a bumpkin at the genteel dinner table of good English. But it has full membership and will get you out of many tight corners.*

—William Zinsser

Dashes, like colons, signal readers to expect a conclusive statement about something mentioned earlier in the sentence, and, like parentheses and commas, they demarcate the beginning and end of a piece of gossip. However, dashes are more dramatic than these other punctuation marks—they delineate abrupt shifts in tone, and they mark definitive interruptions in the narrative flow.

### ➤ Simulate dashes with double hyphens

Before getting to the business of *using* dashes, allow me to clear up the business of *typing* them. If your computer can produce a dash (—) that is distinguishable from a hyphen (-), then you are in fine shape. If it can't, *simulate* a dash by typing two hyphens back to back with no spaces between or on either side of them:

✓ The biker's associates--he didn't consider them friends--pulled the ethnographer off his Suzuki and roughed him up.

✗ The biker's associates -- he didn't consider them friends -- pulled the ethnographer off his Suzuki and roughed him up.

✗ The biker's associates- -he didn't consider them friends- - pulled the ethnographer off his Suzuki and roughed him up.

✗ The biker's associates - he didn't consider them friends - pulled the ethnographer off his Suzuki and roughed him up.

✗ The biker's associates-he didn't consider them friends-pulled the ethnographer off his Suzuki and roughed him up.

### ➤ Use paired dashes to highlight non-essential gossip

As I mentioned a few pages back, dashes allow you to insert gossip into a sentence without minimizing its importance.

✓ For Freud, everything—except, at times, a good cigar—was imbued with sexually symbolic meaning.

✓ When the book fell out of the ethnographer's pocket, the biker froze. The title—*Participant Observation*—told him the imposter wasn't an undercover cop after all. Who but a social scientist would be reading Spradley (1980)?

**➼ Use paired dashes to clarify the beginning and end of complexly punctuated gossip**

The following sentence is punctuated correctly, but readers may struggle a little to sort out the kinds and levels of relationship created by the gaggle of commas:

- The three sisters, Jenny, 10, Melissa, 8, and Kate, 5, played among themselves while I talked with the parents.

A pair of dashes (and a few semicolons) can make a significant difference:

✓ The three sisters—Jenny, 10; Melissa, 8; and Kate, 5—played among themselves while I talked with the parents.

**➼ Use a dash to create anticipation**

Like a colon, a dash can tell readers to prepare for an upcoming statement about or conclusive comment on the earlier part of the sentence.

✓ As blood trickled into the ethnographer's mouth, the title of Stoller's (1989) book trickled into his awareness, and he found himself chuckling—"Is this," he wondered, "*The Taste of Ethnographic Things?*"

✓ For my study, I plan to use the Solomon Four-Group design (Campbell & Stanley, 1963)—it will allow me to account for the effects of the pretest on the independent variable.

✓ Gazing upon the prone, bleeding man at his feet, the biker was seized by a vision—a vivid memory of one of his own anthropological adventures in Northern Mexico.

**➼ Insert dashes with a drummer's sensitivity**

I grew up playing drums in a pop/rock band with my musical-genius friend, Michael. Drums figured prominently in the tunes we played together, so I initially had trouble accepting the advice of my percussion teacher, a lounge-act drummer who occasionally performed with the local symphony orchestra. "If you are playing well," he said, "you should blend so completely with the other instruments that the audience forgets you exist. Do your best not to be noticed."

"What about drum solos?" I asked.

"Fitting in is more important than standing out," he persisted. "Your primary job is to provide rhythmic support for the other musicians, not to draw attention to yourself. The occasional solo can nicely accent the melodic and harmonic patterns of the others, but don't overshadow them."

Punctuation marks in a well-written sentence are like the drums and cymbals in a well-balanced piece of music—when they fit with their surroundings, they are seldom noticed. Dashes, though, stand out more than other punctuation marks. The drum solos of sentences, they can nicely accent important phrases; however, if not used with discretion, they can upstage the words they are meant to highlight and make your sentences sound choppy. Don't put dashes in every paragraph, and be careful about using them (singly, or in pairs) more than once in the same sentence. Consider, for illustration, the following sentence. It is grammatically correct, but the two sets of dashes make it disjointed and difficult to follow.

> ✗ Arnold Lazarus—the cognitive behaviorist who coined the term *behavior modification*—uses the acronym *BASIC I.D.*—it stands for Behavior, Affect, Sensation, Imagery, Cognition, Interpersonal Relationships, and *D*rugs/Biology—to separate the self into seven constituent parts or modalities (Lazarus, 1995).

With a little rearranging and a commas-for-dashes substitution, the sentence reads more smoothly:

> ✓ Arnold Lazarus (1995), the cognitive behaviorist who coined the term *behavior modification*, uses the acronym *BASIC I.D.* to separate the self into seven constituent parts—Behavior, Affect, Sensation, Imagery, Cognition, Interpersonal Relationships, and *D*rugs/Biology.

## Question Marks

The questions we pose as social scientists determine what we can invent, construct, and discover. We are, after all, in the business of *inquiry*. Nevertheless, avoid peppering your writing with rhetorical questions.

> ✗ How, then, were the subjects assigned?

✗ What danger is posed by false positives?

✗ How were the interviews structured?

✗ What conclusions can be drawn from the results?

Such queries might help you organize your thinking as you write, but few if any should remain in your manuscript when you have finished your final draft (see p. 244).

If you *do* pose questions in your manuscript, whether rhetorical or not, be sure to punctuate the *direct* variety differently from the *indirect*. A direct question must be followed by a question mark; an indirect question, by a period (or, less commonly, a colon, semicolon, comma, or dash).

✗ The client wanted to know if I had any experience with dual diagnoses? I asked her which two she had in mind?

✓ The client wanted to know if I had any experience with dual diagnoses; I asked her which two she had in mind.

✗ I wonder how Lazarus would have conceptualized the self if, in English, the word *basic* were spelled *baesick*?

✓ I wonder how Lazarus would have conceptualized the self if, in English, the word *basic* were spelled *baesick*. With an extra *e* and *k* to account for, he would have needed to subdivide the self into *nine* rather than *seven* modalities. Would he then have included *emotion* and *knowledge* in his multimodal scheme, or would he have used *entropy* and *kin*?

✗ Feeling badly about what had happened, the biker, Carl, knelt beside the ethnographer and asked him if he was okay?

✓ Feeling badly about what had happened, the biker, Carl, knelt beside the ethnographer and asked him if he was okay. He wondered whether it would help to share some of the mistakes *he* had made as a naive doctoral student. "Have you ever read any accounts," he began, "about Yaqui shamans?"

# Periods

Periods put an end to things—but let's save that point until the end. First, I'd like to clarify some details about using periods in Latin abbreviations, in reference lists, and (clustered as ellipses) in quotations.

**•► Use periods with Latin abbreviations**

With the exception of the phrase *et al.* (see below), Latin abbreviations—such as, *i.e., e.g., etc., cf., viz.,* and *vs.*—should only be used within parentheses. The APA *Manual* suggests you use the English equivalents of these terms in running text.

| | | |
|---|---|---|
| i.e. = that is | e.g. = for example | etc. = and so forth |
| cf. = compare | viz. = namely | vs. = versus |

Note that i.e. and e.g. need periods after each of their two letters.

- ✓ Vilfredo Pareto, noting Marx's peculiar and sometimes obscure use of language, likened his words to bats (**i.e.,** they can be seen simultaneously as birds and mice) (Ollman, 1971, p. 3).
  - ✓ Vilfredo Pareto, noting Marx's peculiar and sometimes obscure use of language, likened his words to bats—**that is,** they can be seen simultaneously as birds and mice (Ollman, 1971, p. 3).
- ✓ People in other cultures (**e.g.,** the Yequana Indians of Brazil) appreciate the importance of touch much more than we do (see Berman, 1989, p. 44).
  - ✓ People in other cultures, **for example,** the Yequana Indians of Brazil, appreciate the importance of touch much more than we do (see Berman, 1989, p. 44).

The Latin term et al.—short for *et alii,* "and others"—*can* (and should) be used in running text for certain reference citations. Never use et al. when citing a work with only two authors—

- ✗ **Lakoff et al.** (1980) demonstrated the degree to which our conception of time is shaped by the metaphor of money: It can be saved, lost, spent, budgeted, wasted, etc.
  - ✓ **Lakoff and Johnson** (1980) demonstrated the degree to which our conception of time is shaped by the metaphor of money: It can be saved, lost, spent, budgeted, wasted, etc.

—but always use et al. (following the listing of the first author's name) when citing a work with six or more authors.

- ✓ **Witkin et al.** (1976) determined that men with an extra Y chromosome (XYY) were no more likely to commit crimes than men who were genetically normal (XY).

✗ **Witkin, Mednick, Schulsinger, Bakkestrom, Christiansen, Goodenbough, Hirschhorn, Lunsteen, Owen, Philip, Ruben, and Stocking** (1976) determined that men with an extra Y chromosome (XYY) were no more likely to commit crimes than men who were genetically normal (XY).

If you are citing a source with three to five authors, list all of the author's names the first time you mention it; thereafter, use only the first author's name and et al.

✓ According to **Orne, Whitehouse, Dinges, and Orne** (1988), "Hypnosis may not enhance memory per se; instead, it may simply lower the threshold for reporting uncertain items of information" (p. 24). The hypnotic context "provides a number of nonspecific influences that may underlie the apparent utility of hypnosis in restoring memory" (**Orne et al.**, p. 25).

## •► Give (some of) your periods room to breath

The *APA Manual* (1994) stipulates that all punctuation marks, including periods, should be followed by one space. This means, for example, that when you are typing your reference list, you need to include a space between authors' initials.

✓ Duncan, B. L., Hubble, M. A., & Miller, S. D. (1997).

✗ Duncan, B.L., Hubble, M.A., & Miller, S.D. (1997).

Don't, however, put spaces after the periods in Latin abbreviations.

✗ (i. e. , the rats were sleepy)

✓ (i.e., the rats were sleepy)

✗ (e. g. , Descartes and Bacon)

✓ (e.g., Descartes and Bacon)

Points of ellipsis, which signal readers that you have removed something from a quotation, are typed with spaces between each dot. Three dots indicate that some portion *within* a sentence is missing.

✓ "Although most human sciences have modeled themselves on the physical sciences . . . several disciplines have come to be concerned with the understanding configured through narrative forms" (Polkinghorne, 1988, p. 183).

✗ the physical sciences...several disciplines

✗ the physical sciences ... several disciplines

Because the original sentence's punctuation is retained, four dots (the period and ellipsis) tell readers you have deleted the latter part of a sentence, a complete sentence, or more than a sentence. Notice that the first period of the four serves as an end-of-sentence marker, so don't precede it with a space. Capitalize the first letter of the first word following the four points of ellipsis.

✓ "We organize our experience and our memory of human happenings mainly in the form of narrative. . . . Unlike the constructions generated by logical and scientific procedures, which can be weeded out by falsification, narrative constructions can only achieve "verisimilitude"" (Bruner, 1992, p. 232).

✗ of narrative . . . . Unlike the

✗ of narrative....Unlike the

➥ **Use periods to mark the end of a story**

Periods, or *full stops* as they are called in Britain, alert readers that the story they have been reading has come to an end.

✓ The former ethnographer regaled the beat-up ethnographer with tales of flying.

✓ Listening to the siren on the way to the hospital, the ethnographer made a decision. Getting out his notebook and pen, he scribbled down the title of his new study: *A Stitch in Time: The Culture of the Emergency Room.*

# 5
# Keeping Track of Time

*A story is a narrative of events arranged in a time sequence.*
　　　　　　　　　　　　　　　　　　—E. M. Forster

*If nothing passed, there would be no past time; if nothing
were going to happen, there would be no future time; and if
nothing were, there would be no present time.*
　　　　　　　　　　　　　　　　　　—Saint Augustine

For a sentence to be a sentence, it must tell a story, and for a story to
be a story, it must describe a turn of events. Thus, a sentence is always
a place of action, a place where *something happens* (see Chapter 3). The
action of the sentence may take place in the present, past, or future; it
may occur before, during, or after some other event; and it may be in
process or already complete. The various tense forms help readers keep
track of such temporal complexities.

**•◦ Know the intra-story time relations each tense defines**
In every sentence, something happens, happened, or will happen;
something is, was, or will be happening; something has, had, or will
have happened; or something has been, had been, or will have been
happening. You need to be able to hear the nuances of meaning communicated by each of these tense forms. Knowing what grammarians
call them won't contribute to your writing ability, but it may help your
cross-referencing efforts, so I'll include each tense's traditional designa-
tion, in parentheses, following my descriptive name.

☞ **Something happens (present)**

Use this tense form when describing one of the following:

(a) a present action or state of affairs,

- ✓ Orthogonal rotation is most appropriate in this instance.
- ✓ She teaches at Princeton.
- ✓ His research explores the complex relationships between capitalism and democracy.

(b) something generally or universally true,

- ✓ For scientists, type I errors are often more serious than type II: Hubris is usually more dangerous than humility.
- ✓ Language categorizes experience.

(c) something regularly true,

- ✓ I see clients Tuesday evenings.

or (d) something set to occur at a specified time in the future.

- ✓ The take-home exam is due next week.

You should also use this tense form when writing about works of art and literature. Grammarians call this usage the *historic present*.

- ✓ Humpty Dumpty tells Alice, "When I use a word, it means just what I choose it to mean."
- ✓ Hamlet speaks and maneuvers with ironic detachment; everything he says and does resonates with double meanings.

☞ **Something is happening (present progressive)**

Use this form when describing a present, ongoing action or circumstance.

- ✓ The GNP is hindering the GOP.
- ✓ My client is finding her sense of humor.
- ✓ I am still waiting for the results.

☞ **Something has happened (present perfect)**

This tense form covers an action or state of affairs that began at some point in the past and has either recently been completed or has continued into the present. The action or state of affairs may or may not continue into the future.

- ✓ Leary (1990, p. 44) mentioned a number of writers (including Derrida, Richards, and Wilden) who have closely examined Freud's use of metaphor.

✓ To date, no subjects have lodged complaints about how or where we administered the electric shocks.

✓ The recent behavior of the stock market has perplexed the pundits.

☞ **Something has been happening** (present perfect progressive)

This tense form allows you to describe an ongoing action or circumstance that began in the past and has continued up to the recent past or present. Like the previous tense, it leaves the question of the future ambiguous—the action or circumstance may or may not continue.

✓ The U.N. has been struggling financially for some time.

✓ The boy has been setting fires in and around his grandparent's house.

✓ In recent years, qualitative researchers have been developing new software for data analysis.

☞ **Something happened** (past)

Use this tense for an action or circumstance that was completed or finished at some point in the past.

✓ Goffman (1961) argued that the identity of a mental-hospital patient is more influenced by the institution than the person's illness.

✓ Tyler (1987) pointed out that discourse analysis "must first destroy what it seeks to analyze" (p. 104).

✓ Of the 114 items, 72 achieved unimodal chi-square scores above 25.

☞ **Something was happening** (past progressive)

Use this tense to describe an action or circumstance that was ongoing at some point in the past.

✓ About the time Bach was stretching the limits of contrapuntal harmony, Newton was laying the foundation of the scientific method.

✓ The professor worked out the last glitch in her novel while her class was taking their end-of-term exam.

✓ Is it possible that Alzheimer's was affecting Reagan's judgment while he was still in office?

☞ **Something had happened (past perfect)**

This tense form allows you to describe a past action or circumstance that was completed or finished before some later past action or circumstance.

> ✓ After seeing Sergei Pankeev, the so-called "Wolf Man," for psychoanalysis for five years, Freud claimed that he had removed all of his patient's symptoms and inhibitions. However, according to Crews (1995), "Freud knew perfectly well . . . that psychoanalysis had not helped the depressed and obsessive Pankeev at all" (p. 43).

Freud's claim followed the purported cure:

> • . . . Freud claimed that he had removed all of his patient's symptoms and inhibitions.

Similarly, Freud's knowledge of his failure followed the failure itself:

> • . . . Freud knew . . . that psychoanalysis had not helped. . . .

> ✓ As I thanked my research informant for the interview, I wondered how many questions I had forgotten to ask.

The wondering followed the possible forgetting.

☞ **Something had been happening (past perfect progressive)**

Use this tense to describe a past, ongoing action or circumstance that was completed before, or interrupted by, another past action or circumstance.

> ✓ East Asian peoples who crossed the Bering Strait land bridge had been living in America for centuries when Columbus made landfall in 1492.

The living, which followed the crossing, was interrupted by Columbus's arrival.

> ✓ Until the Gulf War, we had been nurturing close economic and political ties with Saddam Hussein.

The nurturing of ties was interrupted by Hussein's invasion of Kuwait.

> ✓ Chinese students had been protesting in Tiananmen Square for six weeks prior to the June 4th, 1989, massacre.

The protesting was interrupted by the army's massacre.

☞ **Something will happen (future)**

This tense covers actions or circumstances that are yet to happen.

✓ By 2030, 20% of Americans will be sixty-five or older.

✓ She will graduate next year.

✓ I will discuss the implications of these results in the final section of the paper.

☞ **Something will be happening** (future progressive)

Use this tense for describing an action or circumstance that will be ongoing at some point in the future.

✓ I will be sending out questionnaires over the next three weeks.

✓ The ethics board will be meeting next week to discuss her research proposal.

✓ "Sorry," she said, "I will be studying Friday night."

☞ **Something will have happened** (future perfect)

This tense form allows you to describe an action or circumstance—already begun, presently beginning, or about to begin—that will be completed or finished before some later future action or circumstance.

✓ By 2030, the ratio of elderly people to working-age people in America will have tripled from what it was in 1950.

✓ By the end of the semester, they will have written eight papers and three take-home exams.

The papers and exams, which the students may not yet have started writing, will be finished before the end of the semester.

✓ By the time the typical American child turns 18, he or she will have witnessed some 200,000 acts of television violence.

☞ **Something will have been happening** (future perfect progressive)

Use this tense form to describe an ongoing action or circumstance—already begun, presently beginning, or about to begin—that will be completed or finished before some later future action or circumstance.

✓ By this time tomorrow, the patient will have been hiccoughing non-stop for two weeks.

✓ When the agreement finally goes through, the negotiators for the two sides may find it difficult to shake hands. By then, they will have been arguing over the small details for more than a year.

✓ As of next summer, he will have been researching AIDS for ten years.

☞ Something happens / is happening / has happened / has been happening / happened / was happening / had happened / had been happening / will happen / will be happening / will have happened / will have been happening to happen (present infinitive)

If you put *to* in front of an action word (a verb), you create an *infinitive*—a verb that can act like a noun, an adjective, or an adverb. The action indicated by a present infinitive happens at the same time or at a later time than the action in the main part of the story. Consider each of the following examples:

✓ She prepares to gather her data via the Internet.

✓ She is preparing to gather her data via the Internet.

✓ She has prepared to gather her data via the Internet.

✓ She has been preparing to gather her data via the Internet.

✓ She prepared to gather her data via the Internet.

✓ She was preparing to gather her data via the Internet.

✓ She had prepared to gather her data via the Internet.

✓ She had been preparing to gather her data via the Internet.

✓ She will prepare to gather her data via the Internet.

✓ She will be preparing to gather her data via the Internet.

✓ She will have prepared to gather her data via the Internet.

✓ She will have been preparing to gather her data via the Internet.

☞ Something happens / happened / will happen to have happened (perfect infinitive)

In this case, the action or circumstance described by the infinitive (*to* + have + action) has *already finished*—is already complete—by the time indicated by the main action of the story. Consider each of the following examples:

✓ The paper appears to have been plagiarized.

The paper appears now to have been plagiarized then.

✓ The crime rate seems to have dropped.

Between some point in the past and now, the crime rate seems to have dropped.

✓ The paper appeared to have been plagiarized; however, I now know it wasn't.

At some point in the past, the paper appeared to have been plagiarized (at a still earlier time); however, that conclusion is now known to be incorrect.

✓ The crime rate seemed to have dropped.

Between some time in the past and a later time in the past (the point at which the evaluation was made), the crime rate seemed to have dropped.

✓ Let me warn you: The paper will appear to have been plagiarized; however, I assure you it wasn't.

In the future when the paper is read, it will, at first, appear to have been plagiarized.

✓ The crime rate will seem to have dropped.

At some point in the future, the crime rate will appear to have dropped from some earlier, higher level.

Don't make the mistake of using the following clumsy constructions; your readers will get lost inside the labyrinthine time relationships. As a grammarian might put it, too much perfection can ruin a perfectly good perfect infinitive.

**✗ Something has happened / had happened / will have happened to have happened**

✗ The paper has appeared to have been plagiarized.

✓ The paper appears to have been plagiarized.

✗ The crime rate has seemed to have dropped.

✓ The crime rate seems to have dropped.

✗ The paper had appeared to have been plagiarized.

✓ The paper appeared to have been plagiarized.

✗ The crime rate had seemed to have dropped.

✓ The crime rate seemed to have dropped.

✗ The paper will have appeared to have been plagiarized.

✓ The paper will appear to have been plagiarized.

✗ The crime rate will have seemed to have dropped.

✓ The crime rate will seem to have dropped.

**➺ Choose the appropriate tense for the task at hand**

Following the *APA Manual* (1994), I suggest you use past tense for describing the actions performed and the results obtained in your study.

✓ All subjects completed an initial 125-item inventory.

✓ We randomly assigned subjects to one of three groups.

✓ The independent variable showed statistically significant effects on three of the four dependent variables.

Use the present tense for discussing results and conclusions: "By reporting conclusions in the present tense, you allow readers to join you in deliberating the matter at hand" (*APA Manual*, p. 25).

✓ The findings of this study support Hare-Mustin's (1987) contention that our construction of gender stresses differences, polarity, and hierarchy.

✓ This study documents some of the unfortunate consequences of reification.

✓ The data can be interpreted in (at least) two ways.

For literature reviews, the *APA Manual* advises you to use past tense or present perfect ("something has happened") tense. Past tense is particularly suited for noting research findings.

✓ Loftus and Pickrell (1995) reported that approximately 25% of research participants formed false memories of childhood events.

✓ Miller (1995) demonstrated how sociology researchers simultaneously exalt and derogate the rural English countryside.

Present perfect tense underscores

(a) the hot-off-the-presses status of a cited work,

✓ Flemons (1998) has described three different ways writers can use present perfect tense in their literature reviews.

(b) the development and continued relevance of a single author's (or of co-authors') work,

✓ Tannen, in both academic (1989, 1993) and popular (1990, 1995) texts, has explored dialogic process in a wide range of contexts.

or (c) the development and continued relevance of an area of study via the work of a variety of authors.

✓ A number of scholars have recognized the importance of narrative for the study of cognition and identity (Bruner, 1986; Cochran, 1986; Gergen & Gergen, 1986; Mishler, 1986; Polkinghorne, 1988; Sarbin, 1986).

The Modern Language Association (MLA) considers either past or present tense appropriate for discussing what an author has written (Cook, 1985).

✓ Skinner (1992) argued that the mind is not "what the brain does"; rather, "the mind is what the *body* does. It is what the *person* does. In other words, it is behavior" (p. 111).

✓ Skinner (1992) argues that the mind is not "what the brain does"; rather, "the mind is what the *body* does. It is what the *person* does. In other words, it is behavior" (p. 111).

Present tense, like present perfect tense, emphasizes the current relevance of a cited work.

✓ Ogden and Richards (1923/1989) remind us that "underlying all communication, and equally fundamental for any account of scientific method, are the rules or conventions of symbolism" (p. 246).

✓ Zerubavel (1991) explains how the drawing of distinctions shapes our relationships with ourselves, our friends and enemies, and our environment.

If you wish to use present tense in your literature review, check the editorial policy of the person(s) or organization (department, graduate school, journal) responsible for assessing your manuscript. If the policy is "strictly APA," you will need to stick to past and present perfect tenses. If you *are* able to use present tense, don't flip flop back and forth between it and past tense. As Cook (1985, p. 194) put it, "If you write *Neitzsche claims* but *Kant argued*, readers may wonder why you are making a distinction."

Sometimes, of course, moving back and forth between tenses is entirely appropriate. The following sentence, for example, does *not* flip flop.

✓ Freud claimed that conscious insight of repressed traumas is necessary for a neurosis to be cured.

Freud's claim was made in the past, but he was proposing something he believed to be generally or universally true—his proposition, then, belongs in the present tense.

## ➡ Write in relationship to the time frame of your readers

When a newspaper journalist writes about an event that occurred, say, three days in the past, he can refer to it as having happened "four days *ago*" because he knows that most people will be reading his article the next day. And a paleontologist can write about an event that occurred "100 million years *ago*," confident that readers who encounter her article in five or ten years will still be 100 million years away from the time described. You, however, don't share the luck of journalists and paleontologists. Given the potential lag time between when you write your paper and when it is read, you can't assume that you and your readers share the same time relationship to the events in your narrative.

✗ Five years ago, I worked with a teenager who had recently attempted suicide.

"Five years ago" for whom? You can either provide a date for the event or offer a reference point within the story itself.

✓ In 1993, I worked with a teenager who had recently attempted suicide.

✓ During my internship, I worked with a teenager who had recently attempted suicide.

**•• Keep track of time relationships within and between sentences**
Writing a coherent narrative—whether encapsulated within a sentence or extended over paragraphs or pages—requires you to keep track of the time relationships between each of the events you describe. For example, in the last illustrative sentence above, the time frame established by the phrase *I worked with a teenager* helps determine the tense form you need for the description of the earlier attempted suicide.

something happened

• During my internship, I worked with a teenager who had recently attempted suicide.

something had happened

Because the suicide attempt happened *at a specific point in time* (i.e., it wasn't an ongoing process, and it came to an end) *prior to the time the teenager was seen in therapy*, it needs to be described as *something* that *had happened*.

When you tell a story longer than a sentence or two, the tense relationships among the various events can get easily tangled. To keep them knot-free, make sure you know how the time frame and state of completion of each event relates to that of the others. The commentary accompanying the following two paragraphs demonstrates a way of checking the narrative integrity of your stories.

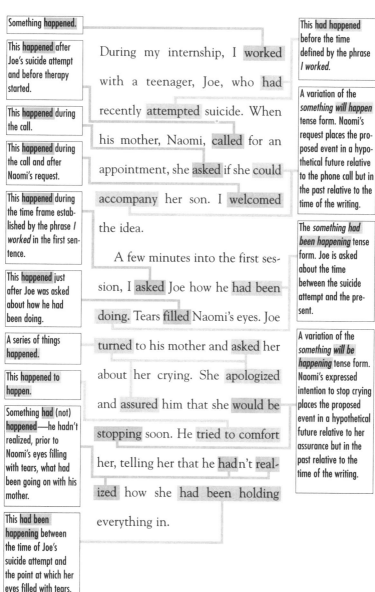

Something **happened.**

This **happened** after Joe's suicide attempt and before therapy started.

This **happened** during the call.

This **happened** during the call and after Naomi's request.

This **happened** during the time frame established by the phrase *I worked* in the first sentence.

This **happened** just after Joe was asked about how he had been doing.

A series of things **happened.**

This happened to **happen.**

Something **had** (not) **happened**—he hadn't realized, prior to Naomi's eyes filling with tears, what had been going on with his mother.

This **had been happening** between the time of Joe's suicide attempt and the point at which her eyes filled with tears.

This **had happened** before the time defined by the phrase *I worked.*

A variation of the *something will happen* tense form. Naomi's request places the proposed event in a hypothetical future relative to the phone call but in the past relative to the time of the writing.

The *something had been happening* tense form. Joe is asked about the time between the suicide attempt and the present.

A variation of the *something will be happening* tense form. Naomi's expressed intention to stop crying places the proposed event in a hypothetical future relative to her assurance but in the past relative to the time of the writing.

During my internship, I **worked** with a teenager, Joe, who **had** recently **attempted** suicide. When his mother, Naomi, **called** for an appointment, she **asked** if she **could accompany** her son. I **welcomed** the idea.

A few minutes into the first session, I **asked** Joe how he **had been doing.** Tears **filled** Naomi's eyes. Joe **turned** to his mother and **asked** her about her crying. She **apologized** and **assured** him that she **would be stopping** soon. He **tried to comfort** her, telling her that he **hadn't realized** how she **had been holding** everything in.

# 6
# Idea Development

*What is true is the relations within the story.*
                                        —Gregory Bateson

*[According to Aristotle,] a beginning is what requires nothing to precede it, an end is what requires nothing to follow it, and a middle needs something both before and after it.*
                                        —David Lodge

*A good paragraph resembles a good essay: it has unity by virtue of being organized around a single major point.*
                                        —John Trimble

*Paragraph = Issue + Discussion*
                                        —Joseph Williams

*Instead of viewing the opening sentence of each paragraph as a thesis sentence, as you've probably been taught to do, try this: View it as a bridge sentence whose prime function is to convey the reader over into the new paragraph.*
                                        —John Trimble

Dr. West, my first English teacher in my first year at university, was critical of my paragraphs. She liked my ideas and was satisfied with my sentence structure, but she couldn't figure out my strategy for making paragraph breaks—how was I, she asked, deciding when to end one paragraph and start the next? I didn't tell her I had been wrestling with that problem since the age of nine.

I was first introduced to paragraphs by my fourth grade teacher, Mrs. Truran. Quick to anger and hard to please, she demanded more of me and my classmates than we were able to give. I remember a particular day when she told us to write a page-long description of something. When we finished, she said, she would be grading the neatness of our work, the accuracy of our spelling, and the correctness of our sentences and paragraphs. She didn't want us using two paragraphs if one would do, but neither did she want us lumping all our sentences into one if two were called for.

Midway through my little essay, I froze. Should the sentence I was about to write conclude the present paragraph or introduce the next? I didn't know how to decide. My distress mounting, I looked inward for inspiration. It came to me in the form of a scheme.

The end of the sentence I had just written had taken me to the edge of the page, so the first word of my next one would need to be placed on a fresh line. I wrote down the first word beside the left margin, scribbled over it until it was indecipherable, and then restarted the sentence to the right of it. I smiled at the tidy little mess on the page, at the perfect ambiguity I had created. Now Mrs. Truran wouldn't know whether I had deleted the word because of a spelling error or because I had realized too late that the new line should have been indented (to start a new paragraph). I predicted I would get criticized for sloppiness—she'd recently taken everyone's new ballpoint pens away because of "poor penmanship"—but I gambled on her approving whichever "correction" she thought I had made. A win-win situation. Or so I thought.

Had I spent less time trying to hoodwink Mrs. Truran and more time learning her principles of proper paragraphing, I may have been in better shape, nine years later, when faced with the task of writing essays for English 101. Dr. West was an inspiring teacher, but I'm not sure my paragraphing improved under her guidance, either. I wish she, or, better, Mrs. Truran, had told me what I'm about to tell you; it would have helped me, I think, get the hang of cross-sentence idea development much earlier in my academic career. The notion is simple, and if you have already read Chapters 3 and 4, it won't surprise you: A paragraph is nothing more—and, just as importantly, nothing less—than a story.[1]

If you approach the task of writing a paragraph as an opportunity to compose a story, you can then draw on your already refined narrative sensibility to help you construct your descriptions and explanations and to assess the clarity and flow of your ideas. With all the novels you have read, with all the movies and television shows you have seen, you are, whether you know it or not, a story connoisseur. You easily recognize the seamless transitions and airtight logic of well-crafted novels and films and, conversely, you can spot the clumsy transitions and the leaps in logic of contrived novels and B-grade movies. Bring this same narrative expertise to bear on your writing, and you will be well-prepared to spot transition and logic problems within and between your paragraphs.

This way of approaching composition invites you to *think relationally* about idea development, to look closely at the continuities and discontinuities between your sentences and paragraphs. As you write, continually pose the narrative-coherence questions listed in the box on page 171. They are designed to focus your scrutiny on your idea development at three different levels of the text: the relationships between words, the relationships between sentences, and the relationships between paragraphs.[2] After briefly describing the purpose of each of the questions, I will illustrate how you can use them to locate and revise narrative problems in your writing.

[1]Allow me to finish my story about Mrs. Truran. My risk-avoidance ruse successfully duped her; she never suspected my ploy. Of course, I never found out whether my little essay required a second paragraph. Intent on not being judged wrong, I missed the opportunity to learn.

[2]As I discuss in Chapter 2, you also need to consider the continuities and discontinuities between each of your sections. Your Abstract is not your Introduction; your Literature Review should follow logically from your Introduction and provide the context for your Method, Analysis, and Discussion; your Discussion and Conclusions should build on and go a step beyond your Literature Review and Data Analysis; and so on.

> ### Narrative-Coherence Questions
> **Relationships between words**
> - Any rough (awkward/meandering/incomplete) sentences?
> - Any vague or confusing ideas?
>
> **Relationships between sentences**
> - Are new terms or ideas introduced appropriately? Are previously mentioned terms or ideas revisited appropriately?
> - Do the ideas progress, step by step, from sentence to sentence? Any leaps between sentences? Any detours? Any treadmills?
>
> **Relationships between paragraphs**
> - Do the ideas progress, step by step, from paragraph to paragraph? Any leaps between paragraphs? Any detours? Any treadmills?

## Narrative-Coherence Questions

In Chapter 1, I explained the importance of your hallucinating an ideal reader—an intelligent, reasonably well-read person in your field who is encountering your work for the first time. Actually, *this* is who should be asking and answering these narrative-coherence questions, not you. You are the *worst* person to be judging whether the idea development on the page in front of you is worth anything, for you also have the ideas floating around in your head. You know too well what you *want* to say to adequately assess whether your sentences manage to say it. Give your imaginary reader a red pen and ask him or her to find the glitches in your progression of ideas. (See Chapter 1 for suggestions on how to read your work in edit-mode.)

### *Relationships between words*

**• Any rough (awkward/meandering/incomplete) sentences?**
You can't build a coherent paragraph out of incoherent sentences. Use the ideas from Chapters 3-5 (or your own knowledge of grammar, punctuation, and tenses) to evaluate and correct each of the component parts of the paragraph.

• **Any vague or confusing ideas?**

You can have a grammatically correct sentence that says nothing or makes no sense:

> ✗ The dialectic of motive and action collapses if proprioceptive cues are proscribed by the simulacrum of Skinnerian metaphysics.

Watch for fuzzy stories and high-sounding, empty abstractions.

### Relationships between sentences

• **Are new terms or ideas introduced appropriately? Are previously mentioned terms or ideas revisited appropriately?**

Shortly after my son, Eric, turned four, he, my wife, and I went out for dinner at an upscale restaurant. When the hostess approached us, smiling, Eric looked up at her and casually intoned, "Have we met before?" This is precisely the question your readers will ask if they unexpectedly stumble on an unfamiliar idea or term. Don't force them to handle such introductions themselves—that's *your* job.

• **Do the ideas progress, step by step, from sentence to sentence? Any leaps between sentences? Any detours? Any treadmills?**

If you try to assess your narrative coherence merely by listening to the flow of your sentences, your connecting words (see Chapter 3)—*and, but, or, for, yet, so, although, because, if, since, whereas, while, however, conversely, moreover, similarly, therefore, thus, further, also,* and so on— can help make your sentences seem more integrated than they actually are. To keep from being deceived, read each sentence over until you can describe its content. What is it about? What does it mean? How does it relate to the sentences preceding and following it? Once you can answer these questions, go on to the next sentence and ask them all again. If you get mired in complexity, grab a piece of paper and keep notes. Write down a short description of each of the sentences of a paragraph and then read through the sequence several times. Can you follow the story development? Can you find any gaps in the narrative? Do you notice any sharp turns (detours) partway through the paragraph? Any unnecessary repetitions (treadmills)?

### Relationships between paragraphs

• **Do the ideas progress, step by step, from paragraph to paragraph? Any leaps between paragraphs? Any detours? Any treadmills?**

The gaps between paragraphs should be wider than the gaps between intra-paragraph sentences, but readers shouldn't have to strain themselves trying to leap them. Each paragraph should work as a stand-alone story *and* as an episode or installment in the more encompassing story (the section or subsection) of which it is a part. Make sure that the first sentence of each paragraph appreciates where it came from and that the last sentence looks forward to what will happen next.

You can also check your paragraph development the same way you check the progression of your sentences. Write down theme or plot descriptions for each paragraph, arrange them in order, and then read through them, looking for unbridgeable gaps, unpredictable shifts, and unpleasant repetitions. This will help you judge whether your paragraphs develop a clearly-definable line of thought over a series of pages.

# Illustration

On the following page, I demonstrate how you can use narrative-coherence questions to evaluate and reorganize the relationships within and between your sentences and paragraphs. For the sake of clarity, I have concentrated on only one organizational level at a time: first, on within-sentence relationships; second, on between-sentence relationships; and third, on between-paragraph relationships. In actual practice, you may find it easier and more efficient to attend to multiple levels simultaneously. After all, making a change within a sentence can alter the flow of ideas between sentences and even between paragraphs.

Imagine you have written the following disheveled introduction to a paper on death and dying.[3] Read it through a few times, noting sentences and sentence sequences in need of help.

[3]Kristin Wright generously allowed me to draw from and play with the first chapter of her dissertation, and she checked to make sure that my statements and citations were appropriate. The scholarship is hers; the sentences are mine.

## The Experience of Dying

Hinton (1963) was the first researcher to interview dying patients. On the other hand Saunders (1965) is responsible for founding the modern hospice movement, for dying patients. But it was the publication of *On Death and Dying* (Kübler-Ross, 1969) that helped the advancement of medical treatments for dying patients, and encouraged the public and health care personnel alike to intimately understand the experiences of them (Corr, 1993; Kastenbaum, 1975; McAteer, 1990; Schulz & Schlarb, 1987-88), thereby making possible significant changes in their treatment in hospitals (Kastenbaum, 1981). Dying patients, who were also interviewed by Kübler-Ross (1969) required four stages of response before acceptance, the final stage is finally reached.

The five stages included: (a) shock and denial, which is the first response to news of impending death; (b) anger; (c) bargaining with fate; (d) when the bargaining doesn't work, depression; (e) followed by acceptance (mentioned above) that happens when the patients themselves are able to look directly into the shadow of mystery. However, follow-up studies have failed to support Kübler-Ross's original findings (e.g., Metzger, 1979-80; Schulz & Aderman, 1974; Wright, in preparation). Researchers have used them to explain grief reactions to every conceivable loss (Levine, 1982); including the loss of a job (Winegardner, Simonetti, & Nykodym, 1984), losses due to closed-head injuries (Groveman & Brown, 1985), or by a college athlete who had to quit involvement in sports (Blinde & Stratta, 1992), or by patients who have received artificial organs (Fertziger, 1991), or, in addition, who can't get pregnant (Kronen, 1994).

Freud is the most well-known and influential of all the psychiatrists. Kübler-Ross's concepts have also; however, influenced our culture significantly. Freudian concepts, such as dreaming, repression, and the unconscious, have become part of how we make sense of our lives. Whereas, Kübler-Ross focused on dying and death, on the process of grieving. The five stages, like the id, ego, and superego, are considered by the lay general public to not be theoretical constructs but objective truths.

I have organized the following discussion as if my hallucinated (i.e., ideal) reader, Katherine, were talking to me about the idea development (or lack thereof) in these three paragraphs. I'll let you listen in while she identifies glitches and suggests revisions. To best help you adapt this process to your own needs, I (or, I guess, Katherine) will demonstrate it in slow-motion detail, erring on the side of thoroughness. You can speed things up for yourself once you understand the principles involved.

### Relationships between words

• **Any rough (awkward/meandering/incomplete) sentences?**[4]

Let's first go through all three paragraphs, sentence by sentence.

> ✓ Hinton (1963) was the first researcher to interview dying patients.

Fine—no problem.

> ✗ On the other hand Saunders (1965) is responsible for founding the modern hospice movement, for dying patients.

Does responsibility endure? Saunders *was* responsible for founding the modern hospice movement, but is she still? She undertook her actions in the past, so you should locate her responsibility back then too.

> ✓ . . . Saunders was responsible . . .

Your introductory suspense phrase—*on the other hand*—also needs attention. I will discuss later the inter-sentence problem this phrase sets up, but let's concentrate first on the relationship problems *within* the sentence. You need a comma after *hand* to cue readers that the suspense has, by that point, reached a peak and is ready to be resolved.

> ✓ On the other hand, . . .

You also need to delete the comma after *movement*. If you don't, it will tell readers to treat the word following it—*for*—as a retrace cue. Remember that retrace cues help readers quickly recognize parallel or referential relationships within a sentence. If the word *for* is turned into a retrace cue by the misplaced comma, it will signal readers to go back (in their memory) to an earlier twin word in the sentence (in this case,

---

[4]The discussion of intra-sentence problems uses the ideas and terminology set forth in Chapters 3-5.

## The Experience of Dying

Hinton (1963) was the first researcher to interview dying patients. On the other hand Saunders (1965) is responsible for founding the modern hospice movement, for dying patients. But it was the publication of On Death and Dying (Kübler-Ross, 1969) that helped the advancement of medical treatments for dying patients, and encouraged the public and health care personnel alike to intimately understand the experiences of them (Corr, 1993; Kastenbaum, 1975; McAteer, 1990; Schulz & Schlarb, 1987-88), thereby making possible significant changes in their treatment in hospitals (Kastenbaum, 1981). Dying patients, who were also interviewed by Kübler-Ross (1969) required four stages of response before acceptance, the final stage is finally reached.

The five stages included: (a) shock and denial, which is the first response to news of impending death; (b) anger; (c) bargaining with fate; (d) when the bargaining doesn't work, depression; (e) followed by acceptance (mentioned above) that happens when the patients themselves are able to look directly into the shadow of mystery. However, follow-up studies have failed to support Kübler-Ross's original findings (e.g., Metzger, 1979-80; Schulz & Aderman, 1974; Wright, in preparation). Researchers have used them to explain grief reactions to every conceivable loss (Levine, 1982); including the loss of a job (Winegardner, Simonetti, & Nykodym, 1984), losses due to closed-head injuries (Groveman & Brown, 1985), or by a college athlete who had to quit involvement in sports (Blinde & Stratta, 1992), or by patients who have received artificial organs (Fertziger, 1991), or, in addition, who can't get pregnant (Kronen, 1994).

Freud is the most well-known and influential of all the psychiatrists. Kübler-Ross's concepts have also; however, influenced our culture significantly. Freudian concepts, such as dreaming, repression, and the unconscious, have become part of how we make sense of our lives. Whereas, Kübler-Ross focused on dying and death, on the process of grieving. The five stages, like the id, ego, and superego, are considered by the lay general public to not be theoretical constructs but objective truths.

an identical twin—an earlier occurrence of the word *for*). Given the way sentences work, readers will expect the phrase beginning with the retrace cue to be parallel with the earlier phrase beginning with its twin, and they will read the first part of the sentence (the part preceding the first *for*) as the stem for both phrases.

✗    On the other hand, Saunders was responsible
    → for founding the modern hospice movement[,]
    → for dying patients.

Once readers get to the word *dying*, they will realize the two phrases *aren't* parallel. Saunders undertook the action of founding the hospice movement; she *didn't* undertake the action of dying patients.

You could correct the muddle by adding a word after the second *for*—this would render the two phrases properly parallel.

✓    On the other hand, Saunders was responsible
    → for founding the modern hospice movement[,]
    → for helping dying patients.

Or, alternatively, you could remove the comma.

✓    On the other hand, Saunders was responsible for founding the modern hospice movement for dying patients.

Let's go with this second option and continue on.

✗    But it was the publication of *On Death and Dying* (Kübler-Ross, 1969) that helped the advancement of medical treatments for dying patients, and encouraged the public and health care personnel alike to intimately understand the experiences of them (Corr, 1993; Kastenbaum, 1975; McAteer, 1990; Schulz & Schlarb, 1987-88), thereby making possible significant changes in their treatment in hospitals (Kastenbaum, 1981).

The comma after *patients* creates confusion. When you have a comma together with a coordinating conjunction—in this case, a comma and an *and*—the two of them in combination tell readers to expect either an upcoming complete story (an independent clause, parallel with an earlier independent clause) or the last in a series of parallel phrases. But, in this case, the part of the sentence following the *and* is neither, so you need to do something with the comma. If you were to delete it, the retrace cue following the conjunction—*encouraged*—

### The Experience of Dying

Hinton (1963) was the first researcher to interview dying patients. On the other hand Saunders (1965) is responsible for founding the modern hospice movement, for dying patients. But it was the publication of *On Death and Dying* (Kübler-Ross, 1969) that helped the advancement of medical treatments for dying patients, and encouraged the public and health care personnel alike to intimately understand the experiences of them (Corr, 1993; Kastenbaum, 1975; McAteer, 1990; Schulz & Schlarb, 1987-88), thereby making possible significant changes in their treatment in hospitals (Kastenbaum, 1981). Dying patients, who were also interviewed by Kübler-Ross (1969) required four stages of response before acceptance, the final stage is finally reached.

The five stages included: (a) shock and denial, which is the first response to news of impending death; (b) anger; (c) bargaining with fate; (d) when the bargaining doesn't work, depression; (e) followed by acceptance (mentioned above) that happens when the patients themselves are able to look directly into the shadow of mystery. However, follow-up studies have failed to support Kübler-Ross's original findings (e.g., Metzger, 1979-80; Schulz & Aderman, 1974; Wright, in preparation). Researchers have used them to explain grief reactions to every conceivable loss (Levine, 1982); including the loss of a job (Winegardner, Simonetti, & Nykodym, 1984), losses due to closed-head injuries (Groveman & Brown, 1985), or by a college athlete who had to quit involvement in sports (Blinde & Stratta, 1992), or by patients who have received artificial organs (Fertziger, 1991), or, in addition, who can't get pregnant (Kronen, 1994).

Freud is the most well-known and influential of all the psychiatrists. Kübler-Ross's concepts have also; however, influenced our culture significantly. Freudian concepts, such as dreaming, repression, and the unconscious, have become part of how we make sense of our lives. Whereas, Kübler-Ross focused on dying and death, on the process of grieving. The five stages, like the id, ego, and superego, are considered by the lay general public to not be theoretical constructs but objective truths.

would then signal a parallel relationship between the phrase it begins and the phrase its similar twin, the word *helped*, begins.

✓ But it was the publication of *On Death and Dying* that
→ helped the advancement of medical treatments for dying patients [and]
→ encouraged the public and health care personnel alike to intimately understand the experiences of them. . . .

The publication did two things: It helped the advancement of medical treatments and it encouraged people to understand.

The sentence now works better, but further problems remain. The parallel relationship *within* the second parallel phrase is also clumsy:

✗ But it was the publication of *On Death and Dying* that . . . encouraged the public and health care personnel alike to intimately understand the experiences . . . .

Every time I read it through, my ear connects the *the* both to *public* and to *health care personnel*—

✗ But it was the publication of *On Death and Dying* that . . . encouraged the
→ public [and]
→ health care personnel alike
to intimately understand the experiences . . .

—and when I hear *the health care personnel*, I ask, "What health care personnel?" The definitive article (*the*) doesn't fit. What happens if you reverse the order?

• But it was the publication of *On Death and Dying* that . . . encouraged health care personnel and the public alike to intimately understand the experiences . . . .

This solves the definitive-article problem—

✓ But it was the publication of *On Death and Dying* that . . . encouraged
→ health care personnel [and]
→ the public alike
to intimately understand the experiences . . .

—but it creates a funny-sounding phrase: *the public alike*. Try replacing both terms.

## The Experience of Dying

Hinton (1963) was the first researcher to interview dying patients. On the other hand Saunders (1965) is responsible for founding the modern hospice movement, for dying patients. But it was the publication of *On Death and Dying* (Kübler-Ross, 1969) that helped the advancement of medical treatments for dying patients, and encouraged the public and health care personnel alike to intimately understand the experiences of them (Corr, 1993; Kastenbaum, 1975; McAteer, 1990; Schulz & Schlarb, 1987-88), thereby making possible significant changes in their treatment in hospitals (Kastenbaum, 1981). Dying patients, who were also interviewed by Kübler-Ross (1969) required four stages of response before acceptance, the final stage is finally reached.

The five stages included: (a) shock and denial, which is the first response to news of impending death; (b) anger; (c) bargaining with fate; (d) when the bargaining doesn't work, depression; (e) followed by acceptance (mentioned above) that happens when the patients themselves are able to look directly into the shadow of mystery. However, follow-up studies have failed to support Kübler-Ross's original findings (e.g., Metzger, 1979-80; Schulz & Aderman, 1974; Wright, in preparation). Researchers have used them to explain grief reactions to every conceivable loss (Levine, 1982); including the loss of a job (Winegardner, Simonetti, & Nykodym, 1984), losses due to closed-head injuries (Groveman & Brown, 1985), or by a college athlete who had to quit involvement in sports (Blinde & Stratta, 1992), or by patients who have received artificial organs (Fertziger, 1991), or, in addition, who can't get pregnant (Kronen, 1994).

Freud is the most well-known and influential of all the psychiatrists. Kübler-Ross's concepts have also; however, influenced our culture significantly. Freudian concepts, such as dreaming, repression, and the unconscious, have become part of how we make sense of our lives. Whereas, Kübler-Ross focused on dying and death, on the process of grieving. The five stages, like the id, ego, and superego, are considered by the lay general public to not be theoretical constructs but objective truths.

✔ But it was the publication of *On Death and Dying* that . . .
encouraged both professional and family caregivers to intimately understand the experience . . .

This works better. But problems persist.

✗ But it was the publication of *On Death and Dying* that helped
the advancement of medical treatments for dying patients
and encouraged both professional and family caregivers to
intimately understand the experience of them, . . .

When you wrote this sentence, you used the pronoun *them* so you
wouldn't have to repeat the term *dying patients*. You had the right idea
(clumsy repetition is unpleasant), but readers could initially interpret
the *them* as a stand-in for *medical treatments*, not for *dying patients*. You
could try substituting the phrase *understand their experience* for *understand
the experience of them*, but readers might then interpret the sentence as
saying that caregivers intimately understand *their own* experience.

✗ But it was the publication of *On Death and Dying* that helped
the advancement of medical treatments for dying patients
and encouraged both professional and family caregivers to
intimately understand their experience, . . .

Before exploring other options, let's take a look at the last phrase of the
sentence. Notice that it invokes a causal relationship.

✗ But it was the publication of *On Death and Dying* that helped
the advancement of medical treatments for dying patients
and encouraged both professional and family caregivers to
intimately understand their experience, thereby making possible significant changes in their treatment in hospitals.

Significant changes in treatment were made possible, but by what?
With the pronoun ambiguity still floating in the air, the sentence
remains muddled and the question remains unanswered. But even if
you cleared up the ambiguity, the sentence would still suffer from
redundancy. The last phrase repeats the point you made earlier about
positive changes in medical treatment. I must say, the best thing about
this sentence is the period. "At last!" I said to myself when I saw it, "the
sentence is over!"

Here is a rewrite that eliminates the redundancy, keeps most of the
content intact, and fixes many of the sentence's other internal glitches. I will address the external (inter-sentence) problems later.

## The Experience of Dying

Hinton (1963) was the first researcher to interview dying patients. On the other hand Saunders (1965) is responsible for founding the modern hospice movement, for dying patients. But it was the publication of *On Death and Dying* (Kübler-Ross, 1969) that helped the advancement of medical treatments for dying patients, and encouraged the public and health care personnel alike to intimately understand the experiences of them (Corr, 1993; Kastenbaum, 1975; McAteer, 1990; Schulz & Schlarb, 1987-88), thereby making possible significant changes in their treatment in hospitals (Kastenbaum, 1981). Dying patients, who were also interviewed by Kübler-Ross (1969) required four stages of response before acceptance, the final stage is finally reached.

The five stages included: (a) shock and denial, which is the first response to news of impending death; (b) anger; (c) bargaining with fate; (d) when the bargaining doesn't work, depression; (e) followed by acceptance (mentioned above) that happens when the patients themselves are able to look directly into the shadow of mystery. However, follow-up studies have failed to support Kübler-Ross's original findings (e.g., Metzger, 1979-80; Schulz & Aderman, 1974; Wright, in preparation). Researchers have used them to explain grief reactions to every conceivable loss (Levine, 1982); including the loss of a job (Winegardner, Simonetti, & Nykodym, 1984), losses due to closed-head injuries (Groveman & Brown, 1985), or by a college athlete who had to quit involvement in sports (Blinde & Stratta, 1992), or by patients who have received artificial organs (Fertziger, 1991), or, in addition, who can't get pregnant (Kronen, 1994).

Freud is the most well-known and influential of all the psychiatrists. Kübler-Ross's concepts have also; however, influenced our culture significantly. Freudian concepts, such as dreaming, repression, and the unconscious, have become part of how we make sense of our lives. Whereas, Kübler-Ross focused on dying and death, on the process of grieving. The five stages, like the id, ego, and superego, are considered by the lay general public to not be theoretical constructs but objective truths.

✓ Kübler-Ross's (1969) *On Death and Dying* provided professional and family caregivers with an intimate understanding of the experience of dying (Corr, 1993; Kastenbaum, 1975; McAteer, 1990; Schulz & Schlarb, 1987-88) and, as a result, helped transform the hospital care of terminally ill patients (Kastenbaum, 1981).

Notice how the parallel relationships now line up:

✓ Kübler-Ross's (1969) *On Death and Dying*
→ provided
→ professional [and]
→ family
caregivers with an intimate understanding of the experience of dying [and, as a result,]
→ helped transform the hospital care of terminally ill patients

Now let's look at the last sentence of the first paragraph. This sentence contains two pieces of non-essential gossip (i.e., non-restrictive phrases), each of which needs to be parenthetically enclosed within commas (or parentheses or dashes). You remembered the first, but not the second, comma for each phrase. In addition, you switched tenses at the end: *is* should be *was*.

✗ Dying patients, who were also interviewed by Kübler-Ross (1969) required four stages of response before acceptance, the final stage is finally reached.

✓ Dying patients, who were also interviewed by Kübler-Ross (1969), required four stages of response before acceptance, the final stage, was finally reached.

The commas help, but I'm still not sure what you are trying to say. Given my familiarity with Kübler-Ross's work, I can guess, but I shouldn't have to. Also, see what happens if you shift the sentence from passive to active voice. That is, instead of telling me what was *done to* someone or something, tell me what someone or something *did*. Passive voice sentences often read like mud.

✓ Kübler-Ross (1969) also interviewed dying patients. She found they passed through four stages of response before reaching a final stage of acceptance.

Okay, that will do for now. Let's go on to the next paragraph.

### The Experience of Dying

Hinton (1963) was the first researcher to interview dying patients. On the other hand Saunders (1965) is responsible for founding the modern hospice movement, for dying patients. But it was the publication of *On Death and Dying* (Kübler-Ross, 1969) that helped the advancement of medical treatments for dying patients, and encouraged the public and health care personnel alike to intimately understand the experiences of them (Corr, 1993; Kastenbaum, 1975; McAteer, 1990; Schulz & Schlarb, 1987-88), thereby making possible significant changes in their treatment in hospitals (Kastenbaum, 1981). Dying patients, who were also interviewed by Kübler-Ross (1969) required four stages of response before acceptance, the final stage is finally reached.

The five stages included: (a) shock and denial, which is the first response to news of impending death; (b) anger; (c) bargaining with fate; (d) when the bargaining doesn't work, depression; (e) followed by acceptance (mentioned above) that happens when the patients themselves are able to look directly into the shadow of mystery. However, follow-up studies have failed to support Kübler-Ross's original findings (e.g., Metzger, 1979-80; Schulz & Aderman, 1974; Wright, in preparation). Researchers have used them to explain grief reactions to every conceivable loss (Levine, 1982); including the loss of a job (Winegardner, Simonetti, & Nykodym, 1984), losses due to closed-head injuries (Groveman & Brown, 1985), or by a college athlete who had to quit involvement in sports (Blinde & Stratta, 1992), or by patients who have received artificial organs (Fertziger, 1991), or, in addition, who can't get pregnant (Kronen, 1994).

Freud is the most well-known and influential of all the psychiatrists. Kübler-Ross's concepts have also; however, influenced our culture significantly. Freudian concepts, such as dreaming, repression, and the unconscious, have become part of how we make sense of our lives. Whereas, Kübler-Ross focused on dying and death, on the process of grieving. The five stages, like the id, ego, and superego, are considered by the lay general public to not be theoretical constructs but objective truths.

✗   The five stages included: (a) shock and denial, which is the first response to news of impending death; (b) anger; (c) bargaining with fate; (d) when the bargaining doesn't work, depression; (e) followed by acceptance (mentioned above) that happens when the patients themselves are able to look directly into the shadow of mystery.

Saunders's responsibility can be located at a particular point in history, so you needed to describe it in the past tense; however, the situation is different here. Kübler-Ross's five stages are theoretical ideas, not historical incidents. She may have invented them on a specific day or during a specific week or year, but the ideas themselves can't be temporally pinned down. They continue to "exist" in a perpetual present:

✓   The five stages include . . .

Your use of a colon at the end of *include* is incorrect.

✗   The five stages include: . . .

You are right to use a colon to set up a list, but you need to precede it with a complete story (an independent clause). Here's a simple, though not a particularly elegant, solution:

✓   The five stages include the following: . . .

Each of the items in a serial list must be grammatically (and conceptually) parallel; yours are, to put it kindly, structurally diverse.

✗   The five stages include the following:
→   shock and denial, which is the first response to news of impending death
→   anger
→   bargaining with fate
→   when the bargaining doesn't work, depression
→   followed by acceptance (mentioned above) that happens when the patients themselves are able to look directly into the shadow of mystery.

Write a list *or* a narrative, or *follow* a list with an elaborating narrative, but don't try to do both simultaneously.

✓   The five stages include the following: (a) initial shock and denial; (b) anger; (c) bargaining with fate; (d) depression; and (e) acceptance. Not everyone is able to reach the final stage prior to death. Acceptance is facilitated by looking directly into the shadow of mystery.

## The Experience of Dying

Hinton (1963) was the first researcher to interview dying patients. On the other hand Saunders (1965) is responsible for founding the modern hospice movement, for dying patients. But it was the publication of *On Death and Dying* (Kübler-Ross, 1969) that helped the advancement of medical treatments for dying patients, and encouraged the public and health care personnel alike to intimately understand the experiences of them (Corr, 1993; Kastenbaum, 1975; McAteer, 1990; Schulz & Schlarb, 1987-88), thereby making possible significant changes in their treatment in hospitals (Kastenbaum, 1981). Dying patients, who were also interviewed by Kübler-Ross (1969) required four stages of response before acceptance, the final stage is finally reached.

The five stages included: (a) shock and denial, which is the first response to news of impending death; (b) anger; (c) bargaining with fate; (d) when the bargaining doesn't work, depression; (e) followed by acceptance (mentioned above) that happens when the patients themselves are able to look directly into the shadow of mystery. However, follow-up studies have failed to support Kübler-Ross's original findings (e.g., Metzger, 1979-80; Schulz & Aderman, 1974; Wright, in preparation). Researchers have used them to explain grief reactions to every conceivable loss (Levine, 1982); including the loss of a job (Winegardner, Simonetti, & Nykodym, 1984), losses due to closed-head injuries (Groveman & Brown, 1985), or by a college athlete who had to quit involvement in sports (Blinde & Stratta, 1992), or by patients who have received artificial organs (Fertziger, 1991), or, in addition, who can't get pregnant (Kronen, 1994).

Freud is the most well-known and influential of all the psychiatrists. Kübler-Ross's concepts have also; however, influenced our culture significantly. Freudian concepts, such as dreaming, repression, and the unconscious, have become part of how we make sense of our lives. Whereas, Kübler-Ross focused on dying and death, on the process of grieving. The five stages, like the id, ego, and superego, are considered by the lay general public to not be theoretical constructs but objective truths.

✓ However, follow-up studies have failed to support Kübler-Ross's original findings (e.g., Metzger, 1979-80; Schulz & Aderman, 1974; Wright, in preparation).

This has no *intra*-sentence relationship problems. Leave it for the time being and go on.

✗ Researchers have used them to explain grief reactions to every conceivable loss (Levine, 1982); including the loss of a job (Winegardner, Simonetti, & Nykodym, 1984), losses due to closed-head injuries (Groveman & Brown, 1985), or by a college athlete who had to quit involvement in sports (Blinde & Stratta, 1992), or by patients who have received artificial organs (Fertziger, 1991), or, in addition, who can't get pregnant (Kronen, 1994).

I suspect you used a semicolon to set up your list because you couldn't figure out whether you needed a colon or a comma.

✗ Researchers have used them to explain grief reactions to every conceivable loss (Levine, 1982);

A semicolon may *look* like a compromise between the two, but it doesn't *function* as one. You can place a semicolon between complex items in a list, but you can't use it to *introduce* the list. In this instance, you can use a comma.

✓ Researchers have used them to explain grief reactions to every conceivable loss (Levine, 1982), including . . .

This introduction now works, but the rest of the sentence doesn't. Once again, your list items are not parallel—they read as if you were comparing apples and Wednesdays.

✗ Researchers have used them to explain grief reactions to every conceivable loss, including
    → the loss of a job[,]
    → losses due to closed-head injuries[, or]
    → by a college athlete who had to quit involvement in sports[, or]
    → by patients
        → who have received artificial organs[, or, in addition,]
        → who can't get pregnant.

## The Experience of Dying

Hinton (1963) was the first researcher to interview dying patients. On the other hand Saunders (1965) is responsible for founding the modern hospice movement, for dying patients. But it was the publication of *On Death and Dying* (Kübler-Ross, 1969) that helped the advancement of medical treatments for dying patients, and encouraged the public and health care personnel alike to intimately understand the experiences of them (Corr, 1993; Kastenbaum, 1975; McAteer, 1990; Schulz & Schlarb, 1987-88), thereby making possible significant changes in their treatment in hospitals (Kastenbaum, 1981). Dying patients, who were also interviewed by Kübler-Ross (1969) required four stages of response before acceptance, the final stage is finally reached.

The five stages included: (a) shock and denial, which is the first response to news of impending death; (b) anger; (c) bargaining with fate; (d) when the bargaining doesn't work, depression; (e) followed by acceptance (mentioned above) that happens when the patients themselves are able to look directly into the shadow of mystery. However, follow-up studies have failed to support Kübler-Ross's original findings (e.g., Metzger, 1979-80; Schulz & Aderman, 1974; Wright, in preparation). Researchers have used them to explain grief reactions to every conceivable loss (Levine, 1982); including the loss of a job (Winegardner, Simonetti, & Nykodym, 1984), losses due to closed-head injuries (Groveman & Brown, 1985), or by a college athlete who had to quit involvement in sports (Blinde & Stratta, 1992), or by patients who have received artificial organs (Fertziger, 1991), or, in addition, who can't get pregnant (Kronen, 1994).

Freud is the most well-known and influential of all the psychiatrists. Kübler-Ross's concepts have also; however, influenced our culture significantly. Freudian concepts, such as dreaming, repression, and the unconscious, have become part of how we make sense of our lives. Whereas, Kübler-Ross focused on dying and death, on the process of grieving. The five stages, like the id, ego, and superego, are considered by the lay general public to not be theoretical constructs but objective truths.

Here's a possible rewrite:

✓ Researchers have used them to explain grief reactions to every conceivable loss (Levine, 1982), including unemployment (Winegardner, Simonetti, & Nykodym, 1984), closed-head injuries (Groveman & Brown, 1985), infertility (Kronen, 1994), quitting college athletics (Blinde & Stratta, 1992), and receiving artificial organs (Fertziger, 1991).

This version maintains parallel relationships.

✓ Researchers have used them to explain grief reactions to every conceivable loss, including

→ unemployment[,]
→ closed-head injuries[,]
→ infertility[,]
→ quitting college athletics[, and]
→ receiving artificial organs.

In the first sentence of your final paragraph, you mistakenly use the definitive article in front of *psychiatrists*.

✗ Freud is the most well-known and influential of all the psychiatrists.

All of *which* psychiatrists? Delete the *the* and you will be fine.

✓ Freud is the most well-known and influential of all psychiatrists.

Have you ever heard the expression, "a little bit of learning is a dangerous thing"? You remembered enough about punctuation rules to precede the *however* in the next sentence with a semicolon and follow it with a comma.

✗ Kübler-Ross's concepts have also; however, influenced our culture significantly.

Unfortunately, you forgot that you should only do this when such words (i.e., adverbial conjunctions) are placed at the *beginning* of a complete story (independent clause). You could, for example, say this:

✓ Freud is the most well-known and influential of all psychiatrists; however, Kübler-Ross is also an important figure.

If, however, you are using *however* (or some other adverbial conjunction) to add a parenthetical comment *within* a complete story, you should enclose it in commas (as I did earlier in this sentence).

## The Experience of Dying

Hinton (1963) was the first researcher to interview dying patients. On the other hand Saunders (1965) is responsible for founding the modern hospice movement, for dying patients. But it was the publication of *On Death and Dying* (Kübler-Ross, 1969) that helped the advancement of medical treatments for dying patients, and encouraged the public and health care personnel alike to intimately understand the experiences of them (Corr, 1993; Kastenbaum, 1975; McAteer, 1990; Schulz & Schlarb, 1987-88), thereby making possible significant changes in their treatment in hospitals (Kastenbaum, 1981). Dying patients, who were also interviewed by Kübler-Ross (1969) required four stages of response before acceptance, the final stage is finally reached.

The five stages included: (a) shock and denial, which is the first response to news of impending death; (b) anger; (c) bargaining with fate; (d) when the bargaining doesn't work, depression; (e) followed by acceptance (mentioned above) that happens when the patients themselves are able to look directly into the shadow of mystery. However, follow-up studies have failed to support Kübler-Ross's original findings (e.g., Metzger, 1979-80; Schulz & Aderman, 1974; Wright, in preparation). Researchers have used them to explain grief reactions to every conceivable loss (Levine, 1982); including the loss of a job (Winegardner, Simonetti, & Nykodym, 1984), losses due to closed-head injuries (Groveman & Brown, 1985), or by a college athlete who had to quit involvement in sports (Blinde & Stratta, 1992), or by patients who have received artificial organs (Fertziger, 1991), or, in addition, who can't get pregnant (Kronen, 1994).

Freud is the most well-known and influential of all the psychiatrists. Kübler-Ross's concepts have also; however, influenced our culture significantly. Freudian concepts, such as dreaming, repression, and the unconscious, have become part of how we make sense of our lives. Whereas, Kübler-Ross focused on dying and death, on the process of grieving. The five stages, like the id, ego, and superego, are considered by the lay general public to not be theoretical constructs but objective truths.

✓ Kübler-Ross's concepts have also, however, influenced our culture significantly.

Your next sentence is fine—

✓ Freudian concepts, such as dreaming, repression, and the unconscious, have become part of how we make sense of our lives.

—but the one after it is incomplete:

✗ Whereas, Kübler-Ross focused on dying and death, on the process of grieving.

A grammarian would say you were using a subordinating conjunction (i.e., *whereas*) as if it were an adverbial conjunction (e.g., *however, conversely, similarly,* etc.). I agree with this diagnosis but would describe the problem a little differently. The sentence you've written leaves your readers up in the air. When you precede a complete story with a word such as *whereas* (or other subordinating conjunctions, such as *because, although, since,* etc.), you turn it into a suspense clause. Remember— when you create suspense, you must always resolve it before the end of the sentence: Don't leave your readers hanging.

✓ Kübler-Ross focused on dying and death, on the process of grieving.

I'm not sure how much the passive construction of the next sentence contributes to its awkwardness—

✗ The five stages, like the id, ego, and superego, are considered by the lay general public to not be theoretical constructs but objective truths.

—but the easiest way to tell is to recast it in active voice and see how it looks.

✗ The lay general public considers the five stages, like the id, ego, and superego, to not be theoretical constructs but objective truth.

Not much improvement, eh? Oh well, at least it's a start. What else? Delete the word *lay*—it is redundant. And rework your comparison between Kübler-Ross's five stages and Freud's three levels of mental process. I initially took the word *like* to be a synonym of *such as*; thus, when I started reading the words *id, ego, and superego,* I thought you were providing specific names for three of the five stages. If it confused *me,* it will confound your readers. Finally, the last part of the sentence

## The Experience of Dying

Hinton (1963) was the first researcher to interview dying patients. On the other hand Saunders (1965) is responsible for founding the modern hospice movement, for dying patients. But it was the publication of *On Death and Dying* (Kübler-Ross, 1969) that helped the advancement of medical treatments for dying patients, and encouraged the public and health care personnel alike to intimately understand the experiences of them (Corr, 1993; Kastenbaum, 1975; McAteer, 1990; Schulz & Schlarb, 1987-88), thereby making possible significant changes in their treatment in hospitals (Kastenbaum, 1981). Dying patients, who were also interviewed by Kübler-Ross (1969) required four stages of response before acceptance, the final stage is finally reached.

The five stages included: (a) shock and denial, which is the first response to news of impending death; (b) anger; (c) bargaining with fate; (d) when the bargaining doesn't work, depression; (e) followed by acceptance (mentioned above) that happens when the patients themselves are able to look directly into the shadow of mystery. However, follow-up studies have failed to support Kübler-Ross's original findings (e.g., Metzger, 1979-80; Schulz & Aderman, 1974; Wright, in preparation). Researchers have used them to explain grief reactions to every conceivable loss (Levine, 1982); including the loss of a job (Winegardner, Simonetti, & Nykodym, 1984), losses due to closed-head injuries (Groveman & Brown, 1985), or by a college athlete who had to quit involvement in sports (Blinde & Stratta, 1992), or by patients who have received artificial organs (Fertziger, 1991), or, in addition, who can't get pregnant (Kronen, 1994).

Freud is the most well-known and influential of all the psychiatrists. Kübler-Ross's concepts have also; however, influenced our culture significantly. Freudian concepts, such as dreaming, repression, and the unconscious, have become part of how we make sense of our lives. Whereas, Kübler-Ross focused on dying and death, on the process of grieving. The five stages, like the id, ego, and superego, are considered by the lay general public to not be theoretical constructs but objective truths.

contrasts *plural* constructs with a *singular* truth. The point is worth making, so try another way of saying it.

> ✓ People relate to Kübler-Ross's five stages the same way they relate to Freud's concepts—rather than regarding them as theoretical constructs, they embrace them as objective truths.

Okay, put all your revised sentences together and see how you stand so far.

### The Experience of Dying (Draft 2)

Hinton (1963) was the first researcher to interview dying patients. On the other hand, Saunders (1965) was responsible for founding the modern hospice movement for dying patients. Kübler-Ross's (1969) *On Death and Dying* provided professional and family caregivers with an intimate understanding of the experience of dying (Corr, 1993; Kastenbaum, 1975; McAteer, 1990; Schulz & Schlarb, 1987-88) and, as a result, helped transform the hospital care of terminally ill patients (Kastenbaum, 1981). Kübler-Ross (1969) also interviewed dying patients. She found they passed through four stages of response before reaching a final stage of acceptance.

The five stages include the following: (a) initial shock and denial; (b) anger; (c) bargaining with fate; (d) depression; and (e) acceptance. Not everyone is able to reach the final stage prior to death. Acceptance is facilitated by looking directly into the shadow of mystery. However, follow-up studies have failed to support Kübler-Ross's original findings (e.g., Metzger, 1979-80; Schulz & Aderman, 1974; Wright, in preparation). Researchers have used them to explain grief reactions to every conceivable loss (Levine, 1982), including unemployment (Winegardner, Simonetti, & Nykodym, 1984), closed-head injuries (Groveman & Brown, 1985), infertility (Kronen, 1994), quitting college athletics (Blinde & Stratta, 1992), and receiving artificial organs (Fertziger, 1991).

Freud is the most well-known and influential of all psychiatrists. Kübler-Ross's concepts have also, however, influenced our culture significantly. Freudian concepts, such as dreaming, repression, and the unconscious, have become part of how we make sense of our lives. Kübler-Ross focused on dying and death, on the process of grieving. People relate to Kübler-Ross's five stages the same way they relate to Freud's concepts—rather than regarding them as theoretical constructs, they embrace them as objective truths.

- **Any vague or confusing ideas?**

Even with the improvements you've made to the structure and punctuation of your sentences, a few muddy ideas remain.

> ✗ She found they passed through four stages of response before reaching a final stage of acceptance.

I read somewhere that Robert Altman requires all the actors in his films to be competent singers. You, apparently, have similarly decided that all readers of your paper need to be competent mathematicians. I suggest you find another way of saying this.

> ✓ She found that some passed through all five stages before passing on whereas others were unable to reach the final stage of acceptance.

This will work for now; at least I no longer need a hand-held calculator to get through the sentence.

> ✗ Acceptance is facilitated by looking directly into the shadow of mystery.

The shadow of mystery? What is that? I applaud your efforts to sprinkle some color into your writing, but are we taking ourselves a little too seriously? Remember, you are writing a social science paper, not a piece of advertising copy for some new perfume. And *who* is looking directly into this "shadow of mystery," this "enigmatic penumbra"? (Sorry, your sense of drama is infectious.) The passive-voice construction of the sentence contributes to the vagueness. Try this:

> ✓ Those who can face their mortality directly may find a sense of acceptance.

And those who can face their bad writing directly may find a way to change it.

✗   Freudian concepts, such as dreaming, repression, and the unconscious, have become part of how we make sense of our lives.

Wait a minute. I can accept *repression* as a Freudian concept, and
even though the notion of the unconscious was around long before
Freud started using it (see Whyte, 1962), I will give him that one too.
But *dreaming*? I didn't know Freud held the patent on that. You may
have Freudian dreams, but dreaming is not a Freudian concept. Try
*catharsis* or *sublimation* or something. I'm also not sure it works to say
these concepts "have become part of how we make sense of our lives."
You mean they have been incorporated into our psychological understanding of ourselves, right? How about something like the following?

✓   We see ourselves through a Freudian lens, interpreting our
motivations, symptoms, and desires through concepts such as
catharsis, repression, and the unconscious.

### Relationships between sentences

• **Are new terms or ideas introduced appropriately? Are previously
mentioned terms or ideas revisited appropriately?**

You have three idea-introduction glitches, all of them in the first paragraph.

✗   Hinton (1963) was the first researcher to interview dying
patients.

Your paper is on dying and death, and Kübler-Ross figures prominently. Why then start your discussion off with a sentence about
Hinton? You never mention him again. The information about him is
relevant to your topic, but in using it like this, you throw the rest of your
paragraph off kilter. Don't delete the sentence, but look for an opportunity to use it, or a rewritten version of it, elsewhere in the paragraph.

✗   On the other hand, Saunders was responsible for founding the
modern hospice movement for dying patients.

You make reference here to *the other hand*—the second of two, no?
What happened to the first hand? Perhaps a Zen Buddhist made off
with it. In any event, if you are going to use this expression, you need
to have earlier introduced a point with the phrase *On the one hand*. I
will applaud your decision if you just drop the expression altogether.

✓   Saunders was responsible for founding the modern hospice
movement for dying patients.

### The Experience of Dying (Draft 2)

Hinton (1963) was the first researcher to interview dying patients. On the other hand, Saunders (1965) was responsible for founding the modern hospice movement for dying patients. Kübler-Ross's (1969) *On Death and Dying* provided professional and family caregivers with an intimate understanding of the experience of dying (Corr, 1993; Kastenbaum, 1975; McAteer, 1990; Schulz & Schlarb, 1987-88) and, as a result, helped transform the hospital care of terminally ill patients (Kastenbaum, 1981). Kübler-Ross (1969) also interviewed dying patients. She found they passed through four stages of response before reaching a final stage of acceptance.

The five stages include the following: (a) initial shock and denial; (b) anger; (c) bargaining with fate; (d) depression; and (e) acceptance. Not everyone is able to reach the final stage prior to death. Acceptance is facilitated by looking directly into the shadow of mystery. However, follow-up studies have failed to support Kübler-Ross's original findings (e.g., Metzger, 1979-80; Schulz & Aderman, 1974; Wright, in preparation). Researchers have used them to explain grief reactions to every conceivable loss (Levine, 1982), including unemployment (Winegardner, Simonetti, & Nykodym, 1984), closed-head injuries (Groveman & Brown, 1985), infertility (Kronen, 1994), quitting college athletics (Blinde & Stratta, 1992), and receiving artificial organs (Fertziger, 1991).

Freud is the most well-known and influential of all psychiatrists. Kübler-Ross's concepts have also, however, influenced our culture significantly. Freudian concepts, such as dreaming, repression, and the unconscious, have become part of how we make sense of our lives. Kübler-Ross focused on dying and death, on the process of grieving. People relate to Kübler-Ross's five stages the same way they relate to Freud's concepts—rather than regarding them as theoretical constructs, they embrace them as objective truths.

If necessary, you can rewrite the sentence later, once you have figured out a different organization for the paragraph.

✗ She found that some passed through all five stages before passing on whereas others were unable to reach the final stage of acceptance.

Hello, have we met before? All *what* five stages? All five stages of *what*? I feel like I just walked into the middle of a conversation. You haven't yet introduced the fact that Kübler-Ross invented (or derived, or whatever) a five-stage model for categorizing the experience of dying people. Don't assume readers will know what you are talking about. Who was it who said, "Give me context or give me death"? I suggest you not waste your time rewriting this sentence right now. Come back to it later (if you still need it) after you have rethought the story of the paragraph as a whole.

- **Do the ideas progress, step by step, from sentence to sentence? Any leaps between sentences? Any detours? Any treadmills?**

As a first step toward assessing and improving your narrative coherence, you need to be able to describe and keep track of the content of each of your sentences. The left column, below, lists the revised versions of your sentences; the right column provides a synopsis of each.

| | |
|---|---|
| Hinton was the first researcher to interview dying patients. | Hinton: first researcher to interview dying pts. |
| Saunders was responsible for founding the modern hospice movement for dying patients. | Saunders: founded hospice. |
| Kübler-Ross's (1969) *On Death and Dying* provided professional and family caregivers with an intimate understanding of the experience of dying and, as a result, helped transform the hospital care of terminally ill patients. | K-R's book: insight into dying and helped change treatment for terminally ill. |
| Kübler-Ross also interviewed dying patients. | K-R also interviewed dying pts. |
| She found that some passed through all five stages before passing on whereas others were unable to reach the final stage of acceptance. | K-R found: some pts. passed through all 5 stages before death; others didn't get to #5. |

## The Experience of Dying (Draft 2)

Hinton (1963) was the first researcher to interview dying patients. On the other hand, Saunders (1965) was responsible for founding the modern hospice movement for dying patients. Kübler-Ross's (1969) *On Death and Dying* provided professional and family caregivers with an intimate understanding of the experience of dying (Corr, 1993; Kastenbaum, 1975; McAteer, 1990; Schulz & Schlarb, 1987-88) and, as a result, helped transform the hospital care of terminally ill patients (Kastenbaum, 1981). Kübler-Ross (1969) also interviewed dying patients. She found they passed through four stages of response before reaching a final stage of acceptance.

The five stages include the following: (a) initial shock and denial; (b) anger; (c) bargaining with fate; (d) depression; and (e) acceptance. Not everyone is able to reach the final stage prior to death. Acceptance is facilitated by looking directly into the shadow of mystery. However, follow-up studies have failed to support Kübler-Ross's original findings (e.g., Metzger, 1979-80; Schulz & Aderman, 1974; Wright, in preparation). Researchers have used them to explain grief reactions to every conceivable loss (Levine, 1982), including unemployment (Winegardner, Simonetti, & Nykodym, 1984), closed-head injuries (Groveman & Brown, 1985), infertility (Kronen, 1994), quitting college athletics (Blinde & Stratta, 1992), and receiving artificial organs (Fertziger, 1991).

Freud is the most well-known and influential of all psychiatrists. Kübler-Ross's concepts have also, however, influenced our culture significantly. Freudian concepts, such as dreaming, repression, and the unconscious, have become part of how we make sense of our lives. Kübler-Ross focused on dying and death, on the process of grieving. People relate to Kübler-Ross's five stages the same way they relate to Freud's concepts—rather than regarding them as theoretical constructs, they embrace them as objective truths.

The five stages include the following: (a) initial shock and denial; (b) anger; (c) bargaining with fate; (d) depression; and (e) acceptance.

Five stages include: a,b,c,d,e.

Not everyone is able to reach the final stage prior to death.

Not everyone reaches stage 5.

Those who can face their mortality directly may find a sense of acceptance.

Those who can face mortality can find acceptance.

However, follow-up studies have failed to support Kübler-Ross's original findings.

However, follow-up studies don't support K-R's findings.

Researchers have used them to explain grief reactions to every conceivable loss, including unemployment, closed-head injuries, infertility, quitting college athletics, and receiving artificial organs.

Researchers have used them to explain grief reactions: [a list].

Freud is the most well-known and influential of all psychiatrists.

Freud: most well-known and influential.

Kübler-Ross's concepts have also, however, influenced our culture significantly.

K-R's concepts: also a sign. influence.

We see ourselves through a Freudian lens, interpreting our motivations, symptoms, and desires through concepts such as repression, unconscious mentation, and catharsis.

We see ourselves through a Freudian lens: [examples].

Kübler-Ross focused on dying and death, on the process of grieving.

K-R focused on d & d: grieving.

People relate to Kübler-Ross's five stages the same way they relate to Freud's concepts—rather than regarding them as theoretical constructs, they embrace them as objective truths.

People relate to K-R's 5 stages like they relate to Freud's concepts: as truths.

### The Experience of Dying (Draft 2)

Hinton (1963) was the first researcher to interview dying patients. On the other hand, Saunders (1965) was responsible for founding the modern hospice movement for dying patients. Kübler-Ross's (1969) *On Death and Dying* provided professional and family caregivers with an intimate understanding of the experience of dying (Corr, 1993; Kastenbaum, 1975; McAteer, 1990; Schulz & Schlarb, 1987-88) and, as a result, helped transform the hospital care of terminally ill patients (Kastenbaum, 1981). Kübler-Ross (1969) also interviewed dying patients. She found they passed through four stages of response before reaching a final stage of acceptance.

The five stages include the following: (a) initial shock and denial; (b) anger; (c) bargaining with fate; (d) depression; and (e) acceptance. Not everyone is able to reach the final stage prior to death. Acceptance is facilitated by looking directly into the shadow of mystery. However, follow-up studies have failed to support Kübler-Ross's original findings (e.g., Metzger, 1979-80; Schulz & Aderman, 1974; Wright, in preparation). Researchers have used them to explain grief reactions to every conceivable loss (Levine, 1982), including unemployment (Winegardner, Simonetti, & Nykodym, 1984), closed-head injuries (Groveman & Brown, 1985), infertility (Kronen, 1994), quitting college athletics (Blinde & Stratta, 1992), and receiving artificial organs (Fertziger, 1991).

Freud is the most well-known and influential of all psychiatrists. Kübler-Ross's concepts have also, however, influenced our culture significantly. Freudian concepts, such as dreaming, repression, and the unconscious, have become part of how we make sense of our lives. Kübler-Ross focused on dying and death, on the process of grieving. People relate to Kübler-Ross's five stages the same way they relate to Freud's concepts—rather than regarding them as theoretical constructs, they embrace them as objective truths.

Let's take a look at the inter-sentence relationships within each paragraph.

1 Hinton: first researcher to interview dying pts.

2 Saunders: founded hospice.

3 K-R's book: insight into dying and helped change treatment for terminally ill.

4 K-R also interviewed dying pts.

5 K-R found: some pts. passed through all 5 stages before death; others didn't get to #5.

What is the connection between the first and second sentence? You are asking your readers to follow as you jump from Hinton the researcher to Saunders the hospice founder, but you don't provide any logic for the leap. What do these two people have in common?

Between the second and third sentence, you leap again, not to a third *person*, which would have been problem enough, but to a *book*. I feel like I'm inside a pinball machine. Even so, I now have an inkling of what you are wanting to say: "Kübler-Ross made a big splash, but Hinton and Saunders were already playing in the pool when she dove in." Something like that, right?

You finally introduce Kübler-Ross in your fourth sentence, and you attempt—using the word *also*—to link her back to Hinton. But this creates confusion, not a connection. The word *also* can join two ideas within the same sentence or between two successive sentences, but it can't construct a bridge spanning *three* sentences. If you want to link Kübler-Ross and Hinton, you will need to mention them in the same, or almost the same, breath. You also should create a stronger narrative tie between Kübler-Ross, Hinton, and Saunders. Don't force your readers to guess why all three are in the same story: Spell it out, saying something like the following:

> Kübler-Ross wasn't the first researcher to interview dying patients—Hinton deserves that credit. Nor did she found the hospice movement—the nod on that goes to Saunders. Nevertheless, she has done much to illuminate the experience of dying people and to improve their medical treatment.

In the last sentence of the original paragraph, you introduce the notion of Kübler-Ross's five stages, and, in the process, create still more

### The Experience of Dying (Draft 2)

Hinton (1963) was the first researcher to interview dying patients. On the other hand, Saunders (1965) was responsible for founding the modern hospice movement for dying patients. Kübler-Ross's (1969) *On Death and Dying* provided professional and family caregivers with an intimate understanding of the experience of dying (Corr, 1993; Kastenbaum, 1975; McAteer, 1990; Schulz & Schlarb, 1987-88) and, as a result, helped transform the hospital care of terminally ill patients (Kastenbaum, 1981). Kübler-Ross (1969) also interviewed dying patients. She found they passed through four stages of response before reaching a final stage of acceptance.

The five stages include the following: (a) initial shock and denial; (b) anger; (c) bargaining with fate; (d) depression; and (e) acceptance. Not everyone is able to reach the final stage prior to death. Acceptance is facilitated by looking directly into the shadow of mystery. However, follow-up studies have failed to support Kübler-Ross's original findings (e.g., Metzger, 1979-80; Schulz & Aderman, 1974; Wright, in preparation). Researchers have used them to explain grief reactions to every conceivable loss (Levine, 1982), including unemployment (Winegardner, Simonetti, & Nykodym, 1984), closed-head injuries (Groveman & Brown, 1985), infertility (Kronen, 1994), quitting college athletics (Blinde & Stratta, 1992), and receiving artificial organs (Fertziger, 1991).

Freud is the most well-known and influential of all psychiatrists. Kübler-Ross's concepts have also, however, influenced our culture significantly. Freudian concepts, such as dreaming, repression, and the unconscious, have become part of how we make sense of our lives. Kübler-Ross focused on dying and death, on the process of grieving. People relate to Kübler-Ross's five stages the same way they relate to Freud's concepts—rather than regarding them as theoretical constructs, they embrace them as objective truths.

muddle. The problem here lies in your referring to all five stages. The word *all* provides the same degree of specificity as the word *the*—it points to something *previously* mentioned. But you *haven't* already introduced the five stages, so your specificity is disorienting.

6  Five stages include a,b,c,d,e.
7  Not everyone reaches stage 5.
8  Those who can face mortality can find acceptance.
9  However, follow-up studies don't support K-R's findings.
10 Researchers have used them to explain grief reactions: [a list].

This paragraph doesn't zigzag around like the first, but it too suffers from continuity problems. Sentence 6, a stilted list, attempts, but fails, to clarify the last sentence in the previous paragraph. It says, in effect, "Oh, woops, sorry—I got ahead of myself back there in the last paragraph. I only just realized that I got to talking about the five stages, but I neglected to mention what they are, so here, before we go any further, let me fill you in." Don't play catch-up in this way; it makes you look disorganized and it will confuse your readers.

Sentence 7 restates what you already said in the latter part of sentence 5: "Not everyone gets to a place where they accept their impending death." Avoid boring your readers with unnecessary repetition: Treadmills are tedious.

Sentence 8 doesn't smoothly follow sentence 7, despite the fact that both sentences talk about the final stage of acceptance. Readers make a leap, only to find themselves on a treadmill.

   ✗  (7) Not everyone is able to reach the final stage prior to death. (8) Those who can face their mortality directly may find a sense of acceptance.

The transition between the two sentences and the flow of ideas would both work better if you were to place the new information offered in sentence 8—that is, what it takes to find acceptance—in the final, rather than the first, part of the sentence:

   ✓  (7) Not everyone is able to reach the final stage prior to death. (8) Finding a sense of acceptance requires people to first face their mortality directly.

When a sentence (or a complete story within a sentence) begins with the word *however*, it promises to offer a contrasting position or per-

## The Experience of Dying (Draft 2)

Hinton (1963) was the first researcher to interview dying patients. On the other hand, Saunders (1965) was responsible for founding the modern hospice movement for dying patients. Kübler-Ross's (1969) *On Death and Dying* provided professional and family caregivers with an intimate understanding of the experience of dying (Corr, 1993; Kastenbaum, 1975; McAteer, 1990; Schulz & Schlarb, 1987-88) and, as a result, helped transform the hospital care of terminally ill patients (Kastenbaum, 1981). Kübler-Ross (1969) also interviewed dying patients. She found they passed through four stages of response before reaching a final stage of acceptance.

The five stages include the following: (a) initial shock and denial; (b) anger; (c) bargaining with fate; (d) depression; and (e) acceptance. Not everyone is able to reach the final stage prior to death. Acceptance is facilitated by looking directly into the shadow of mystery. However, follow-up studies have failed to support Kübler-Ross's original findings (e.g., Metzger, 1979-80; Schulz & Aderman, 1974; Wright, in preparation). Researchers have used them to explain grief reactions to every conceivable loss (Levine, 1982), including unemployment (Winegardner, Simonetti, & Nykodym, 1984), closed-head injuries (Groveman & Brown, 1985), infertility (Kronen, 1994), quitting college athletics (Blinde & Stratta, 1992), and receiving artificial organs (Fertziger, 1991).

Freud is the most well-known and influential of all psychiatrists. Kübler-Ross's concepts have also, however, influenced our culture significantly. Freudian concepts, such as dreaming, repression, and the unconscious, have become part of how we make sense of our lives. Kübler-Ross focused on dying and death, on the process of grieving. People relate to Kübler-Ross's five stages the same way they relate to Freud's concepts—rather than regarding them as theoretical constructs, they embrace them as objective truths.

spective to the sentence (or part thereof) immediately preceding it. You begin sentence 9 with *however*, but you don't live up to the expectation the word creates. The sentence provides important information about follow-up studies, but it doesn't contrast in any way with the information in sentence 8.

✗ (8) Finding a sense of acceptance requires people to first face their mortality directly. (9) However, follow-up studies have failed to support Kübler-Ross's original findings.

Sentence 9 doesn't follow #8, and sentence 10 reads as if it follows #6, not sentences 7, 8, and 9:

✗ (6) The five stages include the following: (a) initial shock and denial; (b) anger; (c) bargaining with fate; (d) depression; and (e) acceptance. (7) Not everyone is able to reach the final stage prior to death. (8) Finding a sense of acceptance requires people to first face their mortality directly. (9) However, follow-up studies have failed to support Kübler-Ross's original findings. (10) Researchers have used them to explain grief reactions to . . . .

When you used the pronoun *them* in sentence 10, you obviously thought it would serve as a recall device, cuing readers to remember your discussion of the five stages back in sentence 6. But you have created the same problem here as you did when you used the word *also* in sentence 4: You are trying to make impossibly long connections, connections that can reach across several sentences at a time. In sentence 9, you talked about follow-up stud*ies*; readers will thus be far more likely to assume, at least until they get confused, that the *them* in sentence 10 refers to the *studies* in the previous sentence, not the five stages in sentence 6. Do them (the readers) a favor: Keep the relationships between sentences clear.

✓ (10) Researchers have used Kübler-Ross's five stages to explain grief reactions to . . . .

11  Freud: most well-known and influential.

12  K-R's concepts: also a sign. influence.

13  We see ourselves through a Freudian lens: [examples].

14  K-R focused on d & d: grieving.

15  People relate to K-R's 5 stages like they relate to Freud's concepts: as truths.

### The Experience of Dying (Draft 2)

Hinton (1963) was the first researcher to interview dying patients. On the other hand, Saunders (1965) was responsible for founding the modern hospice movement for dying patients. Kübler-Ross's (1969) *On Death and Dying* provided professional and family caregivers with an intimate understanding of the experience of dying (Corr, 1993; Kastenbaum, 1975; McAteer, 1990; Schulz & Schlarb, 1987-88) and, as a result, helped transform the hospital care of terminally ill patients (Kastenbaum, 1981). Kübler-Ross (1969) also interviewed dying patients. She found they passed through four stages of response before reaching a final stage of acceptance.

The five stages include the following: (a) initial shock and denial; (b) anger; (c) bargaining with fate; (d) depression; and (e) acceptance. Not everyone is able to reach the final stage prior to death. Acceptance is facilitated by looking directly into the shadow of mystery. However, follow-up studies have failed to support Kübler-Ross's original findings (e.g., Metzger, 1979-80; Schulz & Aderman, 1974; Wright, in preparation). Researchers have used them to explain grief reactions to every conceivable loss (Levine, 1982), including unemployment (Winegardner, Simonetti, & Nykodym, 1984), closed-head injuries (Groveman & Brown, 1985), infertility (Kronen, 1994), quitting college athletics (Blinde & Stratta, 1992), and receiving artificial organs (Fertziger, 1991).

Freud is the most well-known and influential of all psychiatrists. Kübler-Ross's concepts have also, however, influenced our culture significantly. Freudian concepts, such as dreaming, repression, and the unconscious, have become part of how we make sense of our lives. Kübler-Ross focused on dying and death, on the process of grieving. People relate to Kübler-Ross's five stages the same way they relate to Freud's concepts—rather than regarding them as theoretical constructs, they embrace them as objective truths.

Whoa! Where did Freud come from? You have done nothing to prepare your readers for his appearance on the scene. Sentence 12, like sentence 6, provides catch-up contextualizing information; it helps readers understand, too late, the relevance of what you said in the previous sentence. Comparing Kübler-Ross's influence to that of Freud is not a bad idea, but this is not the way to go about doing it.

If the zigzag shifts in the first paragraph mimic the action of a pinball machine, those here resemble the play in a ping-pong match. Sentence by sentence, readers are bounced back and forth between Freud and Kübler-Ross. Sentence 13 says something interesting about Freud's influence in our society, but how is it relevant? How does it relate to Kübler-Ross or, more generally, to dying and death?

Sentence 14 overstates the obvious—yes, your readers know by now (even if they hadn't known before) that Kübler-Ross focused on dying and death—but it also makes the useful point that Kübler Ross was concerned with the process of grieving. Why didn't you mention this earlier?

Finally, in sentence 15, I can see why you might have introduced Freud five sentences ago. But why have you kept me in the dark for so long? I like the idea you are offering here, but is it relevant? If you want to keep it, or some version of it, you had better rethink what you are wanting to say in all three of these paragraphs.

## Relationships between paragraphs

- **Do the ideas progress, step by step, from paragraph to paragraph? Any leaps between paragraphs? Any detours? Any treadmills?**

Paragraph 1 is about early research with the terminally ill and the founding of the hospice movement, and it introduces Kübler-Ross's five stages. Paragraph 2 delineates the five stages, explains the last one (acceptance), mentions the failure of follow-up studies to confirm Kübler-Ross's findings, and introduces some of the applications of the five-step model. Paragraph 3 compares Kübler-Ross's influence to that of Freud's, making the point that people often treat both authors' theoretical constructs as if they were concrete truths.

I have already discussed how the first sentences in paragraphs 2 and 3 ineffectively link back to the last sentences in paragraphs 1 and 2. But the lack of coherence between paragraphs isn't concentrated only in the transitional sentences. Reading over the synopses of the three paragraphs,

I have trouble recognizing any idea progression at all between them. This isn't surprising, given the idea-development problems *within* them.

You could, at this point, tinker with what you've written, revising the idea development with each paragraph so you could clarify the relationships between them, but I recommend, instead, that you read the three paragraphs through several times, set them aside, and then try a new, fresh draft. You are now in a position to think much more clearly (on paper) about what you want to say.

### The Experience of Dying (Draft 3)

Prior to the publication of Elisabeth Kübler-Ross's *On Death and Dying* in 1969, terminally-ill patients were little understood, and, if they lived their remaining days in a hospital, their needs were seldom met (Kastenbaum, 1981). Kübler-Ross was not the first researcher to interview dying patients (see, for example, Hinton, 1963), and she was not the first medical doctor to champion the hospice movement (Saunders, 1965). But she, more than anyone, made it possible for families and health-care professionals to stop recoiling from death, to listen to and learn from the experiences of dying people (Corr, 1993; Kastenbaum, 1975; McAteer, 1990; Schulz & Schlarb, 1987-88).

Based on her conversations with terminally ill patients, Kübler-Ross (1969) put forward a five-stage model of grieving. She noted that news of impending death typically throws people into a state of shocked denial. This response gives way to anger, which, in turn, evolves into impassioned efforts to bargain with fate. As death, unrelenting, looms ever closer, depression sets in. Some people never move beyond this stage, but others—those able to look their mortality in the eye—manage to achieve a final state of acceptance prior to their death.

Although follow-up studies have failed to support Kübler-Ross's original findings (e.g., Metzger, 1979-80; Schulz & Aderman, 1974; Wright, in preparation), her five stages—denial, anger, bargaining, depression, acceptance—have become part of our culture's common currency. Researchers have adopted the five stages to explain grief reactions to every conceivable loss (Levine, 1982), from getting fired (Winegardner, Simonetti, & Nykodym, 1984) to infertility (Kronen, 1994); hospice workers use the stages to guide their counseling work; and the general public has embraced them not as theoretical constructs but as objective truths. If we dream and live under the spotlight of Freud, we grieve and die in the shadow of Kübler-Ross.

Okay, let's once again use the narrative coherence questions to organize an assessment.

### Relationships between words

- **Any rough (awkward/meandering/incomplete) sentences?**

The sentences flow well, and they are clear and structurally sound. Each story unfolds without a hitch, and the parallel and referential relationships are well-defined and easy to follow.

- **Any vague or confusing ideas?**

You might have someone else take a look, but I don't see any problems.

### Relationships between sentences

- **Are new terms or ideas introduced appropriately? Are previously mentioned terms or ideas revisited appropriately?**

I want to comment first on a few of the sentences that did a particularly effective job of introducing ideas. I'll then discuss one—the last sentence of paragraph 3—that may present a problem for some readers.

✓ Kübler-Ross was not the first researcher to interview dying patients (see, for example, Hinton, 1963), and she was not the first medical doctor to champion the hospice movement (Saunders, 1965).

By making Kübler-Ross the focus of the sentence, you manage smooth (leapless) references to Hinton and Saunders. These citations, in turn, provide a way to identify Kübler-Ross as both a researcher and a medical doctor.

✓ Based on her conversations with terminally ill patients, Kübler-Ross (1969) put forward a five-stage model of grieving.

This sentence introduces Kübler-Ross's five stages, defines them in terms of a grieving process, and explains where they came from. The sentence is simple and clear.

## The Experience of Dying (Draft 3)

Prior to the publication of Elisabeth Kübler-Ross's *On Death and Dying* in 1969, terminally-ill patients were little understood, and, if they lived their remaining days in a hospital, their needs were seldom met (Kastenbaum, 1981). Kübler-Ross was not the first researcher to interview dying patients (see, for example, Hinton, 1963), and she was not the first medical doctor to champion the hospice movement (Saunders, 1965). But she, more than anyone, made it possible for families and health-care professionals to stop recoiling from death, to listen to and learn from the experiences of dying people (Corr, 1993; Kastenbaum, 1975; McAteer, 1990; Schulz & Schlarb, 1987-88).

Based on her conversations with terminally ill patients, Kübler-Ross (1969) put forward a five-stage model of grieving. She noted that news of impending death typically throws people into a state of shocked denial. This response gives way to anger, which, in turn, evolves into impassioned efforts to bargain with fate. As death, unrelenting, looms ever closer, depression sets in. Some people never move beyond this stage, but others—those able to look their mortality in the eye—manage to achieve a final state of acceptance prior to their death.

Although follow-up studies have failed to support Kübler-Ross's original findings (e.g., Metzger, 1979-80; Schulz & Aderman, 1974; Wright, in preparation), her five stages—denial, anger, bargaining, depression, acceptance—have become part of our culture's common currency. Researchers have adopted the five stages to explain grief reactions to every conceivable loss (Levine, 1982), from getting fired (Winegardner, Simonetti, & Nykodym, 1984) to infertility (Kronen, 1994); hospice workers use the stages to guide their counseling work; and the general public has embraced them not as theoretical constructs but as objective truths. If we dream and live under the spotlight of Freud, we grieve and die in the shadow of Kübler-Ross.

✓ She noted that news of impending death typically throws people into a state of shocked denial. This response gives way to
anger, which, in turn, evolves into impassioned efforts to bargain
with fate. As death, unrelenting, looms ever closer, depression
sets in. Some people never move beyond this stage, but others—those able to look their mortality in the eye—manage to
achieve a final state of acceptance prior to their death.

This narrative description of the five stages is much less abrupt than
the list you used in the previous draft.

✓ Although follow-up studies have failed to support Kübler-Ross's
original findings, her five stages—denial, anger, bargaining,
depression, acceptance—have become part of our culture's
common currency.

Your parenthetical naming of the five stages is a helpful reminder, particularly since you haven't previously grouped them together in a succinct list.

✓ Researchers have adopted the five stages to explain grief reactions to every conceivable loss (Levine, 1982), from getting
fired (Winegardner, Simonetti, & Nykodym, 1984) to infertility (Kronen, 1994); hospice workers use the stages to guide their
counseling work; and the general public has embraced them
not as theoretical constructs but as objective truths.

Since your last draft, you have winnowed down your examples of
grief studies from five to two. I appreciate the smooth reading afforded
by this version, but I liked the rich diversity covered in the last draft.
Perhaps you can make brief mention of the other three studies without
ruining the flow of your sentence.

• If we dream and live under the spotlight of Freud, we grieve and
die in the shadow of Kübler-Ross.

You need to get another opinion on this one. I think the sentence
works, but I'm not sure. You haven't mentioned Freud before now (in
this draft), so your claim about the ubiquity of his influence, which you
are treating in this sentence as a commonly-held fact, comes out of the
blue. I rather like the freshness of his unanticipated cameo appearance
and the way you contrast his influence with Kübler-Ross's, but some
readers may get confused. Will they know Freud well enough to get
your point? I also like your use of the *shadow* metaphor. In your first

### The Experience of Dying (Draft 3)

Prior to the publication of Elisabeth Kübler-Ross's *On Death and Dying* in 1969, terminally-ill patients were little understood, and, if they lived their remaining days in a hospital, their needs were seldom met (Kastenbaum, 1981). Kübler-Ross was not the first researcher to interview dying patients (see, for example, Hinton, 1963), and she was not the first medical doctor to champion the hospice movement (Saunders, 1965). But she, more than anyone, made it possible for families and health-care professionals to stop recoiling from death, to listen to and learn from the experiences of dying people (Corr, 1993; Kastenbaum, 1975; McAteer, 1990; Schulz & Schlarb, 1987-88).

Based on her conversations with terminally ill patients, Kübler-Ross (1969) put forward a five-stage model of grieving. She noted that news of impending death typically throws people into a state of shocked denial. This response gives way to anger, which, in turn, evolves into impassioned efforts to bargain with fate. As death, unrelenting, looms ever closer, depression sets in. Some people never move beyond this stage, but others—those able to look their mortality in the eye—manage to achieve a final state of acceptance prior to their death.

Although follow-up studies have failed to support Kübler-Ross's original findings (e.g., Metzger, 1979-80; Schulz & Aderman, 1974; Wright, in preparation), her five stages—denial, anger, bargaining, depression, acceptance—have become part of our culture's common currency. Researchers have adopted the five stages to explain grief reactions to every conceivable loss (Levine, 1982), from getting fired (Winegardner, Simonetti, & Nykodym, 1984) to infertility (Kronen, 1994); hospice workers use the stages to guide their counseling work; and the general public has embraced them not as theoretical constructs but as objective truths. If we dream and live under the spotlight of Freud, we grieve and die in the shadow of Kübler-Ross.

draft, the *shadow of mystery* made me cringe, but this toned-down version fits well.

• **Do the ideas progress, step by step, from sentence to sentence? Any leaps between sentences? Any detours? Any treadmills?**
Let's check your idea development in the same way as last time. Write a synopsis of each sentence, and then we'll take a look at the inter-sentence relationships within each of the paragraphs.

| | |
|---|---|
| Prior to the publication of Elisabeth Kübler-Ross's *On Death and Dying* in 1969, terminally ill patients were little understood, and, if they lived their remaining days in a hospital, their needs were seldom met. | Before K-R's book, terminally ill patients weren't understood or helped. |
| Kübler-Ross was not the first researcher to interview dying patients (see, for example, Hinton, 1963), and she was not the first medical doctor to champion the hospice movement (Saunders, 1965). | K-R: not the first researcher to interview dying pts.; not the first M.D. to champion hospice. |
| But she, more than anyone, made it possible for families and health-care professionals to stop recoiling from death, to listen to and learn from the experiences of dying people (Corr, 1993; Kastenbaum, 1975; McAteer, 1990; Schulz & Schlarb, 1987-88). | But she helped fam. and prof. to stop recoiling from death, to listen and learn. |
| Based on her conversations with terminally ill patients, Kübler-Ross (1969) put forward a five-stage model of grieving. | Based on conversations with the dying, K-R put forward a 5-stage model. |
| She noted that news of impending death typically throws people into a state of shocked denial. | She noted: News of impending death produces shocked denial. |
| This response gives way to anger, which, in turn, evolves into impassioned efforts to bargain with fate. | Then comes anger, then bargaining. |

### The Experience of Dying (Draft 3)

Prior to the publication of Elisabeth Kübler-Ross's *On Death and Dying* in 1969, terminally-ill patients were little understood, and, if they lived their remaining days in a hospital, their needs were seldom met (Kastenbaum, 1981). Kübler-Ross was not the first researcher to interview dying patients (see, for example, Hinton, 1963), and she was not the first medical doctor to champion the hospice movement (Saunders, 1965). But she, more than anyone, made it possible for families and health-care professionals to stop recoiling from death, to listen to and learn from the experiences of dying people (Corr, 1993; Kastenbaum, 1975; McAteer, 1990; Schulz & Schlarb, 1987-88).

Based on her conversations with terminally ill patients, Kübler-Ross (1969) put forward a five-stage model of grieving. She noted that news of impending death typically throws people into a state of shocked denial. This response gives way to anger, which, in turn, evolves into impassioned efforts to bargain with fate. As death, unrelenting, looms ever closer, depression sets in. Some people never move beyond this stage, but others—those able to look their mortality in the eye—manage to achieve a final state of acceptance prior to their death.

Although follow-up studies have failed to support Kübler-Ross's original findings (e.g., Metzger, 1979-80; Schulz & Aderman, 1974; Wright, in preparation), her five stages—denial, anger, bargaining, depression, acceptance—have become part of our culture's common currency. Researchers have adopted the five stages to explain grief reactions to every conceivable loss (Levine, 1982), from getting fired (Winegardner, Simonetti, & Nykodym, 1984) to infertility (Kronen, 1994); hospice workers use the stages to guide their counseling work; and the general public has embraced them not as theoretical constructs but as objective truths. If we dream and live under the spotlight of Freud, we grieve and die in the shadow of Kübler-Ross.

| | |
|---|---|
| As death, unrelenting, looms ever closer, depression sets in. | As death looms: depression. |
| Some people never move beyond this stage, but others—those able to look their mortality in the eye—manage to achieve a final state of acceptance prior to their death. | Some people don't move beyond depression; some achieve final acceptance. |
| Although follow-up studies have failed to support Kübler-Ross's original findings (e.g., Metzger, 1979-80; Schulz & Aderman, 1974; Wright, in preparation), her five stages—denial, anger, bargaining, depression, acceptance—have become part of our culture's common currency. | Although follow-up studies don't support K-R's findings, her 5 stages—[list]—have become common currency. |
| Researchers have adopted the five stages to explain grief reactions to every conceivable loss (Levine, 1982), from getting fired (Winegardner, Simonetti, & Nykodym, 1984) to infertility (Kronen, 1994); hospice workers use the stages to guide their counseling work; and the general public has embraced them not as theoretical constructs but as objective truths. | Researchers have adopted 5 stages to explain grief to every loss, from X to Y; hospice workers use them to guide treatment; public has embraced stages as objective truths. |
| If we dream and live under the spotlight of Freud, we grieve and die in the shadow of Kübler-Ross. | If we dream and live under the spotlight of Freud, we grieve and die in the shadow of K-R. |

1  Before K-R's book, terminally ill patients weren't understood or helped.

2  K-R: not the first researcher to interview dying pts.; not the first M.D. to champion hospice.

3  But she helped fam. and prof. to stop recoiling from death, to listen and learn.

This paragraph unfolds nicely, step by step. You begin by giving credit to Kübler-Ross's book for inspiring changes in our understanding and treatment of terminally-ill patients. You then temper the enthusiasm

### The Experience of Dying (Draft 3)

Prior to the publication of Elisabeth Kübler-Ross's *On Death and Dying* in 1969, terminally-ill patients were little understood, and, if they lived their remaining days in a hospital, their needs were seldom met (Kastenbaum, 1981). Kübler-Ross was not the first researcher to interview dying patients (see, for example, Hinton, 1963), and she was not the first medical doctor to champion the hospice movement (Saunders, 1965). But she, more than anyone, made it possible for families and health-care professionals to stop recoiling from death, to listen to and learn from the experiences of dying people (Corr, 1993; Kastenbaum, 1975; McAteer, 1990; Schulz & Schlarb, 1987-88).

Based on her conversations with terminally ill patients, Kübler-Ross (1969) put forward a five-stage model of grieving. She noted that news of impending death typically throws people into a state of shocked denial. This response gives way to anger, which, in turn, evolves into impassioned efforts to bargain with fate. As death, unrelenting, looms ever closer, depression sets in. Some people never move beyond this stage, but others—those able to look their mortality in the eye—manage to achieve a final state of acceptance prior to their death.

Although follow-up studies have failed to support Kübler-Ross's original findings (e.g., Metzger, 1979-80; Schulz & Aderman, 1974; Wright, in preparation), her five stages—denial, anger, bargaining, depression, acceptance— have become part of our culture's common currency. Researchers have adopted the five stages to explain grief reactions to every conceivable loss (Levine, 1982), from getting fired (Winegardner, Simonetti, & Nykodym, 1984) to infertility (Kronen, 1994); hospice workers use the stages to guide their counseling work; and the general public has embraced them not as theoretical constructs but as objective truths. If we dream and live under the spotlight of Freud, we grieve and die in the shadow of Kübler-Ross.

of this claim by putting Kübler-Ross's contribution in historical context, making clear that her research approach and treatment suggestions fit within the emerging Zeitgeist.

4  Based on conversations with the dying, K-R put forward a 5-stage model.

5  She noted: News of impending death produces shocked denial.

6  Then comes anger, then bargaining.

7  As death looms: depression.

8  Some people don't move beyond depression; some achieve final acceptance.

The simple structure of this paragraph makes it easy to follow: The first sentence introduces Kübler-Ross's five-stage model of the grieving process, and the rest of the paragraph offers a narrative describing it.

9  Although follow-up studies don't support K-R's findings, her 5 stages—[list]—have become common currency.

10  Researchers have adopted 5 stages to explain grief to every loss, from X to Y; hospice workers use them to guide treatment; the public has embraced stages as objective truths.

11  If we dream and live under the spotlight of Freud, we grieve and die in the shadow of K-R.

The relationship between sentences 9 and 10 might create some confusion. You start off saying that follow-up studies have failed to support Kübler-Ross's findings, but then, in sentence 10, you talk about researchers adopting the five stages to explain various kinds of loss. I'm sure both statements are accurate—some researchers have critiqued her theory, others have adopted it without question—but, at the moment, they appear to contradict one another. Sentence 11 provides an effective conclusive summary to the paragraph, but it might, instead, work better at the beginning. If you *did* move it up to the top, you could then shift the information about the follow-up studies to the end.

> Kübler-Ross's model has become part of our culture's common currency: If we dream and live under the spotlight of Freud, we grieve and die in the shadow of Kübler-Ross. Researchers have adopted her five stages— denial, anger, bargaining, depression, acceptance—to explain grief reac-

## The Experience of Dying (Draft 3)

Prior to the publication of Elisabeth Kübler-Ross's *On Death and Dying* in 1969, terminally-ill patients were little understood, and, if they lived their remaining days in a hospital, their needs were seldom met (Kastenbaum, 1981). Kübler-Ross was not the first researcher to interview dying patients (see, for example, Hinton, 1963), and she was not the first medical doctor to champion the hospice movement (Saunders, 1965). But she, more than anyone, made it possible for families and health-care professionals to stop recoiling from death, to listen to and learn from the experiences of dying people (Corr, 1993; Kastenbaum, 1975; McAteer, 1990; Schulz & Schlarb, 1987-88).

Based on her conversations with terminally ill patients, Kübler-Ross (1969) put forward a five-stage model of grieving. She noted that news of impending death typically throws people into a state of shocked denial. This response gives way to anger, which, in turn, evolves into impassioned efforts to bargain with fate. As death, unrelenting, looms ever closer, depression sets in. Some people never move beyond this stage, but others—those able to look their mortality in the eye—manage to achieve a final state of acceptance prior to their death.

Although follow-up studies have failed to support Kübler-Ross's original findings (e.g., Metzger, 1979-80; Schulz & Aderman, 1974; Wright, in preparation), her five stages—denial, anger, bargaining, depression, acceptance—have become part of our culture's common currency. Researchers have adopted the five stages to explain grief reactions to every conceivable loss (Levine, 1982), from getting fired (Winegardner, Simonetti, & Nykodym, 1984) to infertility (Kronen, 1994); hospice workers use the stages to guide their counseling work; and the general public has embraced them not as theoretical constructs but as objective truths. If we dream and live under the spotlight of Freud, we grieve and die in the shadow of Kübler-Ross.

tions to every conceivable loss (Levine, 1982), from getting fired (Winegardner, Simonetti, & Nykodym, 1984) to infertility (Kronen, 1994); hospice workers use the stages to guide their counseling work; and the general public has embraced them not as theoretical constructs but as objective truths. Nevertheless, follow-up studies have failed to support Kübler-Ross's original findings (e.g., Metzger, 1979-80; Schulz & Aderman, 1974; Wright, in preparation).

It sounded like a good idea, but, as I read it now, I don't think it works. Repeating Kübler-Ross's name twice in the first sentence sounds clumsy, and everything following the Freud/Kübler-Ross comparison reads like an afterthought. Try again.

Kübler-Ross's model has become part of our culture's common currency. Researchers have adopted her five stages— denial, anger, bargaining, depression, acceptance—to explain grief reactions to every conceivable loss (Levine, 1982), from getting fired (Winegardner, Simonetti, & Nykodym, 1984) to infertility (Kronen, 1994); hospice workers use the stages to guide their counseling work; and the general public has embraced them not as theoretical constructs but as objective truths. If we dream and live under the spotlight of Freud, we grieve and die in the shadow of Kübler-Ross. Nevertheless, follow-up studies have failed to support her original findings (e.g., Metzger, 1979-80; Schulz & Aderman, 1974; Wright, in preparation).

9  K-R's model has become common currency.
10 Researchers have adopted 5 stages—[list]—to explain grief to every loss, from X to Y; hospice workers use them to guide treatment; public has embraced stages as objective truths.
11 If we dream and live under the spotlight of Freud, we grieve and die in the shadow of K-R.
12 Nevertheless, follow-up studies don't support her findings.

Now you've got it. Sentence 10 elaborates on #9; sentence 11 sums up her ubiquitous importance; and sentence 12 provides a qualification (rather than a contradiction, as it did originally) that can be explored in the next paragraph. I'm still unsure about whether sentence 11

### The Experience of Dying (Draft 3)

Prior to the publication of Elisabeth Kübler-Ross's *On Death and Dying* in 1969, terminally-ill patients were little understood, and, if they lived their remaining days in a hospital, their needs were seldom met (Kastenbaum, 1981). Kübler-Ross was not the first researcher to interview dying patients (see, for example, Hinton, 1963), and she was not the first medical doctor to champion the hospice movement (Saunders, 1965). But she, more than anyone, made it possible for families and health-care professionals to stop recoiling from death, to listen to and learn from the experiences of dying people (Corr, 1993; Kastenbaum, 1975; McAteer, 1990; Schulz & Schlarb, 1987-88).

Based on her conversations with terminally ill patients, Kübler-Ross (1969) put forward a five-stage model of grieving. She noted that news of impending death typically throws people into a state of shocked denial. This response gives way to anger, which, in turn, evolves into impassioned efforts to bargain with fate. As death, unrelenting, looms ever closer, depression sets in. Some people never move beyond this stage, but others—those able to look their mortality in the eye—manage to achieve a final state of acceptance prior to their death.

Although follow-up studies have failed to support Kübler-Ross's original findings (e.g., Metzger, 1979-80; Schulz & Aderman, 1974; Wright, in preparation), her five stages—denial, anger, bargaining, depression, acceptance— have become part of our culture's common currency. Researchers have adopted the five stages to explain grief reactions to every conceivable loss (Levine, 1982), from getting fired (Winegardner, Simonetti, & Nykodym, 1984) to infertility (Kronen, 1994); hospice workers use the stages to guide their counseling work; and the general public has embraced them not as theoretical constructs but as objective truths. If we dream and live under the spotlight of Freud, we grieve and die in the shadow of Kübler-Ross.

works, so don't forget to get a second (and probably a third) opinion on
it. I take back my early recommendation, though, about trying in sentence 10 to include more than your two illustrative examples of grief
studies. If you add any more complexity to the sentence, it will collapse
in a heap of confusion.

### Relationships between paragraphs

• **Do the ideas progress, step by step, from paragraph to paragraph?**
**Any leaps between paragraphs? Any detours? Any treadmills?**

The narrative development within your paragraphs is now clear enough
to assess the idea progression between them. Paragraph 1 introduces
Kübler-Ross and discusses her contribution to our understanding and
treatment of dying patients; paragraph 2 introduces and describes her
five-stage model of grieving; and paragraph 3 elaborates on the wide-
spread belief in and influence of the model. Each paragraph tells a story,
a successive installment in the larger story told by the Introduction.
The steps between sentences 3 and 4 and 8 and 9 are larger than those
between the intra-paragraph sentences, but they aren't *too* large. That
is, they don't create gaps in the continuity or logic of the narrative.

1 Before K-R's book, terminally ill patients weren't understood
   or helped.

2 K-R: not the first researcher to interview dying pts.; not the
   first M.D. to champion hospice.

3 But she helped fam. and prof. to stop recoiling from death, to
   listen and learn.

4 Based on conversations with the dying, K-R put forward a 5-
   stage model.

5 She noted: News of impending death produces shocked
   denial.

6 Then comes anger, then bargaining.

7 As death looms: depression.

8 Some people don't move beyond depression; some achieve
   final acceptance.

9 K-R's model has become common currency.

10 Researchers have adopted 5 stages—[list]—to explain grief to
   every loss, from X to Y; hospice workers use them to guide
   treatment; public has embraced stages as objective truths.

### The Experience of Dying (Draft 3)

Prior to the publication of Elisabeth Kübler-Ross's *On Death and Dying* in 1969, terminally-ill patients were little understood, and, if they lived their remaining days in a hospital, their needs were seldom met (Kastenbaum, 1981). Kübler-Ross was not the first researcher to interview dying patients (see, for example, Hinton, 1963), and she was not the first medical doctor to champion the hospice movement (Saunders, 1965). But she, more than anyone, made it possible for families and health-care professionals to stop recoiling from death, to listen to and learn from the experiences of dying people (Corr, 1993; Kastenbaum, 1975; McAteer, 1990; Schulz & Schlarb, 1987-88).

Based on her conversations with terminally ill patients, Kübler-Ross (1969) put forward a five-stage model of grieving. She noted that news of impending death typically throws people into a state of shocked denial. This response gives way to anger, which, in turn, evolves into impassioned efforts to bargain with fate. As death, unrelenting, looms ever closer, depression sets in. Some people never move beyond this stage, but others—those able to look their mortality in the eye—manage to achieve a final state of acceptance prior to their death.

Although follow-up studies have failed to support Kübler-Ross's original findings (e.g., Metzger, 1979-80; Schulz & Aderman, 1974; Wright, in preparation), her five stages—denial, anger, bargaining, depression, acceptance—have become part of our culture's common currency. Researchers have adopted the five stages to explain grief reactions to every conceivable loss (Levine, 1982), from getting fired (Winegardner, Simonetti, & Nykodym, 1984) to infertility (Kronen, 1994); hospice workers use the stages to guide their counseling work; and the general public has embraced them not as theoretical constructs but as objective truths. If we dream and live under the spotlight of Freud, we grieve and die in the shadow of Kübler-Ross.

11 If we dream and live under the spotlight of Freud, we grieve and die in the shadow of K-R.

12 Nevertheless, follow-up studies don't support her findings.

These paragraphs are now ready for Dr. West and Mrs. Truran.

### The Experience of Dying (Draft 4)

Prior to the publication of Elisabeth Kübler-Ross's *On Death and Dying* in 1969, terminally ill patients were little understood, and, if they lived their remaining days in a hospital, their needs were seldom met (Kastenbaum, 1981). Kübler-Ross was not the first researcher to interview dying patients (see, for example, Hinton, 1963), and she was not the first medical doctor to champion the hospice movement (Saunders, 1965). But she, more than anyone, made it possible for families and health-care professionals to stop recoiling from death, to listen to and learn from the experiences of dying people (Corr, 1993; Kastenbaum, 1975; McAteer, 1990; Schulz & Schlarb, 1987-88).

Based on her conversations with terminally ill patients, Kübler-Ross (1969) put forward a five-stage model of grieving. She noted that news of impending death typically throws people into a state of shocked denial. This response gives way to anger, which, in turn, evolves into impassioned efforts to bargain with fate. As death, unrelenting, looms ever closer, depression sets in. Some people never move beyond this stage, but others—those able to look their mortality in the eye—manage to achieve a final state of acceptance prior to their death.

Kübler-Ross's model has become common currency. Researchers have adopted her five stages—denial, anger, bargaining, depression, acceptance—to explain grief reactions to every conceivable loss (Levine, 1982), from getting fired (Winegardner, Simonetti, & Nykodym, 1984) to infertility (Kronen, 1994); hospice workers use the model to guide their counseling work; and the general public has embraced the stages not as theoretical constructs but as objective truths. If we dream and live under the spotlight of

Freud, we grieve and die in the shadow of Kübler-Ross. Nevertheless, follow-up studies have failed to support her original findings (e.g., Metzger, 1979-80; Schulz & Aderman, 1974; Wright, in preparation).

Don't panic. Asking narrative coherence questions (or your own variation of them) is essential if you wish to write clearly, but answering them won't always take this long. As you become more familiar with the process, you should be able to do most of the asking and answering in your head. Still, expect to devote considerable time and concentrated effort to examining and refining the relationships between your words, your sentences, and your paragraphs. I know of no short-cut methods for creating clear, smooth-flowing ideas.

# 7
# Aesthetic Choices

*Reading inexpert writing is deeply exhausting. It is like listening to bad music.*

— Robertson Davies

*The good writer of prose must be part poet. . . . Considerations of sound and rhythm should be woven through everything you write.*

— William Zinsser

*One of the first laws of rhythm is repetition. . . . There is no rhythm without repetition. Once you've observed enough repetitions you can say there's a pattern, and patterns are something we're taught to scan for.*

— Mickey Hart

By aesthetic, *I mean responsive to* the pattern which connects.

— Gregory Bateson

*I do not find that the repetition of an important word a few times—say, three or four times—in a paragraph troubles my ear if clearness of meaning is best secured thereby. But tautological repetition which has no justifying object, but merely exposes the fact that the writer's balance at the vocabulary bank has run short and that he is too lazy to replenish it from the thesaurus—that is another matter.*

—Mark Twain

*Scholarly writing is formal, precise, and allusive. It has to be. It does not have to be wooden, finicking, and cabalistic. . . .*

*The built-in limitations of scholarly prose are no excuse for bad writing. Bad scholarly prose results, as all bad prose does, from laziness and hurry and muddle. Good scholarly prose is probably even harder to produce than other kinds of good prose. All that means is that the scholar must work even harder at it.*

—Mary-Claire van Leunen

If writing is thinking on paper (see Howard & Barton, 1986), then reading is thinking *from* paper. When you hand others a piece of your written work, you are giving them a piece of your mind. And when they read it, they are allowing your words to shape the content and direction of their thinking. Your writing patterns and tickles your readers' imaginations— at least it does if it is clear and evocative. If it is muddled and dull, it will more likely confuse than pattern, more likely scratch than tickle.

Thus, as a writer, you have a twofold responsibility. First, you must ensure that the relationships you create—between words, between sentences, between paragraphs—are clearly articulated. Incoherent writing exhausts and irritates those who attempt to puzzle their way through it. Second, you must invite and hold your readers' captivated attention for the duration of their immersion in your manuscript. To accomplish this, your writing needs more than clarity—it needs *style*. By aesthetically refining your prose, you help your readers enter the flow of your sentences. And once they are there, inside the unfolding of your stories, they can get a participatory understanding of your ideas.

This chapter offers several suggestions for how you can further

develop the quality of your writing, but I should remind you at the outset of something I discussed in Chapter 1. Writing well takes time—
more time, probably, than you will want to devote. A nicely turned
phrase can sometimes take hours to hone; a flowing paragraph, days.
Don't be discouraged, then, if your time-constrained efforts appear less
than refined. For most of us, the speed of production and the elegance
of the result are inversely related.

#### ➥ Balance repetition and variation

As readers make their way through your text, they not only *see* it
arrayed in front of them, but also *hear* it (if only in their heads). They
don't, and can't, separate *what* you say from *how* it sounds. Thus, as you
write, you must attend to issues of both meaning *and* aesthetics: Your
sentences need to make sense *and* make music. No, I'm not suggesting
you start composing in iambic pentameter and rhyming couplets.

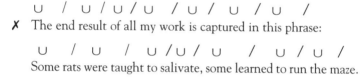

✗   The end result of all my work is captured in this phrase:

Some rats were taught to salivate, some learned to run the maze.

I do suggest, however, that you learn how to refine the rhythm of your
writing. Musicians, choreographers, and poets all know that you create
rhythmic balance by combining *repetition* and *variation*—the warp and
woof of all patterned phenomena.

Take, for example, parallel phrases within sentences (see also
Chapters 3 and 4). Structural repetition provides a foundation for highlighting the content differences (i.e., the variation) between the juxtaposed descriptions.

✓   The researcher articulated a research problem, refined a testable
     hypothesis, and then gathered her empirical data.
     • The researcher
          → articulated a research problem[,]
          → refined a testable hypothesis[, and then]
          → gathered her empirical data.

Notice what happens to the rhythmic precision of the sentence when
you fail to repeat the same structure in each of the phrases.

✗  The researcher articulated a research problem and refined a
   hypothesis that could be tested, and then the empirical data
   were gathered.
          → The researcher
                 → articulated a research problem [and]
                 → refined a hypothesis that could be tested[, and then]
          → the empirical data were gathered.

The changed word order in the second phrase and the shift from active
to passive voice in the third both unravel the rhythmic integrity of the
original version. Parallel phrases work best when the *variation in content*
(in this case, the three different actions undertaken by the researcher)
is balanced by *repetition in structure* (i.e., identical relationships between
words within each phrase).

Used purposefully and judiciously, structural repetition underscores
comparisons and contrasts (variations) within and between sentences.
Used haphazardly, it undermines both content and flow.

✗  This study used a survey research design. I sent a questionnaire
   to 1300 practicing economists. The questionnaire had 80 questions. It was divided into three sections. Most of the questions
   were closed-ended. The first section included 14 demographic
   questions. The second section included 63 Likert-scale questions. These questions required respondents to read statements
   on several different economic issues. The respondents were
   asked to rate their opinions on a five-point scale. Some of the
   issues included the following: NAFTA, universal health care,
   federal reserve strategies, value-added tax, the natural rate of
   unemployment, and the proper measure of the money supply.
   The third section included three open-ended questions. The
   questions were about market trends and public policy.

This paragraph tells a reasonably coherent story, but the relentless
series of simple sentences creates a repetitive, stilted rhythm capable of
irritating the most forgiving of readers. You could make the passage
flow a little better by adding conjunctions, but if this is *all* you do, you
will only replace one kind of monotony with another—sing-song repetition instead of staccato repetition.

✗  This study used a survey research design, and it involved
   sending a questionnaire to 1300 practicing economists. The

questionnaire had 80 questions, and it was divided into three sections. Most of the questions were closed-ended, but three were open-ended. The first section included 14 demographic questions, and the second section included 63 Likert-scale questions. The respondents read statements on several different economic issues, and they rated their opinions on a five-point scale. . . . The third section included the three open-ended questions, so respondents were asked to respond freely. They were asked about market trends, and they were also asked about public policy.

In the following rewrite, each sentence differs in length and shape from one(s) next to it:

✓  For this study, I sent a survey instrument—an 80-item questionnaire—to 1300 practicing economists. The 80 questions, all but three of which were closed-ended, were arrayed in three sections. The first section (14 items) gathered demographic information. The second section required respondents to read 63 statements on a variety of economic issues and to rate their opinions on a five-point Likert scale. This section addressed issues such as NAFTA, universal health care, federal reserve strategies, value-added tax, the natural rate of unemployment, and the proper measure of the money supply. The third section posed three open-ended questions about market trends and public policy.

Structural repetition in this latter version establishes the comparison of the three sections of the questionnaire.

✓  The first section . . . gathered . . .
    The second section required . . .
    The third section posed . . .

However, the repetition is balanced with enough variation to keep the rhythm of the paragraph interesting.

✓  For this study, I sent . . .
    The 80 questions, all but three of which were closed-ended, were . . .
    The second section required respondents to read . . . and to rate . . .

You can also create rhythm problems by inadvertently overusing favored words or phrases. When such expressions occur in close proximity, the repetition will annoy readers, even if the syntactic structure of the sentences is sufficiently varied.

✗   Conversation analysts typically focus their detailed interactive analysis on everyday talk. Interested in typical conversational strategies in the interactions between people, analysts create detailed transcriptions of the interactive process of the conversation, focusing their analysis on the turn-taking process between the conversational participants. Conversation analysts typically make detailed notes of the paralinguistic behavior of the conversing participants; they note instances of overlapping talk, interruptions in the talk, pauses in the talk, audible intakes of breath, and so on.

As you edit your work, listen for and identify too-frequent or too-close repetitions—

- conversation, conversational, conversation, conversational, conversation, conversing
- analysts, analysis, analysts, analysis, analysts
- typically, typical, typically
- focus, focusing
- detailed, detailed, detailed
- interactive, interactions, interactive
- talk, talk, talk, talk
- process, process
- participants, participants
- notes, note

—and eliminate them:

✓   Conversation analysts study everyday talk. Using detailed transcriptions of ordinary conversations, they track verbal and paralinguistic interactions between participants, making note of interruptions, pauses, overlapping talk, audible intakes of breath, and so on. This allows them to illuminate the process and strategies of turn-taking.

This rewrite offers a significant improvement over the first version, but the phrase *overlapping talk* appears too soon after the phrase *everyday talk* (in the previous sentence). You could avoid the repetition of *talk* by replacing the first instance of the word with the term *conversations*, but this solution would create a new problem:

> ✗ Conversation analysts study everyday conversations. Using detailed transcriptions of ordinary conversations, . . .

A better choice would be to replace the second *talk* with the word *dialogue*:

> ✓ Conversation analysts study everyday talk. Using detailed transcriptions of ordinary conversations, they track verbal and paralinguistic interactions between participants, making note of interruptions, pauses, overlapping dialogue, audible intakes of breath, and so on. This allows them to illuminate the process and strategies of turn-taking.

As you can see, the choice of whether to reuse a particular word or phrase depends, in part, on how long it has been since it last appeared. You need to provide readers with enough intervening sentences to allow the memory of it to fade. The more ear-catching the term (such as *ear-catching*), the longer you need to wait before using it again. Indeed, some words and phrases—for example, clichés—draw so much attention to themselves, you should avoid using them altogether. Having already been heard too many times before, clichés generate a monotony born of overfamiliarity, of excessive repetition throughout the culture.

> ✗ Grounded theory, that tried-and-true method of inductively generating categories, . . .
>
> > ✓ Grounded theory, a well-established method of inductively generating categories, . . .
>
> ✗ The interviewee talked my ear off.
>
> > ✓ The interviewee provided thorough, sometimes too thorough, responses to my questions.

While you are listening for overused words, listen too for inadvertent alliterations and rhymes. They can make your prose sound like bad poetry.

> ✗ Incidently, in the interview, . . .
>
> > ✓ Incidently, during the interview, . . .

✗   The forensic investigation focused on the five felons . . .

   ✓   The forensic investigation concentrated on the five men . . .

✗   The mother kept crying about her son's lying, . . .

   ✓   In tears, the mother described how her son's lying had affected . . .

Finally, take care not to overuse distinctive punctuation marks. I once had a dissertation student who became infatuated with semicolons. A clear thinker and technically competent writer, she knew how to punctuate correctly, but her devotion to semicolons knew no bounds, and this threw off her aesthetic judgment. Her sentences were infested with the damn things, and the rhythm of her paragraphs suffered as a result. Despite my comments and corrections on successive drafts of her work, her semicolon count would decrease each time only marginally, and new chapters would show no evidence that my protestations had made a difference.

Late one night, my patience spent, I wrote a diagnosis of her problem in the margins of a particularly unwieldy paragraph: "You must," I speculated, "have been semicolon-deprived as a child." After she read my comment (and after her laughter died down), her infatuation dissipated and her aesthetic sensibilities returned. Today she can go a paragraph, or sometimes even longer, without feeling the urge to insert a semicolon; as a result, her writing appears normal, healthy, and balanced. So can yours.

➥ **Think pattern, not quantity**

Some writers treat their sentences and paragraphs like junk drawers—as repositories for as much stuff as they can cram into them. They try to say too much too fast, tumbling out ideas without attending to order or form.

✗   Ethnographic investigations require (of the ethnographer) perseverance, availability, an involved engagement in the process, effort, ingenuity, and time. However, once they (the investigations) are finished, they are (if well written and thorough) fascinating, instructive, helpful, engaging, edifying, and illuminating to read, opening new vistas for readers. The ethnographer's *emic*, or insider's, approach to learning about culture presents special challenges for the gathering of the data, the analyzing of the data, the interpreting of the results, the displaying of the results, the reliability and validity of the results, the conclusions that can be drawn from the results, etc.

I suggest, instead, that you treat your sentences and paragraphs like Japanese gardens—cultivated landscapes where pattern, balance, and correspondence are everything. Writing with this aesthetic principle in mind will help you bring shape to your offerings of ideas.

> ✓ Ethnographic investigations, as demanding to conduct as they are fascinating to read, require more from researchers than time, effort, and ingenuity: They require *engagement*. Ethnographers immerse themselves in the everyday lives of the people they study, learning about the culture from an insider's, or *emic*, perspective. Such an approach presents special challenges, not only for gathering, analyzing, and interpreting the data, but also for determining their reliability and validity.

Let's compare these two brief paragraphs sentence by sentence.

Ethnographic investigations require (of the ethnographer) perseverence, availability, an involved engagement in the process, effort, ingenuity, and time. However, once they (the investigations) are finished, they are (if well written and thorough) fascinating, instructive, helpful, engaging, edifying, and illuminating to read, opening new vistas for readers.

Ethnographic investigations, as demanding to conduct as they are fascinating to read, require more from researchers than time, effort, and ingenuity: They require *engagement*.

The original version begins with two equally-long, equally-shapeless lists.

- Ethnographic investigations require (of the ethnographer)
  - → perseverence[,]
  - → availability[,]
  - → an involved engagement in the process[,]
  - → effort[,]
  - → ingenuity[, and]
  - → time.

- However, once they (the investigations) are finished, they are (if well written and thorough)
    - → fascinating[,]
    - → instructive[,]
    - → helpful[,]
    - → engaging[,]
    - → edifying[, and]
    - → illuminating
                to read, opening new vistas for readers.

Long lists belong in grocery stores, not in sentences. If you take them with you shopping, they can help you remember to buy milk and orange juice, but if you put them in your manuscripts, they will undermine the shape and movement of your stories.

Readers will easily recognize pattern in your sentences if you limit the number of comparisons you make to two or three—certainly, never more than four—particularly if each compared element is clearly parallel with the other(s). But once a list in a sentence goes beyond three or four items, it devolves from a *pattern of relationships* into a *pile of things*. If the parallel structure of the list is impeccable, as in the second of the two sentences above, it may read as a *tidy* pile, but, unlike a well-told story, it won't capture and hold your readers' interest—it won't invite or carry them forward.

The revised version begins with two comparisons: The first is between two elements (*demanding to conduct* / *fascinating to read*); the second, between three (*time* / *effort* / *ingenuity*):

- Ethnographic investigations, as
    - → demanding to conduct [as they are]
    - → fascinating to read[,]
                require more from researchers than
        - → time[,]
        - → effort[, and]
        - → ingenuity[:]
                They require *engagement*.

This sentence is less exhaustive in its description of reading and conducting ethnographic research than the two long lists, but it is more evocative—what it loses in quantity of details it makes up for in quality of arrangement.

Let's go on.

| The ethnographer's *emic*, or insider's, approach to learning about culture presents special challenges for the gathering of the data, the analyzing of the data, the interpreting of the results, the displaying of the results, the reliability and validity of the results, the conclusions that can be drawn from the results, etc. | Ethnographers immerse themselves in the everyday lives of the people they study, learning about the culture from an insider's, or *emic*, perspective. Such an approach presents special challenges, not only for gathering, analyzing, and interpreting the data, but also for determining their reliability and validity. |
|---|---|

The original paragraph ends with another grocery list of comparisons. It even includes an *etc.*—a promise to the reader that the list would have been still longer if *all* the special challenges had been noted.

- The ethnographers' *emic*, or insider's, approach to learning about culture presents special challenges for
    - → the gathering of the data[,]
    - → the analyzing of the data[,]
    - → the interpreting of the results[,]
    - → the displaying of the results[,]
    - → the reliability and validity of the results[,]
    - → the conclusions that can be drawn from the results[,]
    - → etc.

The revised paragraph breaks this list up into *two groups of comparisons* (of three and two items, respectively).

- Such an approach presents special challenges, not only for
    - → gathering[,]
    - → analyzing[, and]
    - → interpreting
        the data, but also for determining their
            - → reliability [and]
            - → validity.

Again, a few of the details in the original sentence didn't make it into the revision. Adding any more items to the first group of comparisons would undermine the patterned flow of the sentence:

✗   Such an approach presents special challenges, not only for gathering, analyzing, interpreting, displaying, and drawing conclusions from the data, but also for determining their reliability and validity.

Five items is too many.

- Such an approach presents special challenges, not only for
    → gathering[,]
    → analyzing[,]
    → interpreting[,]
    → displaying[, and]
    → drawing conclusions from[,]
            the data, but also for determining their
                    → reliability [and]
                    → validity.

If you were to decide that you *had* to make mention of *displaying* and *drawing conclusions*, you would be better off adding an extra sentence than stuffing them into this one.

### ➥ Sequence juxtaposed items according to length

You will enhance the rhythm of your sentences if you sequence your patterned comparisons—parallel pairs or lists—according to the length of the items you are juxtaposing. Whenever possible and logical, place the shortest item first and the longest item last.

If you are comparing two or more single words, base your sequencing decision on the number of syllables in each.

✓   The sociologist measured and predicted.
- The sociologist
    (2 syllables)  → measured [and]
    (3 syllables)  → predicted

When parallel words have the same number of syllables, arrange the sequence according to the number of letters.

✓   The psychologist was quiet yet friendly.
- The psychologist was
    (2 syllables—5 letters)  → quiet [yet]
    (2 syllables—8 letters)  → friendly

If you are juxtaposing two or more phrases, array them according to the number of words in each.

✓ The anthropologist conducted extensive interviews, participated in daily activities, and observed some of the less sacred rituals.

- The anthropologist
  (3 words) → conducted extensive interviews[,]
  (4 words) → participated in daily activities[,and]
  (7 words) → observed some of the less sacred rituals.

When two or more phrases have the same number of words, base your decision on the number of syllables.

✓ The economist studied the labor tactics of investment houses and the investment strategies of labor unions.

- The economist studied
  (6 words—11 syllables) → the labor tactics of investment houses [and]
  (6 words—12 syllables) → the investment strategies of labor unions.

✓ The political scientist was interested in relationships between the House, the Senate, and the Oval Office.

- The political scientist was interested in relationships between
  (2 words—2 syllables) → the House[,]
  (2 words—3 syllables) → the Senate[, and]
  (3 words—5 syllables) → the Oval Office.

Rhythm is important, but not as important as the customary or logical order of parallel words and phrases.

✗ This quasi-experimental design introduces several threats to validity and reliability.

- This quasi-experimental design introduces several threats to
  (4 syllables) → validity [and]
  (6 syllables) → reliability.

Even though *reliability* has two more syllables than *validity*, it should be mentioned first. Researchers talk about *reliability and validity*, not *validity and reliability*, in part because validity *depends* on reliability. Thus, you should preserve the customary order despite the rhythmic benefits of reversing it.

   ✓  This quasi-experimental design introduces several threats to reliability and validity.

## •➤ Streamline the narrative of your sentences

The best choreographers give dancers the means to carve air with their bodies; the best writers give readers the means to carve their imaginations with words. Both create patterns defined by clear and flowing lines.

As you write, adopt the aesthetic sensibility of a choreographer. Streamline your prose so your readers can "dance" it, so they can execute each spin, step, and gesture with precision and ease. Allow them to read with a dancer's grace.

By streamlining, I mean trimming superfluous words and phrases from the beginnings, middles, and ends of your sentences. Read through your work with the following questions in mind:

- Is this word/phrase necessary for the meaning of the sentence?
- Is this word/phrase necessary for the rhythm of the sentence?
- Can I say this more succinctly? More smoothly?

In some cases, you can simply delete non-essential verbiage; in other cases, you will need to start over and rewrite from scratch.

   ✗  It is important to note that the results arrived at by the researchers are arguably suspect, owing to the fact that the issue of familywise error (Keppel, 1982) was not taken into account at all, despite the fact that in the process of analyzing the data, the researchers ran multiple *t* tests, which, strictly speaking, should not have been done.

Let's walk through this phrase by phrase.

- *It is important to note that*: You wouldn't bother noting what you are about to say if it *weren't* important, right? Don't dictate to readers what they should think; do your best to *demonstrate* the importance of your statement, and then let them decide for themselves whether you succeeded.

   ✓  ~~It is important to note that~~

- *the results arrived at by the researchers*: Who else besides the researchers would have arrived at the results?

   ✓  the results ~~arrived at by the researchers~~

- *are arguably suspect*: If they are *arguably* suspect, they are suspect—you have no need for the qualifier.
  - ✓ are ~~arguably~~ suspect
- *owing to the fact that*: Avoid academese.
  - ✓ ~~owing to the fact that~~ because
- *the issue of familywise error*: No meaning is sacrificed if you cut *the issue of*.
  - ✓ ~~the issue of~~ familywise error
- *was not taken into account*: You can shave off a word by saying, instead, that the family-wise error *was not accounted for*.
  - ✓ ~~was not taken into account~~ was not accounted for

This still sounds awkward, though. We'll come back to it.

- *at all*: This adds nothing ~~at all~~.
  - ✓ ~~at all~~
- *despite the fact that*: More academic fluff.
  - ✓ ~~despite the fact that~~ even though
- *in the process of analyzing the data*: The readers don't need to be told that analyzing is a process.
  - ✓ ~~in the process of analyzing the data~~ while analyzing the data
- *the researchers ran multiple t tests*: No problem.
  - ✓ the researchers ran multiple *t* tests,
- *which, strictly speaking*: Avoid empty qualifiers—the *strictly speaking* sounds impressively scholastic, but it contributes nothing to the meaning of the sentence.
  - ✓ which, ~~strictly speaking,~~
- *should not have been done*: This is redundant. If the researchers hadn't committed an error, you wouldn't be criticizing them.
  - ✓ ~~which should not have been done~~.

Okay, let's see what is left standing:

- The results are suspect because familywise error was not accounted for, even though, while analyzing the data, the researchers ran multiple *t* tests.

This is better than the original, but, as my wife's grandmother, "Mamaw," once said to me when I thought I had finished washing a sinkful of dishes, "You're not done!" (I had neglected to polish the water spots off the faucet.)

- *while analyzing the data*: Have you ever heard of a researcher running *t* tests while *gathering* the data? The phrase isn't necessary.

  ✓ ~~while analyzing the data~~

Now what do we have?

- The results are suspect because familywise error was not accounted for, even though the researchers ran multiple *t* tests.

The sentence is trying to say that the researchers should have known better than to run multiple *t* tests on their data, but it could easily be *misread* as saying that the researchers purposefully ran the multiple *t* tests in a (failed) effort to *correct* the problem of not accounting for familywise error. Recasting the sentence in active voice will clear up the confusion.

  ✓ The researchers ran multiple *t* tests without accounting for familywise error (Keppel, 1982); thus, their results are suspect.

The sentence now works much better, but it dribbles away at the end. It needs a stronger, more dramatic, more rhythmically satisfying conclusion:

  ✓ The researchers ran multiple *t* tests without accounting for familywise error (Keppel, 1982); this oversight throws their results into question.

This has come a long way from the first draft:

  ✗ It is important to note that the results arrived at by the researchers are arguably suspect, owing to the fact that the issue of familywise error (Keppel, 1982) was not taken into account at all, despite the fact that in the process of analyzing the data, the researchers ran multiple *t* tests, which, strictly speaking, should not have been done.

If you can't yet recognize superfluous words and phrases on your own, train your ear with books such as *Edit Yourself* (Ross-Larson, 1996), *Usage and Abusage* (Partridge, 1994), and *The Elements of Style* (Strunk & White, 1979). See the Bibliography for additional references.

### ➥ Don't pontificate and don't gush

New therapists sometimes don't quite know how to dress. Striving to appear professional, they may show up for a therapy session more properly attired for the opera, a cocktail party, or a boardroom meeting. Or, wanting to project an air of casual friendliness, they may look as if they are headed for a pub or a picnic.

When my wife, Shelley, is supervising beginning therapists, she tells them to dress so that nothing about their appearance draws attention to itself. "Your clients," she says, "need to be focusing on your questions and comments, not on your neckline, your hemline, the crease in your suit, or the wrinkles in your shirt."

As a writer, you may benefit from similar advice. Avoid dressing your writing in too formal or too casual a tone of voice: Either will distract your readers' attention from the content of your sentences.

✗   The verbalizations of the 19-year-old female were duly noted. Her languaging revealed noteworthy intrapersonal and contextual factors that have favorably influenced the trajectory of her psychological development and, possibly, her physiological survival.

✗   For the edification of the reader, this researcher will undertake a meticulous itemization and explication of the salient stages in this study's methodological process; however, before such an explanatory elucidation can be realized, it will be essential to render into the light a smattering of the heretofore tacit epistemological underpinnings informing the research tradition utilized for this investigation.

You don't need to pontificate or put on airs for readers to take you seriously, and you don't need to gush or sound like a Hallmark card for them to consider you "reader-friendly."

✗   As the beautiful young woman shared her innermost feelings, I looked deeply into her limpid blue eyes and felt my own brim with tears. How touched I was by her miraculous strength, her breathtaking insights, and her amazing stories of personal and family triumph in the face of certain death.

✗   Before sharing a little about my research method, I'd just like to take a moment to share my personal thoughts on research. So what do I believe? Musing over this question reminds me of something Donald Campbell once said.

Adopt a tone that allows your readers to recognize your competence and clarity.

✓   The client, a mature 19-year-old woman, movingly described the changes she and her family had made since her cancer diagnosis three years earlier.

✓   Several factors influenced my choice of research method.

☞ **Avoid discursive practices that privilege the dominant discourse
   of persons situated in positions of power**

Roughly translated into English, this suggestion means "avoid jargon."
But, in the ironic spirit of William Safire's (1990) *Fumblerules*, it fails
to heed its own advice. Social scientists have similarly failed to listen
to the counsel of style-manual writers who, for many years, have been
pointing out the drawbacks of "specialty vocabularies." Open most any
journal in your discipline and you will be sure to discover several jar-
gon-laden articles.

Like a distinguishing haircut, tattoo, pierced body part, or style of
clothes, the use of jargon announces membership; it bestows a sense of
belonging. By mastering the idiosyncratic terminology of a particular
group, you may get welcomed into the fold. Why, then, should you listen to me or anyone else telling you to strive for jargon-free prose?
Perhaps you shouldn't. As social scientists well know, the lure of the
group is strong. If your colleagues and mentors were all to sport the
same tattoo, could you stand apart? Could you afford *not* to get one too?
How else would you gain acceptance? Of course, the more idiosyncratic your style, the more you will guarantee rejection of your work by
those who *don't* belong to this group.

If you feel caught between the demands for good writing and the
hope for good friends, remember that jargon, like any other fashion
statement, becomes dated. Whenever I become reflexively stimulated
to the presence of a motivating affective state that, in turn, triggers an
instinct-driven urge for propinquity with significant others and a tacit
understanding that such propinquity will only be actualized by my performing languaging practices that are situated in a privileging of local
knowledges in a radical undermining of the institutionalized regulari-
ties of the dominant discourse, . . .

Let me start again: Whenever I feel a fleeting desire to get close to
important people by slinging around some jargon, I remember something my mother told me when I was a teenager: "If you ever feel
impelled to get a tattoo," she warned, "think not just about how great
it will look the next morning, not just about how much your friends
will admire it and you. Think, too, about how foolish you'll feel looking in the mirror at 45, 60, or 75."

## ➥ **Thaw your frozen verbs**

If you take a descriptive verb and freeze it, you create an *abstract thing*—you congeal graphic *action* into an *abstraction*.

   ✓  The committee reconciled the House and Senate versions of the bill.

       ✗  The committee did the reconciliation of the House and Senate versions of the bill.

The *act* of *reconciling* becomes the *fact* of *reconciliation*.

   ✓  SPSS calculates the F score for each independent variable.

       ✗  SPSS's calculation of the F score is done for each independent variable.

The *act* of *calculating* becomes the *fact* of *calculation*.

   ✓  The wife scorned her husband when she saw his tears.

       ✗  The wife's scorn was activated when she saw her husband's tears.

The *act* of *scorning* becomes the *fact* of *scorn*.

If a descriptive verb is in its thawed state—that is, if it is serving in a sentence as an *action* rather than a *thing*—it adds color and specificity to the story. But if it is frozen as an abstraction, then the action of the story (the verb in the sentence) will be colorless and vague. You can breathe life into your sentences (and interest into your readers) by locating and thawing your frozen verbs.

       ✗  Outcome studies of clinical effectiveness have provided a demonstration that shows that the prediction of therapeutic outcome can be made more effectively by the quality of the therapist-client relationship than by the practitioner's specific therapeutic approach. The indication offered by these research results is that the concentration of therapists should be less on techniques and more on the connection of the therapists with their clients (see Miller, Duncan, & Hubble, 1997).

- frozen abstraction: *demonstration*; thawed action: *to demonstrate*
  - ✓  ~~have provided a demonstration that shows~~ have demonstrated
- frozen abstraction: *prediction*; thawed action: *to predict*
  - ✓  ~~the prediction of therapeutic outcome can be made . . . by . . . the therapist-client relationship~~ the therapist-client relationship predicts therapeutic outcome

- frozen abstraction: *indication*; thawed action: *to indicate*
  - ✓ ~~The indication offered by these research results is that~~ Results indicate that
- frozen abstraction: *concentration*; thawed action: *to concentrate*
  - ✓ ~~the concentration of therapists should be less~~ therapists should concentrate less

Readers can more easily warm up to the melted version:

  - ✓ Outcome studies of clinical effectiveness have demonstrated that the quality of the therapist-client relationship predicts therapeutic outcome far better than does the practitioner's specific therapeutic approach. Results indicate that therapists should concentrate less on techniques and more on connecting with their clients (see Miller, Duncan, & Hubble, 1997).

### ➵ Why ask rhetorical questions?

Why do some writers get carried away, posing multiple questions throughout their text? Would their work not read more smoothly if they didn't do this? Could they not use their questions to organize their thinking but then eliminate most (if not all) of them from their manuscript? Would readers not appreciate not having to read annoying queries? How much more could the universe get done if writers stopped asking it so many questions? Need I say more?

### ☞ Read outside your field

When I'm involved in admission interviews for my department's graduate programs, I often ask applicants what they have been reading. Mistaking limited breadth for depth, too many reply with too much pride that they restrict their reading to their chosen field of study.

You can learn much about your discipline by reading outside of it, and if you choose from excellent essayists, novelists, and poets, you can learn even more about the art of writing. As you read, listen to how authors play with words, conjure up rhythms, and tease out ideas. Write down sentences that sing to you, memorize their melodic patterns, and transpose them into your own work.

# Appendix
# Writing Theses and Dissertations

*Out of a human population on earth of four and a half bil-*
*lion, perhaps twenty people can write a book in a year. Some*
*people lift cars, too. Some people enter week-long sled-dog*
*races, go over Niagara Falls in barrels, fly planes through the*
*Arc de Triomphe. Some people feel no pain in childbirth.*
*Some people eat cars. There is no call to take human*
*extremes as norms. . . . Writing a book, full time, can take*
*years.*

—Annie Dillard

*I think it is very, very serious, a very, very serious mistake*
*when you begin to think of yourself as an important writer.*
*It makes you venture into a kind of writing which my wife,*
*who is my most important critic, calls life-workical and mas-*
*terpiecical. And you begin to write rather grandiosely. . . .*
*It's fatal when you begin to approve of yourself and say, by*
*gosh, that's a good piece of work and gloat over your own*
*doing.*

—Robertson Davies

Soon after I started my doctoral program, my friend Craig, who was a
few years ahead of me, told me about two different approaches to
choosing a viable dissertation topic. "One school of thought," he
explained, "says you should pick a topic you love. That way, when you

hit the inevitable wall partway through and all you want to do is quit, your fascination with the area of study and your devotion to your project will help pull you through."

I nodded. "Makes good sense."

"Yeah, maybe," said Craig, "but I'm a devoted follower of the second school of thought. It says you should pick a topic you despise. Since you're bound to hate what you're doing by the time you're finished, you might as well start off in the same frame of mind and avoid the added trauma of disillusionment."

I chose the route proposed by the first school and never regretted my decision, particularly since I never got to the point of hating what I was doing. I doubt Craig regretted his decision, either, but I'm certain I had a better time in front of my computer.

In this Appendix, I offer a few suggestions that may help you avoid having to choose Craig's path. Despair and loathing do not *necessarily* have to accompany you on your journey. You may feel lost and frustrated and anxious from time to time, but you need not hate either your dissertation or the writing of it.

### ➥ Choose a committee chair you can trust and respect

Some students look for a "nice" person to chair their committee, some try to find someone who will be "easy," and others make their choice out of a sense of obligation or pity. I suggest, instead, that you use respect and trust as your primary criteria. Choose a person who thinks clearly and who will talk *with* you, not *at* you—someone who will invite your questions, who will give you the freedom to learn from your mistakes, but who won't leave you dangling when you feel totally lost. You probably won't respond joyfully if he or she says you need to gather more data, rerun an analysis, rethink a category set, or rewrite a chapter, but you can respect the advice if you trust the person offering it.

### ➥ Choose committee members who can work together

Before you choose your committee members, consult with your chair. You need scholars who can contribute academically to your study, but you also need people who can work well with each other. You don't want your manuscript getting caught in the crossfire between warring factions of the faculty. Look your chair in the eyes and ask about possible committee members, one by one. If he or she is appropriately tight-lipped about faculty politics, you might glean some helpful information from blinks and raised eyebrows.

### ⚈ Apply for funding

Take time early on to check out potential funding sources for your research. Grant-writing experience will look good on your curriculum vita (particularly if your efforts prove successful), and financial support will provide you extra freedom and flexibility for your work. Talk to your chair and your university's granting office for ideas of where to start looking.

### ⚈ Get comfortable with uncertainty

When you write a book-length manuscript for the first time, you must adapt your thinking-and-writing skills to the parameters of the project. You can and must provide more detailed information than you would if you were only composing a paper, and you need to learn how to develop and sustain ideas not only across sentences and paragraphs but also across chapters. Faced with the enormity of the undertaking, you may feel at least a little panicked. After all, you have to learn as you go, and you can only be sure you know what you are doing once your committee approves of what you have already done. In the meantime, get used to living with uncertainty, and stay in touch with your chair.

### ⚈ Don't get *too* comfortable

If you have to read background material for your literature review (and you do), you might as well do it in that stuffed chair at the library, while drinking cappuccino at the bookstore down the street, or while lying on your couch, listening to the stereo. But don't adopt all this "scholarly activity" as a way of life; otherwise, you'll never start writing. Unless you want to become the best-read-but-never-defended person on your block, make a regular practice early on of sitting yourself in front of your computer.

### ⚈ Stay in touch with your chair

If you are like some of my students, you may, at times, want to work with minimal guidance. Such an arrangement, if you and your chair are both comfortable with it, can offer an excellent opportunity for learning. However, the longer you stay out of touch, the more you risk writing something your chair will consider tangential to the focus of your study. This is not to say that you should drop off a new draft every time you compose a new paragraph, but you would be wise to keep him or her apprised of your progress and struggles. That way, when your document begins developing in an unanticipated direction, you can decide together whether the change makes sense.

### ➻ Stay in touch with your manuscript

If you have any kind of life outside of the university, any demands on your time other than your thesis or dissertation—a job or career, a spouse, children, friends, eating, sleeping, exercising, relaxing—you will want to assimilate the writing of your document into your already busy schedule. Stealing an hour or two a day to write is better than nothing, but at some point in the process, you will probably need to readjust your priorities, accommodating your life to the demands of your manuscript. Arrange your schedule so you can stay immersed in your project for long stretches of time—long enough, at least, to grasp the problems your manuscript is presenting, to find possible solutions, and to recognize that you are making progress.

### ➻ Only think big when you have to

You can't write a manuscript as long and complex as a thesis or dissertation without continually thinking about the project as a whole. How else can you assess whether you are keeping on track? Nevertheless, you might want to limit the extent to which you keep the "big picture" uppermost in your mind, particularly if you find yourself staring at the ceiling at 2 a.m., hyperventilating, paralyzed by fear, and bathed in a cold sweat. If you keep your focus on the sentence, the paragraph, the section, then your paralysis will melt and your breathing will return to normal. Instead of asking, "O my God, how am I ever going to do this?!" try, "Okay, what am I trying to say with this sentence? What is the paragraph about?" You need an overall plan, but if you don't keep your attention focused on the necessary steps for realizing it, you will trip and fall.

## ❧ Care more than anyone else about the quality of your project

Don't rely on your chair or committee members to find the clumsy errors in your manuscript. Take another week or two before giving them a draft so you can go in search of typos, awkward sentences, tense difficulties, misplaced and missing punctuation marks, and reference-list/citation problems. If you show the committee members you care about the quality of your work, they will read your manuscript with a positive frame of mind; if you give them the impression that you expect editorial services from them, they will read with irritated, perhaps even angry, eyes.

## ❧ Don't set your hopes on a specific defense date

As long as you won't feel too disappointed if you aren't finished as soon as you'd hoped, holding a specific date in mind for defending your thesis or dissertation may help you to keep working when you'd rather just sleep or relax. But don't use your desired date as a way of encouraging (read *pressuring*) your chair and committee to give you a faster turnaround time or to grant premature approval for scheduling your defense. They will likely interpret such requests as an indication that you are more interested in finishing than in producing a quality product.

## ❧ Lose your deference

By the time you finish your research, you will probably know as much or more than most people (including your chair) about your area of study. Let the significance of this fact soak in, and let your appreciation of your developing expertise help you read and write with a greater authority. Just make sure your confidence doesn't devolve into arrogance.

## ❧ Keep yourself and your project in perspective

Conducting an in-depth research study, writing a book-length manuscript about it, and then orally defending it—you may well find these tasks to be among the most difficult and meaningful in your life. It would make sense, then, if you were to imbue your efforts with something approaching cosmic significance. Take it easy, though. If you attribute *too* much importance to them, if you take yourself *too* seriously, you may unduly slow yourself down, whether with writer's block (or "sticky writing"—see Chapter 1) or with an attempt to be comprehensively, thoroughly, fully encompassing.

Instead of considering your thesis or dissertation to be the culmination of your life's work, think of it as the first of a series of publications. That way, you don't have to write an everything-but-the-kitchen-sink document, and you don't have to try to be profound. Settle for clear, thoughtful, and interesting, and your task will become far more manageable.

# Bibliography of Books and Internet Resources

## Style Manuals

American Psychological Association. (1994). *The publication manual of the American Psychological Association* (4th ed.). Washington, DC: Author.

*Chicago manual of style* (14th ed.). (1993). Chicago: University of Chicago Press.

Cook, C. K. (1985). *The MLA's Line by line.* Boston: Houghton Mifflin.

Fowler, H. R., & Aaron, J. E. (1995). *The Little, Brown handbook* (6th ed.). New York: HarperCollins.

Fowler, H. W. (1996). *The new Fowler's modern English usage* (3rd ed.) (R. W. Burchfield, Ed.). Oxford: Oxford University Press.

Gordon, K. E. (1993). *The deluxe transitive vampire.* New York: Pantheon.

Gordon, K. E. (1993). *The new well-tempered sentence.* New York: Ticknor & Fields.

Gowers, E. (1988). *The complete plain words* (Rev. ed.) (S. Greenbaum & J. Whitcut, Ed.). Boston: David R. Godine.

Ivers, M. (1991). *The Random House guide to good writing.* New York: Random House.

Partridge, E. (1994). *Usage and abusage* (Rev. ed.) (J. Whitcut, Ed.). New York: Norton.

Ross-Larson, B. (1996). *Edit yourself.* New York: Norton.

Safire, W. (1990). *Fumblerules.* New York: Doubleday.

Strunk, W., & White, E. B. (1979). *The elements of style* (3rd ed.). New York: Macmillan.

Trimble, J. R. (1975). *Writing with style.* Englewood Cliffs, NJ: Prentice-Hall.

Turabian, K. L. (1996). *A manual for writers* (6th ed.). Chicago: University of Chicago Press.

Van Leunen, M. (1992). *A handbook for scholars* (Rev. ed.). New York: Oxford University Press.

Williams, J. M. (1990). *Style: Toward clarity and grace.* Chicago: University of Chicago Press.

# Writing Guides

Barzun, J. (1985). *Simple and direct.* Chicago: University of Chicago Press.

Becker, H. (1986). *Writing for social scientists.* Chicago: University of Chicago Press.

Brown, R. M. (1988). *Starting from scratch.* New York: Bantam.

Dillard, A. (1989). *The writing life.* New York: HarperPerennial

Goldberg, N. (1986). *Writing down the bones.* Boston: Shambhala.

Graves, R., & Hodge, A. *The use and abuse of the English language.* New York: Marlowe & Co.

Howard, V. A., & Barton, J. H. (1986). *Thinking on paper.* New York: William Morrow.

Lamott, A. (1994). *Bird by bird.* New York: Anchor.

Ueland, B. (1987). *If you want to write.* Saint Paul: Graywolf.

Zinsser, W. (1988). *Writing to learn.* New York: Harper & Row.

Zinsser, W. (1985). *On writing well.* New York: Harper & Row.

# Internet Resources

*Inkspot*—Writing resources on the Web:
    http://www.inkspot.com/

*National Writing Centers Association*—comprehensive list of online writing centers:
    http://www2.colgate.edu/diw/NWCAOWLS.html

*National Writing Centers Association*—resources for writers:
    http://www2.colgate.edu/diw/NWCA/Resources.html

*Purdue Writing Lab:*
    http://owl.english.purdue.edu/

Randall Hansen's index of writing-related Internet sites:
    http://www.stetson.edu/~rhansen/writweb.html

*Research-it! language tools*—dictionary, thesaurus, word translator, etc.:
    http://www.itools.com/research-it/

*Yahoo!* WWW index of Internet sites related to grammar and style:
    http://www.yahoo.com/Social_Science/
        Linguistics_and_Human_Languages/
            Languages/English/Grammar__Usage__and_Style/

# References

American Psychological Association. (1994). *The publication manual of the American Psychological Association* (4th ed.). Washington, DC: Author.

Arendt, H. (1968). *Between past and future.* New York: Penguin Books.

Baker, R. A. (1990). *They call it hypnosis.* Amherst, NY: Prometheus Books.

Bartlett, F. C. (1932). *Remembering: A study in experimental and social psychology.* Cambridge, England: Cambridge University Press.

Bateson, G. (1979). *Mind and nature: A necessary unity.* New York: Bantam.

Bateson, G. (1991). *A sacred unity* (R. Donaldson, Ed.). New York: Harper-Collins.

Benedict, R. (1989). *Patterns of culture.* Boston: Houghton Mifflin. (Original work published 1934)

Berman, M. (1989). *Coming to our senses.* New York: Simon and Schuster.

Birdwhistell, R. L. (1970). *Kinesics and context.* Philadelphia: University of Pennsylvania Press.

Blinde, E. M., & Stratta, T. M. (1992). The "sport career death" of college athletes: Involuntary and unanticipated sports exits. *Journal of Sport Behavior, 15*(1), 3-20.

Brown, N. O. (1959). *Life against death.* Middletown, CT: Wesleyan University Press.

Bruner, J. (1986). *Actual minds, possible worlds.* Cambridge, MA: Harvard University Press.

Bruner, J. (1990). *Acts of meaning.* Cambridge, MA: Harvard University Press.

Bruner, J. (1992). Narrative construction of reality. In H. Beilin & P. B. Pufall (Eds.), *Piaget's theory: Prospects and possibilities* (pp. 229-248). Hillsdale, NJ: Lawrence Erlbaum Associates.

Campbell, D. T., & Stanley, J. C. (1963). *Experimental and quasi-experimental designs for research.* Boston: Houghton Mifflin.

Cebula, R. J. (1997). An empirical note on the impact of the federal budget deficit on ex ante real long-term interest rates, 1973-1995. *Southern Economic Journal, 63,* 1094-1099.

Chenail, R., & Gale, J. (1993). Practicing research. Proceedings from the seventh annual conference of the Qualitative Interest Group, held at the Georgia Center for Continuing Education, Athens, Georgia, January, 1994, College of Education, The University of Georgia, Athens, Georgia 30602.

*Chicago manual of style* (14th ed.). (1993). Chicago: University of Chicago Press.

Cochran, L. (1986). *Portrait and story.* New York: Greenwood Press.

Connolly, W. E. (1991). *Identity\Difference.* Ithica, NY: Cornell University Press.

Cook, C. K. (1985). *The MLA's line by line.* Boston: Houghton Mifflin.

Corr, C. (1993). Coping with dying: Lessons that we should and should not learn from the work of Elisabeth Kübler-Ross. *Death Studies, 17,* 69-83.

Crews, F. (1995). *The memory wars.* New York: The New York Review of Books.

Dunbar, R. (1996). *Grooming, gossip, and the evolution of language.* Cambridge, MA: Harvard University Press.

Duncan, B. L., Hubble, M. A., & Miller, S. D. (1997). *Psychotherapy with "impossible" cases.* New York: Norton.

Erickson, M. H., Rossi, E. L., & Rossi, S. I. (1976). *Hypnotic realities.* New York: Irvington.

Erikson, E. (1968). *Identity: Youth and crisis.* New York: Norton.

Fertziger, A. P. (1991). Artificial organs, organ transplantation, and dealing with death. *Loss, Grief & Care, 5*(1-2), 69-75.

Flemons, D. G. (1987). Zucchini mush as a misguided way of knowing. *Canadian Journal of Counselling, 21*(2 & 3), 161-164.

Flemons, D. G. (1998). *Writing between the lines.* New York: Norton.

Fowler, H. W. (1965). *Fowler's modern English usage* (E. Gowers, Ed.). Oxford: Oxford University Press.

Fulghum, R. L. (1988). *All I really need to know I learned in kindergarten.* New York: Villard Books.

Garry, M. & Loftus, E. (1994). Pseudomemories without hypnosis. *International Journal of Clinical and Experimental Hypnosis, 42,* 363-378.

Gergen, M. M., & Gergen, K. J. (1986). Narrative form and the construction of psychological science. In T. R. Sarbin (Ed.), *Narrative psychology* (pp. 22-44). New York: Praeger.

Gioia, T. (1988). *The imperfect art.* Oxford: Oxford University Press.

Glaser, B. G. (1992). *Emergence vs. Forcing: Basics of grounded theory.* Mill Valley, CA: Sociology Press.

Glaser, B. G., & Strauss, A. L. (1967). *The discovery of grounded theory.* Chicago: Aldine.

Goffman, E. (1959). *The presentation of self in everyday life.* Garden City, NY: Doubleday Anchor Books.

Goffman, E. (1961). *Asylums.* Garden City, NY: Anchor.

Gordon, D. M. (1974). Capitalism, class and crime in America. In C. E. Reasons (Ed.), *The criminologist: Crime and the criminal* (pp. 66-88). Pacific Palisades, CA: Goodyear Publishing.

Gould, S. J. (1981). *The mismeasure of man.* New York: Norton.

Groveman, A. M., & Brown, E. W. (1985). Family therapy with closed head injured patients: Utilizing Kubler-Ross' model. *Family Systems Medicine, 3*(4), 440-446.

Hare-Mustin, R. T. (1987). The problem of gender in family therapy theory. *Family Process, 26,* 15-27.

Harré, R., & Secord, P. F. (1972). *The explanation of social behaviour.* Totowa, NJ: Littlefield, Adams, & Co.

Haug, A. A. (1995). Has federal budget deficit policy changed in recent years? *Economic Inquiry, 33,* 104-118.

Hillman, J. (1983). *Healing fiction.* Barrytown, New York: Station Hill Press.

Howard, V. A., & Barton, J. H. (1986). *Thinking on paper.* New York: William Morrow.

Kastenbaum, R. J. (1975). Is death a life crisis? On the confrontation with death in theory and practice. In N. Datan & L. Ginsberg (Eds.), *Life-span developmental psychology: Normative life crises* (pp. 19-50). New York: Academic Press.

Kastenbaum, R. J. (1981). *Death, society, and human experience* (2nd ed.). St. Louis: The C. V. Mosby Company.

Kelly, G. A. (1955). *The psychology of personal constructs* (Vol.1). New York: Norton.

Keppel, G. (1982). *Design and analysis* (2nd ed.). Englewood Cliffs, NJ: Prentice-Hall.

Kihlstrom, J. F. (1994). Hypnosis, delayed recall, and the principles of memory. *International Journal of Clinical and Experimental Hypnosis, 42,* 337-345.

Kingsolver, B. (1995). *High tide in Tucson.* New York: HarperCollins.

Kronen, J. (1995). Infertility and psychotherapy. *Issues in Psychoanalytic Psychology, 17*(1), 52-64.

Kübler-Ross, E. (1969). *On death and dying.* New York: Macmillan.

Laing, R. D. (1969). *The divided self.* New York: Penguin.

Lakoff, G. (1987). *Women, fire, and dangerous things.* Chicago: University of Chicago Press.

Lakoff, G., & Johnson, M. (1980). *Metaphors we live by.* Chicago: University of Chicago Press.

Lazarus, A. (1995). Multimodal therapy. In R. J. Corsini & D. Wedding (Eds.), *Current psychotherapies* (5th ed.) (pp. 322-355). Itasca, IL: F. E. Peacock.

Leary, D. E. (1990). Psyche's muse: The role of metaphor in the history of psychology. In D. E. Leary (Ed.), *Metaphors in the history of psychology* (pp. 1-78). Cambridge, England: Cambridge University Press.

Levine, S. (1982). *Who dies?* New York: Anchor Books.

Lincoln, Y. S., & Guba, E. G. (1985). *Naturalistic inquiry.* Thousand Oaks, CA: Sage.

Loftus, E. F., & Pickrell, J. E. (1995). The formation of false memories. *Psychiatric Annals, 25,* 720-725.

Lovejoy, A. O. (1964). *The great chain of being.* Cambridge, MA: Harvard University Press.

Mancias, P. T. (1986). Whither psychology? In J. Margolis, P. T. Mancias, R. Harre, & P. F. Secord, *Psychology: Designing the discipline.* New York: Basil Blackwell.

Marsalis, W. (1995). *Marsalis on music.* New York: Norton.

McArthur, T. (Ed.). (1992). *The Oxford companion to the English language.* Oxford: Oxford University Press.

McAteer, M. (1990). Reactions to terminal illness. *Physiotherapy, 76*(1), 9-12.

Mead, G. H. (1962). *Mind, self, and society* (C. W. Morris, Ed.). Chicago: University of Chicago Press.

Metzger, A. (1979-80). A Q-methodological study of the Kübler-Ross stage theory. *Omega—The Journal of Death and Dying, 10,* 291-301.

Miller, S. (1995). Land, landscape and the question of culture: English urban hegemony and research needs. *Journal of Historical Sociology, 8*(1), 94-107.

Miller, S. D., Duncan, B. L., & Hubble, M. A. (1997). *Escape from Babel.* New York: Norton.

Mishler, E. G. (1986). *Research interviewing: Context and narrative.* Cambridge, MA: Harvard University Press.

Ogden, C. K., & Richards, I. A. (1989). *The meaning of meaning.* San Diego, CA: Harcourt Brace Jovanovich. (Original work published 1923)

Ollman, B. (1971). *Alienation.* Cambridge, England: Cambridge University Press.

Orne, M. T., Whitehouse, W. G., Dinges, D. F., & Orne, E. C. (1988). Reconstructing memory through hypnosis: Forensic and clinical implications. In H. M. Pettinati (Ed.), *Hypnosis and memory* (pp. 21-63). New York: Guilford.

Osborne, L. (1997, April/May). Does man eat man? *Linguafranca, 70,* 28-38.

Parsons, T. (1954). *Essays in sociological theory* (Rev. ed.). New York: The Free Press.

Partridge, E. (1994). *Usage and abusage* (Rev. ed.) (J. Whitcut, Ed.). New York: Norton.

Patton, M. Q. (1990). *Qualitative evaluation and research methods.* Newbury Park, CA: Sage.

Pettinati, H. M. (1988). Hypnosis and memory: Integrative summary and future directions. In H. M. Pettinati (Ed.), *Hypnosis and memory* (pp. 277-291). New York: Guilford.

Polkinghorne, D. E. (1988). *Narrative knowing and the human sciences.* Albany, NY: SUNY.

Polanyi, M. (1962). *Personal knowledge*. Chicago: University of Chicago Press.

Reps, P. (1957). *Zen flesh, zen bones*. Rutland, VT: Charles E. Tuttle.

Ross, L., & Nisbett, R. E. (1991). *The person and the situation*. Philadelphia: Temple University Press.

Ross-Larson, B. (1996). *Edit yourself*. New York: Norton.

Safire, W. (1990). *Fumblerules*. New York: Doubleday.

Sarbin, T. R. (Ed.). (1986). *Narrative psychology*. New York: Praeger.

Schacter, D. L. (1996). *Searching for memory: The brain, the mind, and the past*. New York: BasicBooks.

Scherman, T. (1996). Liner notes. In *Bobby McFerrin & Chick Corea: The Mozart sessions* [CD]. New York: Sony Music.

Schlesinger, A. M., Jr. (1968). *The bitter heritage* (Rev. ed.). Greenwich, CT: Fawcett.

Schulz, R., & Aderman, D. (1974). Clinical research and the stages of dying. *Omega—The Journal of Death and Dying, 5*, 137-143.

Schulz, R., & Schlarb, J. (1987-88). Two decades of research on dying: What do we know about the patient? *Omega—The Journal of Death and Dying, 18*, 299-317.

Skinner, B. F. (1953). *Science and human behavior*. New York: The Free Press.

Skinner, B. F. (1992). Whatever happened to psychology as the science of behavior? In R. B. Miller (Ed.), *The restoration of dialogue* (pp. 105-114). Washington, DC: American Psychological Association.

Soja, E. W. (1989). *Postmodern geographies*. London: Verso.

Spradley, J. P. (1980). *Participant observation*. New York: Holt, Rinehart, & Winston.

Stoller, P. (1989). *The taste of ethnographic things*. Philadelphia: University of Pennsylvania Press.

Strauss, A. L., & Corbin, J. (1990). *Basics of qualitative research: Grounded theory procedures and techniques*. Newbury Park, CA: Sage.

Strunk, W., & White, E. B. (1979). *The elements of style* (3rd ed.). New York: Macmillan.

Tannen, D. (1989). *Talking voices*. Cambridge: Cambridge University Press.

Tannen, D. (1990). *You just don't understand*. New York: William Morrow.

Tannen, D. (1993). *Framing in discourse*. New York: Oxford University Press.

Tannen, D. (1995). *Talking from 9 to 5*. New York: Avon.

Turner, J., & Fine, M. (1995). Postmodern evaluation in family therapy supervision. *Journal of Systemic Therapies, 14*(2), 57-69.

Turner, V. (1986). *The anthropology of performance*. New York: PAJ Publications.

Tyler, S. A. (1987). *The unspeakable*. Madison, WI: University of Wisconsin Press.

Walker, L. (1979). *The battered woman*. New York: Harper & Row.

Watson, R. I., & Evans, R. B. (1991). *The great psychologists* (5th ed.). New York: HarperCollins.

Whyte, L. L. (1962). *The unconscious before Freud.* Garden City, NY: Anchor.

Wilden, A. (1980). *System and structure* (2nd ed.). London: Tavistock Publications.

Winegardner, D., Simonetti, J. L., & Nykodym, N. (1984). Unemployment: The living death? *Journal of Employment Counseling, 21*(4), 149-155.

Witkin, H. A., Mednick, S. A., Schulsinger, R., Bakkestrom, E., Christiansen, K. O., Goodenbough, D. R., Hirschhorn, K., Lunsteen, C., Owen, D. R., Philip, J., Ruben, D. B., & Stocking, M. (1976). Criminality in XYY and XXY men. *Science, 193,* 547-555.

Wolcott, H. F. (1994). *Transforming qualitative data: Description, analysis, and interpretation.* Thousand Oaks, CA: Sage.

Wright, K. (in preparation). *Living with dying: Conversations with terminally-ill patients.* Unpublished doctoral dissertation, Nova Southeastern University, Fort Lauderdale, FL.

Yeatman, A. (1990). A feminist theory of social differentiation. In L. J. Nicholoson (Ed.), *Feminism/Postmodernism* (pp. 281-299). New York: Routledge.

Zerubavel, E. (1991). *The fine line.* New York: The Free Press.

# Index